Not All Supermen

Not All Supermen

Sexism, Toxic Masculinity, and the Complex History of Superheroes

Tim Hanley

ROWMAN & LITTLEFIELD
Lanham • Boulder • New York • London

Published by Rowman & Littlefield
An imprint of The Rowman & Littlefield Publishing Group, Inc.
4501 Forbes Boulevard, Suite 200, Lanham, Maryland 20706
www.rowman.com

86-90 Paul Street, London EC2A 4NE, United Kingdom

British Library Cataloguing in Publication Information Available

Library of Congress Cataloging-in-Publication Data
Names: Hanley, Tim, author.
Title: Not all supermen : sexism, toxic masculinity, and the complex
  history of superheroes / Tim Hanley.
Description: Lanham : Rowman & Littlefield, 2022. | Includes
  bibliographical references and index. | Summary: "Not All Supermen
  explores the complex history of the superhero genre, with its troubling
  undercurrent of sexism and toxic masculinity while supposedly espousing
  truth, justice, and valor for generations of fans"—Provided by
  publisher.
Identifiers: LCCN 2021048027 (print) | LCCN 2021048028 (ebook) | ISBN
  9781538152737 (cloth) | ISBN 9781538152744 (epub)
Subjects: LCSH: Comic books, strips, etc.—United States—History and
  criticism. | Superheroes in literature. | Masculinity in literature. |
  Sexism in literature. | LCGFT: Literary criticism.
Classification: LCC PN6725 .H364 2022 (print) | LCC PN6725 (ebook) | DDC
  741.5/973—dc23/eng/20211223
LC record available at https://lccn.loc.gov/2021048027
LC ebook record available at https://lccn.loc.gov/2021048028

Contents

Introduction   vii

1   Origins   1
2   Codification   13
3   Marvelous   23
4   Mania   35
5   Divergence   45
6   Overpowered   57
7   Despair   67
8   Caliber   77
9   Exaggeration   89
10 Breakdown   101
11 Frozen   111
12 Barriers   123
13 Pride   133
14 Supremacy   143
15 Assemble   153
16 Power   165
17 Instigate   175

Conclusion   185

Acknowledgments   189

Notes   191

Bibliography   227

Index   229

About the Author   239

Introduction

Superheroes are amazing. For over eighty years, caped champions have saved the world countless times across myriad universes in comic books that continually push the limits of artistry and imagination. On the big screen, whether it's Wonder Woman defiantly crossing No Man's Land to end a war or Captain America wielding Mjölnir for one last valiant stand against Thanos, superhero movies have uplifted and inspired audiences all around the world. Their iconography is instantly recognizable and holds a special sort of power. Wearing Superman's shield makes us feel strong. A Green Lantern logo reminds us that we can overcome fear. Captain Marvel's Hala star motivates us to go higher, further, faster.

In many ways, superhero stories are our modern mythology. These larger-than-life figures give us morality tales that reflect our world in fantastical ways. While we don't need to worry about alien invasions, interdimensional monsters, or maniacal clowns in our day-to-day lives, superheroes nonetheless show us the value of being courageous, believing in ourselves, and standing up for what we think is right.

Superheroes have been inspirational from their earliest days too. Superman established himself as a defender of the downtrodden in his very first appearance in 1938, Captain America took on Hitler and the Nazis before America even entered the war, and Wonder Woman advocated female strength and self-reliance in an era when women's rights were few. In the decades since, legions of characters have provided a heroic example to generations of fans, young and old, across comics, film, television, and more.

However, as great as superheroes are, there is a troubling undercurrent to the genre. Superheroes were for everyone originally, popular adventures sold for a dime that were read by boys and girls alike. The vast majority of the writers, artists, and editors behind the stories were men, though, as were the bulk of the heroes who starred in these comics. Over time, the readership began to shift. Boys became the dominant audience, and publishers catered to their interests. They continued to do so as the readership changed further, from boys to teenagers to young men. Today, superhero media remains a male-dominated affair, whether in comic book production or among those who write, produce, and direct their blockbuster film franchises. The narrow perspectives offered in these decades of stark gender divides have enshrined certain attitudes and values and conditioned the fandom to accept skewed, often sexist gender dynamics as commonplace.

This pervasive sexism colors the genre, limiting who can be a hero and which heroic traits are valued. It also restricts the roles of female characters and characters of marginalized genders, often devaluing them through omission and objectification. Ultimately, such an environment can lead to the rise of toxic masculinity, an attitude that promotes aggression and violence, stifles empathy, and denigrates women. It does not mean that all masculinity is toxic, but rather that rigidly held ideas about masculinity that uphold male dominance and toughness above all else can be harmful to everyone, male or otherwise. Toxic masculinity is based in a disdain for femininity that often manifests in misogyny and homophobia, promotes anger while punishing other expressions of emotion, and fosters defensive animosity toward anything outside of one's narrow perspective.

Sexism and toxic masculinity are not unique to the world of superheroes. Male-dominated media and sexism tend to go hand in hand, especially in nerd communities, and we've seen it manifest to varying degrees time and again. Insular fandoms are resistant to change, and the biggest change they tend to face, especially when niche media goes mainstream, is an influx of characters and fans outside of the typical straight, white male mold they're used to. Gatekeeping and harassment are common outcomes, unfortunately.

But while sexism and toxic masculinity are common across many fandoms, the superhero community is especially susceptible. First, the genre is deeply rooted in nostalgia. Although superhero media has evolved and expanded, their narratives have been continuously told for over eighty years, with the original stories upheld as sacred texts. They are foundational and bring with them all manner of outdated, problematic elements that continue to influence new superhero work today. Everything is canon, to one degree or another, leading to negative tropes and attitudes that date back decades becoming enshrined as essential to the genre.

This penchant for nostalgia combines with a level of defensiveness and arrested development that's been woven into the framework of superhero media. Many boys who got bullied for reading comics grew up to make comics, and they've held positions of power in major publishers for some time. These creators remain closely connected to the stories of their youth, inclined to promote their preferred heroes to their similarly inclined fan base rather than expand the universe in new ways to new readers. They valorize the old comics they grew up with, fetishize female characters, and generally adhere to the way that things used to be as their primary publishing strategy.

The history of superhero comics and its fandom is littered with bad actors that embody toxic masculinity. There are all manner of sexist, homophobic, and racist stories, many of which remain influential today. Several creators have also been outed as sexual harassers and bigots, and intolerant fan movements have highlighted the darker corners of the community. But beyond this horrific behavior, a bigger, treacherously subtle issue permeates the genre.

While it's easy to point out the obvious villains who attack and belittle others, there's a more insidious side to the sexism and toxic masculinity that pervades the superhero genre and its fandom. Misogynistic gender dynamics are so woven into the industry that they feel commonplace, an underlying constant that the male-dominated fan community has unknowingly internalized. Although not all men, or in this case not all supermen, are sexist bigots or harassers, we've all absorbed the genre's tropes and tendencies. We accept skewed representation, outmoded attitudes, and harmful messaging as normal, allowing them to go unchecked because it doesn't seem unusual. It's just the way superheroes have always been. We focus on what's good about the stories instead, but in doing only that we allow pernicious aspects of the genre to carry on and flourish. What we've been conditioned to consider normal isn't necessarily so.

This is not a screed, or some sort of performative exercise in wokeness. This is a discussion about the nature of superheroes, what they've become, and what they will be moving forward. Superheroes can be a force for good, but the industry is laden with excessive baggage. The future of the genre and its fandom depends on what elements of the past we choose to celebrate and what we choose to leave behind. As superhero media continues to grow in popularity, we have the opportunity to reconcile with this past and the deeply ingrained, lingering effects thereof. Only by unraveling the complex history of the genre can we find the good, excise the bad, and begin to move forward in a meaningful, authentically representative way that champions a broader approach to heroism and a more inclusive fan community.

CHAPTER 1

Origins

Comic books had only been around for a few years when *Action Comics* #1 hit newsstands in 1938. Most comics consisted of newspaper strips bundled together into cheap, disposable magazines, but *Action Comics* was part of a new trend with all original material. The cover of the first issue featured a strongman in a red cape and blue tights with an "S" insignia emblazoned across his chest, holding a car over his head and smashing it into a rock. Inside the book, the lead story explained that the character was Superman, a survivor of a distant, destroyed planet. Sent to Earth as a baby, he grew up to develop strength and speed beyond that of mortal men. He lived as Clark Kent, a reporter for the *Daily Star*, but when danger arose he donned his costume to become the "champion of the oppressed, the physical marvel who had sworn to devote his existence to helping those in need!"

In his first story, Superman strong-armed his way into the governor's mansion and demanded the pardon of a wrongly convicted woman on death row, broke into an apartment to stop a man from abusing his wife, and accosted a lobbyist for a war profiteer who'd just bribed a senator. From the head of a state to the head of a household, Superman didn't care who he was up against. When innocent people were in danger, he was there to be a voice for those who couldn't speak up and to step in for those who couldn't fight back. It was a remarkably progressive first outing that quickly established Superman as the defender of the powerless.

Superman was created by two young men, writer Jerry Siegel and artist Joe Shuster, and their upbringing influenced every aspect of the feature. They grew up in a poor, predominantly Jewish neighborhood in Cleveland, Ohio, and were intimately familiar with feeling powerless. The sons of Jewish immigrants from Europe, they were bullied often, and Siegel's father was killed during a robbery at his store when Siegel was a teenager. Ohio was also a hotbed for hate groups

Action Comics #1, art by Joe Shuster, DC Comics, 1938. The debut of Superman launched the superhero genre.

like the Ku Klux Klan, and they saw anti-Semitism grow to horrific extremes after Adolf Hitler came to power in Germany in 1933. Siegel and Shuster lived in fear for their relatives in Europe, while at home groups like America First and its prominent members, including Charles Lindbergh and Walt Disney, lobbied for the country to stay out of German affairs. From poverty to loss to racist hatred, the duo faced a litany of suffering, and they channeled their experiences into Superman.

Siegel and Shuster couldn't fix the world, but Superman could. Over the next several issues, Superman dealt with poverty on several fronts. He stood up for workers' rights, confronting a wealthy mine owner after a cave-in and convincing him to treat his employees better. He also evacuated and then demolished a city slum, knowing that the government would have to step in and build new, modern housing projects for the displaced residents. Superman stopped swindlers, corrupt politicians, and cruel judges as well, all in the interest of protecting the nation's most impoverished citizens. He was a New Deal Democrat with superpowers, battling the lingering effects of the Great Depression wherever he could.

Harry Donenfeld, the owner of DC Comics, didn't care for Superman initially and took him off the cover of *Action Comics* after the first issue, but then the sales reports came in. Readers loved Superman, and they wanted more of the "friend of the helpless and oppressed" who waged a "one-man battle against evil and injustice." Donenfeld gave the people what they wanted, and Superman became the permanent headliner of *Action Comics* before launching his own eponymous series soon after.

By 1940, Superman was so popular that *Look* magazine hired Siegel and Shuster to do a special comic strip in which Superman addressed the conflict in Europe called "How Superman Would End the War." The Man of Steel smashed German cannons and punched their planes out of the sky as he raced across the continent; then he grabbed Hitler and Stalin and delivered the dictators to the League of Nations in Geneva where they were found guilty of "modern history's greatest crime—unprovoked aggression against defenseless countries." America hadn't entered the war yet, but Siegel and Shuster used their fictional creation to take a strong stand against Nazi aggression.

Their fellow creators followed suit. After Superman became a hit, other publishers wanted heroes of their own and flooded the newsstands with caped marvels, many from Jewish writers and artists. The publishing business was a tough game for Jewish creators, who were often shut out of highbrow, established outlets, and some of the only places to find consistent work were less respectable fields like pulp magazines and the emerging comic book industry. The latter became a haven for Jewish writers and artists, and they took advantage of the new medium to take a stand against fascism.

At MLJ Magazines, Harry Shorten and Irv Novick created the Shield, a star-spangled hero who fought thinly veiled Nazi analogues just short months after the war began. At Quality Comics, Will Eisner and Dave Berg introduced Uncle Sam, the spirit of America reborn in physical form to take on American fascist groups at home and fight German forces abroad. More patriotic heroes followed, but one stood above the rest as he pushed an interventionist message to the forefront of American popular culture.

Jack Kirby liked to draw, he liked to fight, and he hated Nazis. He found a way to combine all three with his friend Joe Simon when they created Captain America for Timely Comics. Their hero was Steve Rogers, a scrawny young man who developed a muscular physique and superhuman strength after he was injected with the military's supersoldier serum. A Nazi agent killed the serum's inventor and destroyed the remaining vials, leaving Steve as the nation's only supersoldier. He donned a blue costume with red boots and gloves, sported a white star on his chest and a white "A" on his forehead, and carried a round shield as he took on missions for the military.

Timely publisher Martin Goodman loved the pitch and gave Captain America his own series straightaway rather than following the usual procedure of introducing a character in an anthology book. Simon wrote the debut issue, and Kirby drew it all on a tight deadline, showcasing his distinctive, bombastic style throughout, but nothing was more quintessentially Kirby than the cover. *Captain America Comics* #1 hit the newsstands in December 1940, a full year before America entered the war, yet the cover showed Captain America smashing his way into a Nazi stronghold and punching Adolf Hitler square on the jaw.

While other publishers pitted their heroes against vaguely German foes, Kirby did away with any subtlety and took the fight straight to the top. Captain America fought domestic Nazi spies and saboteurs in the first outing, then raided a German concentration camp in the next issue and fought Hitler and one of his top lieutenants, Hermann Göring. Simon and Kirby's anti-Nazi stance sparked strong reactions, both from fans who loved the book and angry Nazi supporters who called into the Timely offices to threaten the staff. One of the threats came when Kirby was there, and the caller claimed there was a gang in the lobby spoiling for a fight. Kirby rolled up his sleeves and went down to take them on, but they'd left, no doubt to his great disappointment.

Early comic book creators addressed their fears through their characters, often directly, but even more conventional crimefighters followed a similar pattern. At DC Comics, Batman debuted in *Detective Comics* #27 in 1939. Created by Bill Finger and Bob Kane, millionaire Bruce Wayne dressed as a bat to strike fear into the hearts of crooks as he patrolled Gotham City each night to avenge the murder of his parents. His adventures were less blatantly politically conscious than Superman or Captain America, but the same themes were present between

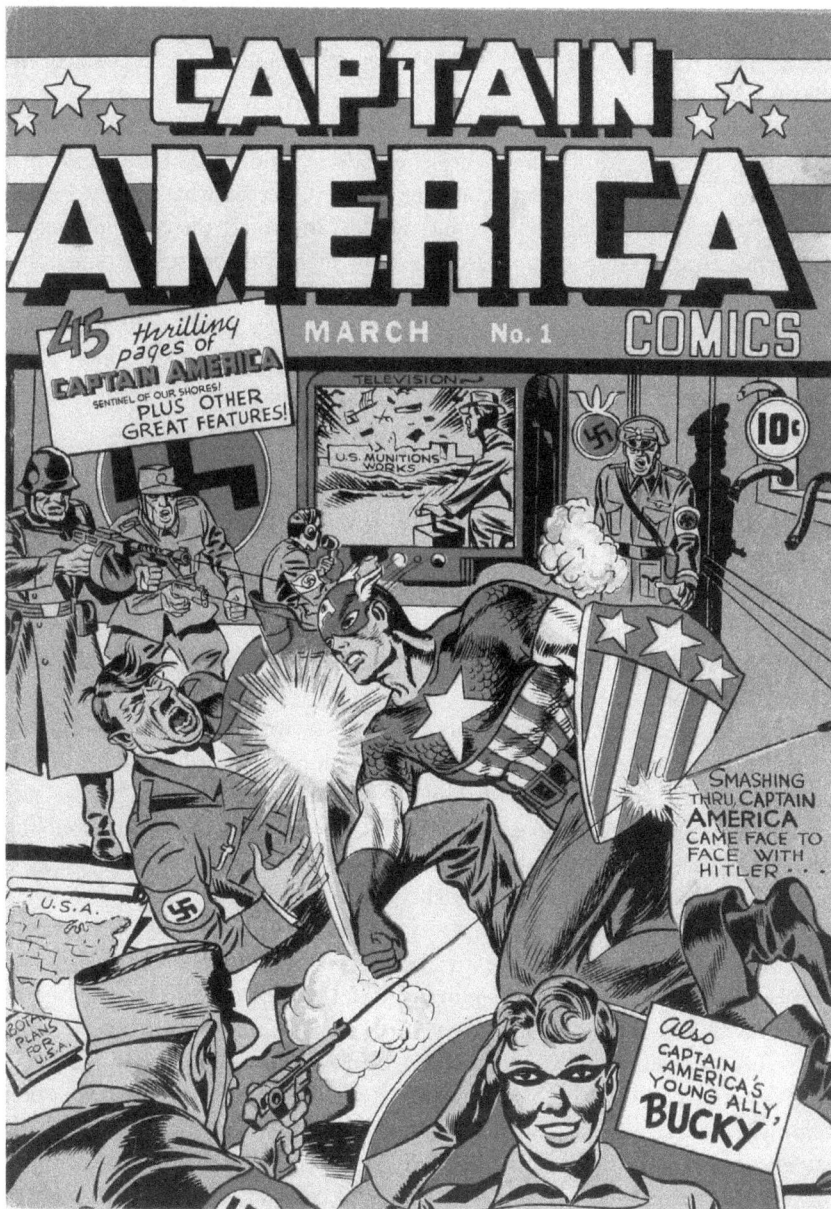

Captain America Comics #1, art by Jack Kirby, Timely Comics, 1941. Captain America punched his way through Nazi foes, including Hitler himself.

the lines. Like Superman, Batman disdained authority figures, most notably the police as he engaged in vigilantism in his crusade to stop crime. Like Captain America, he protected the country from invaders, facing off against villains like the Scarlet Horde and its leader, Carl Kruger, who aimed to be "dictator of the world."

These young Jewish creators crafted heroes who addressed issues they were powerless to do anything about, both realistically and fantastically, and their characters' values were clear and consistent. Early heroes in what became known as the Golden Age of superhero comics worked to protect the common people from any and all dangers, opposed powerful men who oppressed or ignored them, and tore down fascism at home and abroad. This was the core foundation of the genre, and it was a noble one. Even though their work was in disposable funny books, the founders of the genre were doing their best to showcase the values of courage and compassion to their readers, to great effect. By the early 1940s, superhero titles were being read by millions across America.

These initial adventures were the pillars upon which the superhero genre was built. For mainstays like Batman, Captain America, and Superman, their classic stories have been reprinted, retold, and reworked countless times across generations. Although continuity has shifted over the decades, these tales remain a cornerstone that still defines the genre today. Enshrining the progressive, altruistic ethics the original superheroes embodied has been essential to the industry's consistent success. These ideals have proven relevant time and again, and they continue to inspire fans even now.

At the same time, however, canonizing these works whole cloth and celebrating them uncritically has allowed less enlightened values to persevere. Superheroes, for all their forward-thinking attitudes, were very much a product of the late 1930s, and these early tales brought with them a host of troubling elements that have influenced the genre ever since.

One of these elements was a dependence on violence. Now, these were action adventure stories. Violence was always going to be part of the equation, and violence isn't always inherently bad. Captain America socking Hitler in the jaw was beyond warranted. However, violence quickly became the go-to response for superheroes in any given situation, establishing an overreliance on aggression that all too often paired with a casual disregard for human life.

Superman wasn't the big blue Boy Scout we know today in his earliest appearances. He was strong and intimidating, and frequently leveraged his superior power to threaten his foes. While he was always on the side of right, his tactics were fear based, rooted in a forceful coercion that bordered on bullying. Batman and Captain America were even more callous, expressing no remorse when lives were lost during their many violent skirmishes. All of the heroes avoided killing their opponents directly, but none of them were upset when an errant kick or stray bullet led to an enemy's death. Instead they scoffed, and often labeled their demise "a fate [they] well deserved." Answering pitiless violence with pitiless violence created a framework that normalized aggressive brutality throughout the genre.

As superheroes caught on with young readers and became mainstream, comic books turned into wholesome entertainment and the violence toned down somewhat. Decades later, though, creators would look back at these initial tales and resurrect a similar tone. Meanwhile, this decrease in violence came with a new political alignment. Superheroes broke into the mainstream just as America entered World War II, and questioning authority as the country pulled together to defeat the Axis was no longer acceptable. Rather than challenging the status quo, superheroes now embraced it, working in lockstep with the police and the government instead of opposing harmful policies. They weren't progressive outsiders anymore. They were part of the establishment, and this shift to complacency over advocating for change has never really gone away.

The war also spurred a rash of bigotry, further fanning racist flames that had already been present in the genre. DC Comics is named after *Detective Comics*, Donenfeld's first series before *Action Comics* kick-started the superhero genre. The cover of the book's first issue featured a harshly stylized Chinese character, with exaggerated features that included prominent fangs and menacing, sharply slanted eyes. He was the antagonist of "The Claws of the Red Dragon," one of several stories in the issue with Chinese villains. The characters spoke in broken, phonetic English that mocked their accents, and a later tale referred to them as "yellow rats." It was an inauspicious beginning to DC's flagship title, and epitomized a common approach to nonwhite characters.

Across early superhero tales, people of color were either villains or curiosities, exoticized and denigrated. They were awash in hackneyed stereotypes as writers and artists put little effort into accurately portraying their cultures. Even when they tried to present characters in a favorable light, it still went poorly. This was especially common with Black characters who, despite the realistic art used for white characters, were often drawn cartoonishly, with big eyes and even bigger lips that encompassed the bottom half of their faces. Case in point, Whitewash Jones, a teammate of Captain America's kid sidekick Bucky in the spin-off book *Young Allies*. After explaining the skills of his other teammates, Bucky said of Whitewash, "[He] can make a harmonica talk!" Whitewash then chimed in, "Yeah man! I is also good on de watermelon!" He was also the most cowardly and ineffective member of the team.

Then America entered the war, and the racial dynamics worsened. The crass stereotypes that had been employed for Chinese villains were now foisted on the Japanese, who became the chief enemies of many superheroes in the wake of Pearl Harbor. Japanese characters were dehumanized, reduced to barbaric warmongers who lusted for the deaths of valiant white Americans with a bestial, almost vampiric rage. German characters, meanwhile, were goofy and over the top but remained recognizably human. This demonization of the Japanese wasn't unique to superhero comics. American propaganda across the board was appalling in its depiction of its Japanese foes, fueling inhumane policies like forcing Japanese Americans into internment camps. But by following suit, superhero comics began a trend of reducing foreign enemies to demeaning caricatures that still continues.

Poor representation of a sizable group continued with the genre's treatment of half of the world's population. Women were not a major factor in early superhero comics. The few that appeared were damsels in distress, love interests or, more commonly, both. In these initial years, Lois Lane wanted to be a great reporter, but her inquisitive nature resulted in her getting captured by villains again and again, then rescued by Superman so she could sing his praises. Her narrative function was to make him look good. The same was true for Betty Ross and Captain America. She was a federal agent, but did little apart from stumble into peril so he could save her. Bruce Wayne's fiancé, Julie Madison, was endangered often then quickly phased out after his young sidekick Robin entered the picture. Apart from these secondary roles, women were rare in their books.

They were also treated poorly. After Superman rescued Lois Lane in *Action Comics* #1, he told her, "I'd advise you not to print this little episode," despite the fact that he knew she was a reporter who was keen for a big story. As Clark Kent, he regularly stole scoops from Lois, and gaslit her time and again in both identities anytime she suspected that Clark Kent was Superman. Batman was dismissive of female characters, like in his first meeting with Catwoman when he infamously exclaimed, "Quiet or papa spank!" Captain America was cordial toward Betty Ross, at least, but he didn't trust her in a fight despite the fact that she was a gun-toting federal agent.

Superhero comics were written, drawn, and edited primarily by men, and their grasp on how to portray women was limited, to say the least. While some of the female characters rose in prominence over the years, most notably Lois Lane, this was due to volume more than any direct intention. Superman became so popular that Lois's role expanded exponentially and she grew into a more well-rounded character, but few female characters were paired with male heroes that reached this level of success.

It wasn't all male creators, though. Fiction House had a handful of female creators working throughout their line, including Lily Renée and Ruth Roche. Barbara Hall worked on *Black Cat* for Harvey Comics, while June Tarpé Mills wrote and drew the comic strip *Miss Fury* that was later collected at Timely Comics. There were female heroes too, like Black Widow, Mary Marvel, and Phantom Lady. Still, women were rare, real or fictional. Female creators worked intermittently, briefly engaging with superhero stories after their male counterparts went off to war, while female superheroes tended to be short-lived derivatives of male heroes in skimpier outfits who faded into obscurity after a few issues.

One of the few female characters to break through was Wonder Woman, and she was very nearly a man. Her creator, William Moulton Marston, was a psychologist who saw comics as an avenue for spreading his feminist theories to young audiences but, following the trend established by early superheroes, he was planning to do so with a male lead. Then his wife, Elizabeth, wisely suggested a heroine instead, and the seed for a legend was planted.

The result was Wonder Woman, who debuted in DC Comics' *All-Star Comics* #8 in December 1941 with an introductory story written by Marston and drawn by his handpicked artist, cartoonist H. G. Peter. She was Diana, princess of the mythical Amazons, hidden away on the utopian, all-female Paradise Island. The Amazons had superhuman strength and speed but they were disinterested in outside affairs until American Air Force pilot Steve Trevor crash-landed near the island and Diana rescued him. Athena and Aphrodite, the chief goddesses of the Amazons, declared, "America, the last citadel of democracy, and of equal rights for women, needs your help!" so Diana took Steve home to the United States and stayed with him to help fight the war.

Wonder Woman was a unique superhero, intentionally eschewing the morbid violence and "blood-curdling masculinity" of her peers in favor of a more loving approach to conflict. Although she fought in the war and tackled all manner of real and mythological villains, her main goal was rehabilitation. She wanted to show her foes the error of their ways, and used her golden lasso to compel them to set aside their evil machinations. Wonder Woman's unusual adventures resonated with young readers, and before long she was one of DC's bestselling characters.

Marston wasn't surprised. His psychological theory, DISC (dominance, inducement, submission, compliance), led him to believe that people were naturally drawn to strong women. When men were in charge, Marston argued, they used harsh dominance to demand compliance. Women, meanwhile, used kind inducement to bring about willing submission. Ultimately, Marston concluded that "women, as a sex, are many times better equipped to assume emotional leadership than are males," and declared that the world was ready for a matriarchal revolution after millennia of male greed and aggression. He created Wonder Woman to prepare the way for this inevitable takeover, calling her "psychological propaganda for the new type of woman who should, I believe, rule the world."

While Marston and Peter were Wonder Woman's primary creators, there were a number of women working behind the scenes. Marston lived in

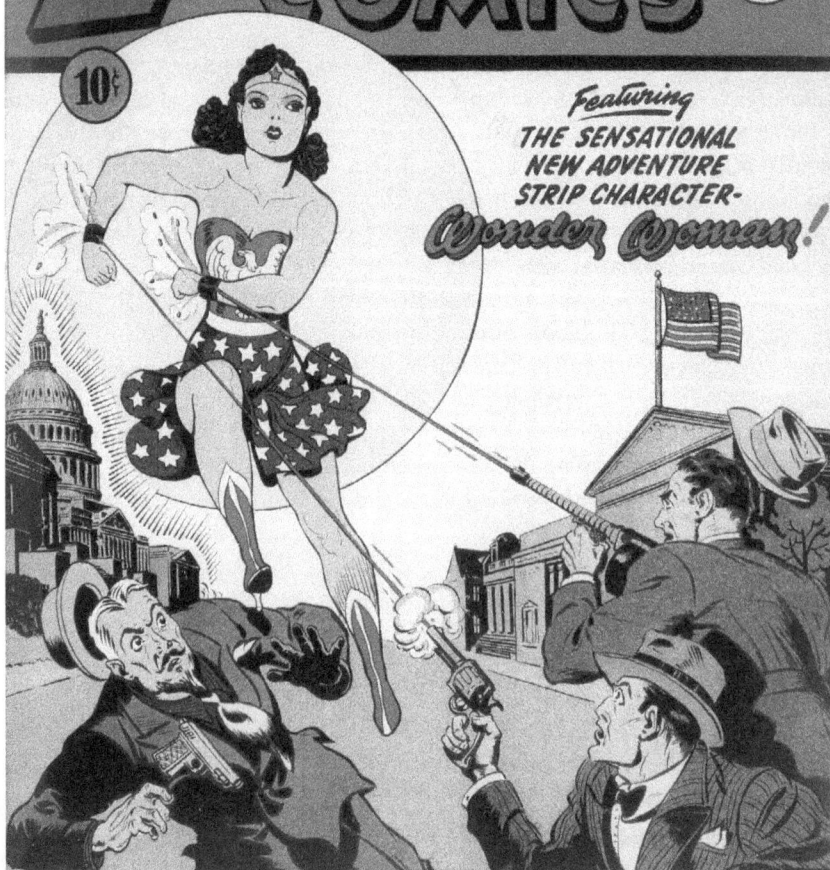

Sensation Comics #1, art by H. G. Peter, DC Comics, 1942. Wonder Woman was a combination of her creator's feminism and fetishism.

a polyamorous relationship with his wife, Elizabeth, and their partner, Olive Byrne, both of whom were well-educated women with ties to the women's suffrage and birth control movements. They influenced Marston's pro-matriarchal worldview, and inspired Wonder Woman for as long as Marston wrote the book. At DC Comics, Dorothy Roubicek served as assistant editor across Wonder Woman's many series, while former tennis star Alice Marble edited a regular "Wonder Women of History" feature that highlighted inspirational women from the past. When Marston fell ill with polio and later cancer, he hired Joye Hummel, a young psychology student, to assist him. Over five years she penned many of Wonder Woman's classic adventures, matching Marston's style while adding her own flair to the books, and although she went uncredited, she was one of only a handful of women with a regular gig on a superhero comic in this era.

However, despite all these remarkably progressive elements, there was another side to Marston's theories. His focus on dominance and submission in his Wonder Woman stories was illustrated through bondage imagery. Wonder Woman and other characters were tied up, chained, or otherwise incapacitated to contrast male and female rule. On Paradise Island, where women were in charge, getting tied up was a fun game as the Amazons willingly submitted to the loving authority of their wise queen. In the world of men, bondage was unpleasant, and when Wonder Woman's bracelets were chained together by a man she lost all her superpowers. The metaphor held, by and large, but the degree to which it was employed highlighted certain fetishistic fixations.

Early issues of *Wonder Woman* contained bondage imagery in over a quarter of the book's panels, with Diana or other characters bound in some capacity. While getting captured was a key feature of the genre, *Wonder Woman* had nearly ten times more bondage imagery than other superhero comics. Also, Wonder Woman was bound and powerless in the world of men far more often than she was happily tied up with her Amazon sisters. Marston had a clear fascination with the harshest, most unpleasant forms of bondage that bordered on the sadistic.

This kinky side of the bondage imagery was also intrinsic to Marston's larger goals. His editors were concerned with the situation, and became even more so when they received fan letters from other bondage enthusiasts. Marston dismissed their qualms, explaining that a kinky interest in bondage was both healthy and common, and that including such imagery was a way to lure in readers and thus expose them to his feminist theories. The sexual allure of women was why men would be willing to submit to their rule. Given that the books were bestsellers, Marston's editors stopped trying to change them and the bondage imagery continued.

The feminism and fetishism in *Wonder Woman* were intertwined, and while the existence of one didn't negate the other, it certainly complicated the message of the books. Even though Marston thought that women should rule the world, he was still happy to sexualize his lead heroine in ways that seemingly correlated with his own kinks and interests. He wasn't the only creator to manifest his lust in comic book form either. Joe Shuster was immediately smitten with the model he hired to pose for Lois Lane, and nearly all the female characters he drew from then on were brunettes patterned on her. Bob Kane based Catwoman on his cousin Ruth, whom he was in love with and would have married if they weren't related. From love interests to villains to the most famous and influential female superhero of all time, female characters served as vehicles for the desires of their male creators, and this pattern became a lasting legacy.

These initial years of the Golden Age of superheroes laid the groundwork for what the genre would become, and it was an exercise in complex dichotomies. Superman stood up for the downtrodden, but he was also a sexist bully. Captain America and other heroes took on the racist Nazi menace directly, but their wartime adventures dehumanized their Japanese foes with bigoted caricatures. Wonder Woman represented female power, but she was deeply rooted in her creator's own sexual fetishes. All of this has carried on in various forms ever since.

One clear constant across all of these superhero comics was the elevation of male fantasy. With predominantly male creators creating predominantly male superheroes, the genre was awash in male fantasy in several respects. The men were male power fantasies, as creators crafted determined, physically imposing characters who could fix the ills of the world. The women were male sexual fantasies, objects of desire for their heroes or for the creators themselves. Every aspect of the genre was cast through the lens of a male-centric perspective, and because these early comics are placed on such a pedestal, this perspective was enshrined as integral to the genre. The positive aspects continued while the negative aspects were allowed to remain and fester over the decades that followed.

CHAPTER 2

Codification

The superhero bubble burst in the mid-1940s as the war neared its end, and other genres quickly filled the space they left behind. Kids' comedy comics, westerns, and romances flourished, while crime and horror comics grew in popularity with each passing year as readers flocked to their violent, gory tales. By the early 1950s, crime and horror series had a considerable presence at newsstands across the country. Books like *Crime Does Not Pay, Vault of Horror,* and *Teen-Age Dope Slaves* stood out from their tamer counterparts with eye-catching titles and lurid artwork.

None of this went unnoticed. Postwar American society consisted of a revolving series of moral panics over any perceived threat to the bland harmony of the white, patriarchal hegemony. From communists to drug fiends to sexual perversion, middle-class Americans felt like they were constantly under attack. One major moral panic centered on a perceived juvenile delinquency epidemic, as parents worried that their kids might be getting up to no good. They weren't. Delinquency levels were no higher than usual. But parents were anxious nonetheless, and on the lookout for nefarious influences that could lead their innocent children astray.

Dr. Fredric Wertham provided a convenient scapegoat with his 1954 book *Seduction of the Innocent.* Wertham was a psychiatrist focused on the care of young Americans, and he'd grown concerned about comics. As he explained in the book's opening chapter, "Slowly, and at first reluctantly, I have come to the conclusion that this chronic stimulation, temptation and seduction by comic books [. . .] are contributing factors to many children's maladjustment." *Seduction of the Innocent* sold well, and was even excerpted in *Ladies' Home Journal* and *Reader's Digest.*

Wertham's popularity was impactful but fleeting. He's a largely forgotten figure today, apart from scores of comic book fans who continue to vilify him and his work. They view *Seduction of the Innocent* as a hit job, an unsubstanti-ated screed against comics that ended a creatively rich era of the medium and led to watered-down content for decades. He's been pilloried as a "self-righteous shrink," the "Josef Mengele of funnybooks," and a "publicity-seeking German quack."

While Wertham was German, he wasn't a quack. After earning his medical doctorate, he immigrated to the United States in 1922 to work at Johns Hopkins Hospital before moving to the Bellevue Mental Hygiene Clinic in New York City in 1932. Much of his work was remarkably progressive for the time. In 1946, he opened the Lafargue Clinic in Harlem to provide low-cost psychiatric care to underserved Black and Latin American youth. His research on the harm-ful effects of segregation was used in the *Brown v. Board of Education* case in the early 1950s, and he also testified on behalf of Soviet spy Ethel Rosenberg in 1953, arguing that solitary confinement was cruel and jeopardized her mental health. Wertham used his work to make a difference in lives that were often forgotten or dismissed.

That's not to say that *Seduction of the Innocent* was good. It was riddled with a host of issues. But it came from good intentions. Wertham genuinely cared about the "mental hygiene" of children and teens, and he believed that the extreme violence in crime and horror comics were harmful to them. Plus, the comics were violent. Some were artfully done while others were intentionally and outlandishly provocative, but they were all graphically gory and gruesome, focused on assault and murder. Wertham also made compelling observations about how children read comics. With the bulk of each story dedicated to crimi-nal activities and brutality and the perpetrator punished only at the very end, he argued that the books served as how-to manuals for misdeeds. Moreover, readers easily missed the moral of the story as the quick resolution was buried under the mass of carnage that preceded it.

But Wertham went overboard, tackling comics from every angle with nearly four hundred pages of fervent, single-minded focus. He clearly had contempt for the medium, arguing that children should be reading "real" literature and that comics could lead to a rise in illiteracy. He also ignored the fact that reading comics wasn't unique to delinquents. Almost every child in America read comic books, with no ill effects for the vast majority of them. Recent research has also shown that in his fervor, Wertham conflated and exaggerated the accounts of his patients, leaving out important details and context that could contradict his critique of the medium. Despite his claim that he "slowly" and "reluctantly" determined that comics were a problem, once he arrived at this conclusion he went full steam ahead in tying every ill to their influence.

Although crime and horror comics were Wertham's main focus, he didn't spare the superhero genre. He stated, "If I were asked to express in a single sentence what has happened mentally to many American children during the last decade I would know no better formula than to say that they were conquered by Superman." For Wertham, superhero comics were a subset of crime comics, rampant with all the same evils and vices and just as harmful for young minds.

Violence and crime were the book's primary concerns, but *Seduction of the Innocent* is best remembered for Wertham's discussion of Batman and Robin. He painted a lush picture of their partnership as he wrote, "At home they lead an idyllic life. [. . .] They live in sumptuous quarters, with beautiful flowers in large vases, and have a butler, Alfred. Batman is sometimes shown in a dressing gown." He then concluded, "It is like a wish dream of two homosexuals living together," and decried the pederastic connotation of the Dynamic Duo when he declared that "only someone ignorant of the fundamentals of psychiatry and of the psychopathology of sex can fail to realize a subtle atmosphere of homo-eroticism which pervades the adventures of the mature 'Batman' and his young friend 'Robin.'" For Wertham, the homoerotic undertones in the comics were clear as day. Batman and Robin were wholly devoted to each other, creating an atmosphere that was "homosexual and anti-feminine."

Wertham provided testimonial evidence for his outlandish claims, citing several patients who were supposedly "influenced" by Batman comics. These queer teens saw themselves in Robin, and were intrigued by the idea of living with someone like Batman. However, Dr. Carol Tilley's recent research into Wertham's records shows that these testimonies were manipulated. Wertham combined different accounts and left out key information. In one glaring omission, he cited a teen who was attracted to Batman but failed to mention that he was actually far more interested in the Sub-Mariner and Tarzan. He also carefully trimmed the words of another patient to make him seem more familiar with Batman comics than he actually was.

Altogether, Wertham made bizarre assumptions about Batman and Robin and then adjusted his patients' statements to support them. It was shoddy work, and shoddier psychiatric care. Clearly his patients were young homosexuals searching for a hint of representation and recognition in a culture that shunned them, but Wertham's homophobia got in the way of him realizing this fact.

He applied the same wrongheaded zeal to Wonder Woman, calling her "a horror type" who was "the Lesbian counterpart of Batman." His distaste for Wonder Woman ran deep, and he wrote, "While she is a frightening figure for boys, she is an undesirable ideal for girls, being the exact opposite of what girls are supposed to want to be." His evidence for this was minimal. With Batman and Robin, Wertham at least presented a series of stereotypes and falsified tes-timonies. With Wonder Woman, who actually had a steady boyfriend in Steve Trevor, Wertham simply quoted an editorial that said her comics portrayed an "extremely sadistic hatred of all males in a framework which is plainly Lesbian," then called Wonder Woman "definitely anti-masculine" because she and her friends, the Holliday Girls, regularly rescued each other.

That was the extent of his argument. He didn't think he needed any more evidence because, as he wrote of female heroes generally, "They do not work. They are not homemakers. They do not bring up a family." That was enough for him to label Wonder Woman a lesbian. Wertham underscored this elsewhere in the book when he stated, "A homoerotic attitude is also suggested by the presentation of masculine, bad, witchlike or violent women." A woman fighting crime instead of staying at home raising a family was inherently unacceptable, so outside of the natural order that clearly she must be a lesbian.

Throughout *Seduction of the Innocent*, Wertham assumed a set of narrow gender norms that affected how he approached these characters. Men could be heroes. As much as Wertham hated crime comics, he was upset with the violence and racism that came with men fighting crime, not men taking on a heroic role. Mistaking familial love for homoeroticism spoke to a limited perspective on male emotion that stripped warmth and affection from masculinity. His vision of men was stalwart and emotionless, very much in line with how men were viewed in the dominant culture of the time.

For women, strength and independence was inherently antifeminine. A woman without a man was a "morbid ideal," and heroism of any sort was entirely out of the question. Women were meant to be homemakers and mothers, calm and gentle and concerned with the domestic sphere rather than the outside world. Again, Wertham's views reflected the standards for women in the mid-1950s. For all his progressive stances elsewhere, he was very much in line with the restrictive gender roles of postwar America.

Seduction of the Innocent came out at an opportune time, just as Senator Estes Kefauver was launching an investigation into juvenile delinquency, and Wertham didn't hold back when he appeared before his Senate subcommittee. He called comics "smut and trash" in his opening statement, and later declared that "Hitler was a beginner compared to the comic book industry" as he outlined his main arguments against the injurious effects of the medium. Wertham was followed by William Gaines, the editor of famed crime comics publisher EC Comics, who performed poorly and painted himself into a corner when he had to defend an EC Comics cover with a severed head and a bloody ax as "within the bounds of good taste." The hearings made the front page of the *New York Times* the next day, and soon there were reports of mass comic book burnings in towns across America.

These developments sent shockwaves through the comic book community. Fearing government reprisal, a consortium of publishers led by Archie Comics and DC Comics banded together to form the Comics Magazine Association of America and deal with their sinking reputation. Publicly, the CMAA planned to implement a content code that would ensure their books were wholesome and unobjectionable. More privately, they wanted to wipe out crime and horror comics entirely and take out several competitors in the process.

The CMAA hired New York magistrate Charles F. Murphy to run the Comics Code Authority, a watchdog group to approve comic books based on a strict content code. Using Archie Comics' in-house regulations as a guide, the preamble to the code promised that "violations of standards of good taste, which might tend toward corruption of the comic book as an instructive and wholesome form of entertainment, will be eliminated." The CCA banned the words "crime" and "horror" from titles, effectively ending the genres, and came down hard on violence. It stated that "if crime is depicted it shall be as a sordid and unpleasant activity," insisted that "scenes of excessive violence shall be prohibited," and emphasized that "in every instance good shall triumph over evil and the criminal punished for his misdeeds."

"Marriage and Sex" garnered its own section of the code, and it was similarly thorough. The new rules included, "illicit sex relations are neither to be hinted at nor portrayed," "passion or romantic interest shall never be treated in such a way as to stimulate the lower and baser emotions," and "sex perversion or any inference to same is strictly forbidden." Most importantly, the CCA declared outright that "the treatment of live-romance stories shall emphasize the value of the home and the sanctity of marriage."

Every comic book issue that passed the agency's close inspection was printed with a small logo on the cover that read "Approved by the Comics Code Authority." This seal of approval became a requirement for distribution across the country. Retailers refused to sell books without it, and any publisher that failed to follow the rules or submit their comics to the CCA didn't last long in this new environment. Many publishers went out of business in the years following the code's implementation, and their competitors quickly swooped in to take over their spots on the newsstands.

Not without major changes, though. At DC Comics, the "Marriage and Sex" portion of the code was of primary interest to the publisher's still-reeling editors. They took Wertham's stance against violence to heart, lessening their violent content and shifting villains from common criminals to more fantastical foes like monsters and aliens, but their biggest concern lay elsewhere. Wertham's allegations of homosexual undertones in their books loomed large, and had long-lasting effects on their lineup.

In 1954, homosexuality was essentially illegal in America. Sodomy was a felony in every state in the union, and the country had just gone through the "Lavender Scare" in which homosexual employees were purged from the federal government. Homosexuality was viewed in the same vein as communism, a subversive element that threatened American society and its values.

No one at DC wanted their characters to be associated with homosexuality in any way. Everyone at the publisher knew Batman, Robin, and Wonder Woman weren't gay, but that wasn't enough. They had to go further to reassert the heterosexuality of their core characters. To do so, they adopted Wertham's narrow view of gender norms as they realigned their entire superhero lineup.

Batman was the publisher's top priority, and editor Jack Schiff made sure readers knew the Caped Crusader was straight in the most direct way possible: by giving him a girlfriend. She was Kathy Kane, an heiress and former circus performer who, inspired by Batman, decided to use her wealth and skills to fight crime as Bat-Woman. The new heroine debuted on the cover of *Detective Comics* #233 in July 1956, racing ahead of the Batmobile on her Bat-cycle as she smiled back at Batman, and the story's opening page heralded her as a "mysterious and glamorous girl." Her debut cemented her purpose twice over. First, she romanced Bruce Wayne as Kathy Kane, dancing with him at a society party as they flirted. Second, she romanced Batman as Bat-Woman, tenderly cradling his head after he was injured in a fight. By the issue's end, both characters were smitten with each other in both of their identities.

There was much more to Bat-Woman than just romance, though. Schiff brought in Edmond Hamilton to write her first issue, an intriguing choice given he usually worked on the Superman line. Hamilton was married to writer Leigh Brackett, a mainstay in science fiction pulp books, and their union had improved his writing enormously. A decade after they wed, his formerly pedestrian work showed new depths and his female characters had far more agency, with his peers crediting Brackett's influence for his growth.

Throughout Bat-Woman's debut, Hamilton established her as a daring and proficient heroine. She built her own Bat-cave and her own gadgets, and showed herself to be a capable crimefighter time and again, even saving Batman a few times. The Dynamic Duo were incredulous about their new female associate, with Batman telling her, "This is no place for a girl—please let me handle it!" and Robin exclaiming to Batman, "A girl saving **you**? It's ridiculous!" But despite their constant disapproval, Bat-Woman proved them wrong at every turn.

She was back a few months later, but the story had a different tone. Hamilton was no longer at the helm, and Bat-Woman became the butt of the joke for the entire outing after she wrongly assumed an amnesiac athlete was Batman and the real Batman told Robin to play along as she nursed him back to health. This became the norm moving forward. Bat-Woman was always a step behind the Dynamic Duo, held at arm's length and kept in the dark, her overconfidence often leading her to folly. She was smart, but not as smart as Batman. Capable, but not as capable as Batman.

Detective Comics #233, art by Sheldon Moldoff, DC Comics, 1956. Bat-Woman was introduced to prove Batman and Robin weren't gay.

That's because, despite Hamilton's best efforts to start her off on the right foot, her original purpose was paramount. She wasn't there to be smart and capable. She was there to be in love with Batman, and he with her. Kathy and Bruce dated regularly, Bat-Woman and Batman flirted often, and a series of "imaginary stories" imagined a future where the two wed and had children. Schiff also went a step further, eliminating any lingering questions about the other half of the Dynamic Duo when he introduced Kathy Kane's niece Bette as Bat-Girl in 1961 to be a romantic interest for Robin.

The Bat-Woman era lasted eight years, until Schiff retired in 1964 and new editor Julius Schwartz decided to take the Bat-line in a more mature direction. Bat-Woman was dropped unceremoniously, having served her purpose by shining a spotlight on Batman's heterosexuality for a full decade after *Seduction of the Innocent* brought it into question. All the while, she also confirmed another tenet of the new DC Comics, that women weren't as good at superheroism as men.

Wonder Woman did the same as part of DC's campaign to counter Wertham's allegations of lesbian undertones. William Moulton Marston died in 1947, and while new writer Robert Kanigher didn't carry on his feminism or fetishism as strongly, *Wonder Woman* didn't change too drastically. Artist H. G. Peter stayed on board as well, furthering this continuity. Peter drew a sturdy Wonder Woman, emphasizing her strength and capturing a classic albeit outdated approach to beauty that grew increasingly flat and static over the years.

This all changed with *Wonder Woman* #98 in May 1958. Peter was replaced by Ross Andru and Mike Esposito, and their modern style left Peter's unique approach behind. Their Wonder Woman was lithe and curvaceous, with long, flowing hair and lots of dynamic posing. Making Wonder Woman conventionally attractive emphasized her femininity in a socially acceptable way, marking a clear break from her earlier, supposedly lesbian incarnation.

The writing emphasized this break. In years previous, Steve Trevor had been madly in love with Wonder Woman, but his feelings weren't wholly reciprocated. She was busy fighting monsters and deities, and Steve was left to admire her from afar. In this new era, they were now an item. Many stories began with them out on a date, and Steve proposed marriage regularly. While he was always rebuffed, Wonder Woman was regretful. She'd explain, "I **can't** marry you—until my services are no longer needed to battle crime and injustice! Only **then** can I think about myself." She wanted to marry Steve, but her annoying superhero gig was in the way.

She further explained, "How can I become your wife 100 percent of the time—and also fulfill my mission as an Amazon and help anyone in distress?" and later added, "It would be unfair to marry you unless I could be a full-time wife!" These weren't empty excuses either. She urged Steve to wait for the day her services would no longer be needed so that they could be together, and went out of her way to soothe his hurt feelings.

The refusals were a key genre convention. Love triangles and romantic hijinks provided great story fodder, and a marriage would bring all of that to a halt. That's why Lois Lane didn't marry Superman and Bat-Woman didn't marry Batman. It would eliminate the tension between them, and all the stories it provided. Wonder Woman was never going to marry Steve, but now her attitude was completely different. She lamented that she couldn't, pining for the day that they could settle down as husband and wife, and spent all of her non-superheroing time with him on romantic outings.

Soon after this shift, Kanigher, Andru, and Esposito introduced a Wonder Girl feature to explore the amazing Amazon's teenage adventures. She got up to hijinks around Paradise Island, tackling an assortment of mythical opponents, but young Diana had time for romance as well. Her regular beau was Ronno the Mer-Boy, who lived in a nearby mer-city. The two went on adventures together, as well as more conventional dates like undersea dances. Wonder Girl's romance made clear that even when she lived in an all-female society, she was still firmly heterosexual.

DC's treatment of Wonder Woman was markedly different from the publisher's approach to Batman. His mission remained the same; he just flirted with Bat-Woman now. He certainly never saw his career as a nuisance or wished he wasn't needed anymore so he could be a good husband. Quitting was never on the table. In fact, the "imaginary stories" that explored his future showed him still fighting crime decades later while Bat-Woman was retired. Meanwhile, Wonder Woman's entire outlook had changed. She was less devoted to her work, preoccupied with proving her love to her boyfriend so he'd stick around long enough for her to be able to marry him. The expectations for men and women were worlds apart, and this continued as DC's superhero line grew.

With many of their competitors now out of business, DC expanded their output rapidly by returning to superheroes. Forgotten characters like the Atom, the Flash, and Green Lantern were updated and reimagined for a new generation, with origins and story lines that tied into modern science as the dawn of the space age began. They were intrepid heroes who battled intergalactic threats and explored new worlds and dimensions. Despite the limitations of the Comics Code, this era is heralded for its creativity and is remembered as the Silver Age of superhero comic books.

The vast majority of these new leads were men, and the only regular female characters in their books were their beleaguered girlfriends. Iris West was left to wonder why Barry Allen was always late for their dates, wholly unaware he was racing around Central City as the Flash. Jean Loring was similarly in the dark about her boyfriend Ray Palmer's gig as the Atom. Carol Ferris occasionally manifested superpowers and became Star Sapphire, but she then used those abilities to try to convince Green Lantern to marry her, unaware that he was actually her frustratingly unreliable employee, Hal Jordan.

Lois Lane launched her own series in 1958, joining Wonder Woman as DC's only female characters to headline books. It was called *Superman's Girl Friend Lois Lane*, and her adventures bore out this title. She spent as much time trying to marry Superman as she did tracking down stories for the *Daily Planet*, and many of her outings ended in tears. Superman's teenage cousin Supergirl debuted in 1959 and launched a backup feature in *Action Comics* soon after, but her activities were limited as well. The Man of Steel kept her hidden away as his secret weapon, leaving her in an orphanage where she spent the bulk of her time helping other children find a good home.

Men could be superheroes full-time with romance as a secondary plotline, if not tertiary. It wasn't a priority, apart from underscoring their heterosexuality. For women, marriage was a constant preoccupation. They were bastions of the nuclear family, and were written explicitly to highlight the CCA's injunction to "emphasize the value of the home and the sanctity of marriage." Even young Supergirl got involved, creating new families from her orphanage because she wasn't yet old enough to have her own.

The Comics Code Authority wasn't solely responsible for this growing discrepancy. Everything happening at DC Comics in the late 1950s was a reflection of American society as a whole. However, the code captured a snapshot of these values in 1955 and wove it into the DNA of the superhero genre. The Comics Code stayed in place, with occasional revisions, for another fifty years, allowing these values to continue on even as the world changed dramatically.

CHAPTER 3

Marvelous

In 1960, DC Comics decided to capitalize on the success of their superhero renaissance and bring the characters together in one all-star series. *Justice League of America* starred Aquaman, Batman, the Flash, Green Lantern, Martian Manhunter, Superman, and Wonder Woman, working together to defeat villains too nefarious for any one member to handle on their own. The book was full of bold, imaginative stories that tested the mettle of the heroes with each issue, but the gender breakdown remained as stale as the rest of DC's line. Wonder Woman was the only female member of the team, outnumbered six to one. The disparity grew as the team expanded over the following years, with the Atom, Green Arrow, and Hawkman added to the ranks. This tokenism continued when the Justice League's blockbuster success inspired a competitor to get back in the superhero business.

Martin Goodman had seen a lot in his twenty-five years as a publisher. He started Timely Comics after Superman and Batman became instant hits, and found winners with the Human Torch, the Sub-Mariner, and Captain America before the superhero bubble collapsed. He chased trends from then on, changing the company name to Atlas Comics as he tried to stay relevant with romance, horror, and western books. Nothing really caught on, and the publisher became a small operation, so small that Goodman's wife's cousin Stanley Lieber wrote most of their comics, using the name Stan Lee. Despite their best efforts, a hit book eluded them.

Then DC's booming superhero relaunch caught Goodman's attention. He wanted a superteam of his own, so he once again renamed the company and gave Lee the task of bringing the genre to Marvel Comics. By this point, Lee was burnt out and considering a career change. He'd been writing comics for nearly two decades and had little to show for it. With a possible exit on the horizon, he decided to go for broke with his latest assignment and turned to artist Jack Kirby for help. Aside from his time overseas during World War II, Kirby had been a workhorse in the comics industry ever since cocreating Captain America twenty years before, bouncing around from publisher to publisher. Marvel was his latest home, and he approached the project with his customary verve.

Reports differ on the exact origins of Lee and Kirby's new superhero team. Lee claimed it was all his idea, that he came to Kirby with a synopsis for a relatable, flawed family of heroes that would contrast well with DC's one-dimensional paragons of virtue. Kirby countered that he was responsible for crafting the bulk of this new concept, which had strong similarities to his work on another team, DC's Challengers of the Unknown. Whatever the case, both Lee and Kirby agreed upon a synopsis for the first issue, which Kirby drew before Lee then added the dialogue. Their new team premiered in November 1961 when *Fantastic Four* #1 hit newsstands across the country.

The core concept was quintessentially Silver Age. Scientist Reed Richards was determined to launch his rocket and beat "the commies" into space, despite the risk from potentially harmful cosmic rays. He was joined by his pilot, Ben Grimm; his girlfriend, Sue Storm; and Sue's brother, Johnny. Their launch was successful, but the rays penetrated the ship and altered the passengers, giving them superpowers. Reed became elastic and took on the name Mister Fantastic, Ben changed into a craggy rocklike being known as the Thing, Sue could turn invisible and was named the Invisible Girl, and Johnny was able to burst into flame and fly so he called himself the Human Torch. Together they decided to use their new abilities to help mankind.

While this origin wouldn't have been out of place in a DC comic book, Lee and Kirby's execution immediately set *Fantastic Four* apart. The members of the Justice League were an amiable group who got along well and met every challenge with poise and professionalism. The Fantastic Four were not. They bickered often, before and even during missions, their personalities clashing constantly. Reed was a know-it-all, Johnny a hotshot, and Ben embittered over being turned into a monster. They were like a real family, loving each other deep down even though they had a history of animosity and squabbles. It was a unique dynamic that made the series something new and different for readers.

The style of the book was surprising as well. There were no colorful costumes, no capes, no masks. The Fantastic Four wore plain clothes for their first few outings before shifting to functional blue uniforms. Kirby's bombastic approach was evident throughout, with fierce arguments and even fiercer battles with their outrageous foes. Every issue was a potent mix of emotion and action, a nonstop roller coaster that bordered on chaos some months.

These displays of emotion were a new development for the genre, especially for male heroes. Batman, Superman, and the rest of DC's men were even keeled and generically pleasant, if casually chauvinistic. They represented what men of the time thought themselves to be, measured and resolute, a shining example for all. Reed, Ben, and Johnny, on the other hand, reflected what men of the time actually were, perhaps unintentionally. Lee saw them as charming heroes, but their foibles highlighted troubling facets of masculinity in this era.

Reed led the team, though he often seemed ill equipped for the job. He was arrogant and rude, hiding his controlling nature under the guise of calm, collected rationality. Because of his genius intellect, he assumed he knew best in every situation and dismissed any form of dissension with cold severity. Ben was Reed's opposite, ruled by his feelings and prone to angry outbursts. His disfigured appearance was a blow to his ego and he lashed out constantly, unable to contain his wounded fury. Johnny was a mix of the two thanks to his youth, both arrogant and quick to anger, caring more about his own desires than the feelings of the group.

And then there was Sue, a grown woman nicknamed the Invisible Girl. It was a fitting title given her role in the book. She was a background player, rarely driving the action. Instead, she served as a mediator between the bickering men, a den mother who tried to keep the volatile team from descending into disorder. She took on matronly duties as well, like domestic tasks at the Fantastic Four's headquarters, though even that came with little peace. When the team returned from a mission and Sue announced, "Hmmm, I think **I'd** better do a little housecleaning!" Reed was quick to bark back, "Just so long as you do it **silently!**"

Sue also served as eye candy, there for the men to fight over. Reed and Ben were her initial suitors, beginning in the book's first issue when Sue called Reed "darling," and Ben angrily shouted, "**Bah!** How can you care for that weakling when **I'm** here?" He then snapped a tree in half and swung the trunk at Reed as he declared, "I'll **prove** to you that you love the wrong man, Susan!"

Ben's jealousy led to more conflict in the months that followed until that love triangle went by the wayside when Namor the Sub-Mariner returned to Marvel Comics. Now a villain bent on ending mankind, Namor was instantly infatuated when he first saw Sue and declared, "Well! **Here** is a prize worth catching! You're the loveliest human I've ever seen!" The boys defeated Namor, but Sue stayed in touch with him from then on, to Reed's regular consternation, cautiously flirting with him and trying to convince the world that he was just misunderstood.

One key component of Marvel's new approach to superheroes was serializing the narrative. Rather than resetting to the established status quo at the end of each issue like DC did, Marvel stories were ongoing sagas that were allowed to grow and change. Thus, unlike DC's heroes, Sue and Reed could get married, and they did in 1965. The marriage did little to change Reed's condescending ways, however. He continued to talk down to Sue, and in one infamous panel he proclaimed, "Wives should be **kissed**—and not heard!"

Fantastic Four #4, art by Jack Kirby and Sol Brodsky, Marvel Comics, 1962. Mister Fantastic, the Human Torch, and the Thing teamed up to save the captured Invisible Girl.

The fight scenes in *Fantastic Four* also highlighted the gender imbalance on the team. Reed was everywhere at once as he stretched himself far and wide to ensnare villains, Ben clobbered everyone in sight, and Johnny blazed through the sky while unleashing fiery attacks on their foes. Sue was there too, off to the side, usually subdued already.

While Sue's invisibility could have been useful, it rarely helped. It was often an indication of fear, like when she first saw footage of the rampaging Hulk and disappeared because "the sight of that monster unnerved me so that I lost control of my visibility power!" Sue also stumbled into traps frequently, leading to her capture. After falling for Dr. Doom's manipulative hallucinations in one issue, she apologized: "Reed . . . dearest! I've been such a **fool**!" Reed helpfully replied, "Not a fool, Sue . . . merely a **female**! You **couldn't** have reacted differently!!"

Sue's limited role didn't go unnoticed by fans. One letter in an early issue read, "I think Susan Storm ought to be thrown out. She never does anything." Other fans disagreed, but they wanted to keep Sue around more for her appearance than her skills. As another fan explained a few issues later, "If you ever throw that doll out, I want to know where you throw her, because I'm making a bee-line for the place!"

Lee and Kirby addressed the topic directly in *Fantastic Four* #11, when Sue read fan letters that said she didn't contribute enough and that the team would be better off without her. Sue was devastated, and Reed and Ben immediately leapt to her defense—sort of. Reed launched into a lengthy monologue about how much Abraham Lincoln admired his mother, who was "the most important person in the world to him" even though "she didn't help him fight the Civil War! She didn't split rails for him! She didn't battle with his enemies!" Basically, Reed argued that Sue was valuable because she inspired the team, even though she did little else. The following issue doubled down on this sentiment. After Sue told General Ross she wasn't sure how she could help capture the Hulk, the general exclaimed, "A pretty young lady can **always** be of help—just by keeping the men's **morale** up!" Reed immediately agreed: "That's the way **we** feel about Sue, General!"

Fantastic Four seemed designed to undercut Sue at every turn in favor of letting the men do all the superhero work, but a closer look at the series shows some discrepancies. After their first issue, Lee and Kirby continued to put the book together in the same manner, with Kirby drawing it before Lee added the dialogue in what is now known as the Marvel method. Most comic books began with a script that had full dialogue and panel descriptions, and the artist worked off of that. The Marvel method began with a synopsis instead, and in Lee and Kirby's case there was rarely even that. As Lee explained in 1968, "Some artists, such as Jack Kirby, need no plot at all. I mean I'll just say to Jack, 'Let's let the next villain be Dr. Doom' . . . or I may not even say that. He may tell me. And then he goes home and does it."

This lack of planning explains why sometimes the text didn't match the pictures. Pop culture historian Kate Willaert's *Kirby Without Words* project showcases this disconnect by pairing printed panels with Kirby's textless artwork. In many instances, Lee worked around Kirby's artwork to make his own take on the story fit better. Sometimes these discrepancies were funny, like when Kirby drew a character with their mouth open, clearly speaking, but Lee's interpretation of the tale required that dialogue go to someone else. The character would be left hanging, unaddressed, their mouth agape. But other times, Lee ignored the artwork to fundamentally change a plot point, and these changes often came at the expense of Sue's agency.

In one example, Kirby showed Sue pointing at the television, seemingly connecting the news report with the Puppet Master's plans she'd witnessed while captured earlier, and the team zoomed off to investigate in the following panel. With dialogue, Sue simply suggested they go help with the unfolding situation, and it was Reed who deduced the connection to the Puppet Master. In another issue, Kirby had Sue sneak up behind the Red Ghost, envelop him in a force field, and knock his gun away to save Reed. She still did the same in the print version, but Lee had Reed explain, "Sue, honey . . . you didn't **have** to! His gun was **empty** . . . though he didn't **know** it!!" thus invalidating her efforts.

There's a degree of interpretation in comparing artwork and finished panels, to be sure, but sometimes Kirby's intentions were crystal clear. A panel in *Fantastic Four* #43 showed Sue lunging forward, obviously furious and spoiling for a fight, with Reed holding her back. Kirby's margin notes on the original inked artwork for this page confirmed this dynamic as Reed cautioned her, "Easy, Sue!" Yet Lee's dialogue told a different story. Instead of taking matters into her own hands, Sue said, "**Stop him**, Reed! They **can't** defeat us again!" Reed became the active party once more, and he solemnly promised, "They **won't**, Sue! I **swear** it!"

Sue's role in *Fantastic Four* was minor regardless of these discrepancies. Her superheroic exploits paled in comparison to Reed, Ben, and Johnny, in the art and in the text. At the same time, it seems clear that Kirby wanted Sue to be more involved while Lee wanted the men to drive all the action and went out of his way to sideline Sue. It's perhaps telling that Lee consistently gave Sue's action to Reed, the controlling, often chauvinistic architect of the team. Lee was the architect of the new Marvel superhero line, with a hand in every series that followed *Fantastic Four*, and his poor handling of female characters continued throughout the growing slate.

Marvel debuted several new solo heroes in the wake of *Fantastic Four*'s success, all of them men. The Incredible Hulk came first, and Spider-Man, Thor, Ant-Man, and Iron Man followed soon after. By late 1963, Goodman and Lee decided it was time for another team book, and they brought several of their new characters together to create the Avengers.

Like *Justice League of America* and *Fantastic Four* before it, *Avengers* had one female character in the mix. While Ant-Man had started in a solo feature, his new partner the Wasp debuted just a few short months before the Avengers united, and Lee and Kirby brought her along. She was Janet van Dyne, a young woman whose scientist father died under mysterious circumstances in *Tales to Astonish* #44, and she reached out to one of his colleagues, Dr. Hank Pym, asking him for help. Unbeknownst to her, Hank was also Ant-Man, and the miniscule hero arrived to help her solve the murder.

Also unbeknownst to Janet, she looked exactly like Hank's deceased wife. Upon meeting her, Hank thought, "So much like Maria! If she were not such a child . . ." Her young age was something he had to remind himself of regularly as his infatuation with Janet led him to reveal his secret identity and ask her to be his crimefighting partner. Janet fell for him instantly, making matters even more complicated. He rebuffed her advances but cautioned himself, "I must be careful lest I **do** fall in love with her!" A middle-aged widower infatuated with a young woman who was "not much more than a child" was an odd dynamic for a children's comic, certainly. Interestingly, two middle-aged men, Stan Lee and Ernie Hart, wrote the issue. There may have been some projection there, in keeping with the genre's history of men identifying with their heroes and bringing their desires to life via their heroines.

Whatever the case, Lee and Hart endeavored to craft a modern young woman, and in doing so only made clear how little they thought of them. Janet was impulsive and headstrong as the Wasp, rushing into dangerous situations that required Ant-Man to come save her. While initially she said she wanted to be the Wasp to avenge her father's death, she admitted a few issues later, "If he thinks I became the **Wasp** because I like to chase criminals, he's **maaad**!! **He** may go for all that adventure jazz, but **I** go for big, wonderful, dreamy **him**! If only Hank could see me as a **girl**, instead of a costumed crime-fighter!"

The Wasp was just as flighty when she joined the Avengers. She wasn't listed in the cover's roll call, and tagged along as Ant-Man's plus-one. The duo was introduced with Hank condescendingly snarking at a tardy Janet, "I can't see why you have to stop and powder your nose every time we have a mission!" He chastised her again when she was far more interested in "that gorgeous Thor" than the mission at hand, telling her to "stop acting like a love-sick female." Janet did name the team at the first issue's end, but that was her sole contribution to the outing.

Avengers revolved around expansive fight scenes with Marvel's heavy hitters showing off their prowess. Between the Hulk's destructive rage, Iron Man's weaponized armor, and Thor's powerful hammer, there wasn't much room left

Avengers #2, art by Jack Kirby and Sol Brodsky, Marvel Comics, 1963. The minuscule Wasp got lost in the fray.

for anyone else. Ant-Man got in on the action when he learned to reverse his shrinking technology and turned into Giant-Man, adding another behemoth to the roster. Captain America also joined the team a few issues in, and became a mainstay in the melees. There was little for the Wasp to do in the midst of these testosterone-fueled battles. She was tiny and easily lost in the action, as well as considerably weaker than her counterparts. In one issue, she tried to help by slipping inside the villain's suit and disabling its electronics, but in typical Stan Lee fashion, her aid proved useless. The villain quickly regained control of his suit, and Thor had to step in and defeat him properly.

Her limited role didn't go unnoticed by fans. In *Avengers* #13, two readers sent in a letter that read, "We are writing to ask you if you would kick the Wasp out of the Avengers. All she can do is go 'buzz-buzz.' Anyone could smear her with a fly swatter and a can of insect repellent. The Avengers would be a better mag without her." It seemed that Lee agreed. The entire configuration of the team changed a few issues later, with only Captain America staying on, and Ant-Man and the Wasp's feature in *Tales to Astonish* ended soon after. They'd failed to find an audience at the same level as the rest of Marvel's superheroes, and the feature became the first casualty of the new line.

Goodman and Lee didn't spend much, if any, time mourning the loss because the hit rate for the rest of their books was high, including yet another team title. The series starred an all-new cast of teen mutants learning to use their powers for good under the tutelage of Professor Charles Xavier. In an odd if revealing choice, despite the presence of a female member, Lee called the book *X-Men*.

Each student took on a superhero identity related to their superpower. Bobby with his freezing abilities was Iceman, the burly yet acrobatic Hank was the Beast, Scott with his optic blasts was Cyclops, and the winged Warren was Angel. Jean, however, was simply Marvel Girl, with her femininity as her only relevant trait.

In their first adventure, the X-Men faced off against Magneto, an "evil mutant" who hated the human race and aimed to make "homo sapiens bow to homo **superior**!" Some histories suggest that Lee was inspired by the civil rights movement, crafting the peaceful Professor X as an analogue for Martin Luther King Jr. and the more radical Magneto as Malcolm X. This was not the case. The prejudice against mutants that was central to later X-Men stories wasn't present in these early years, nor was Magneto written as anything other than an outright villain initially. While *X-Men* writers drew inspiration from the civil rights movement decades later and Lee eventually claimed credit for the civil rights metaphor, it was not part of his original vision in any way.

Like all of Marvel's teams, the book was male led with only one woman in the mix. Jean Grey joined the X-Men in their first issue, and her introduction set the tone for her role moving forward. Professor X told the boys that their new pupil was "a most attractive **young lady**," and the boys responded by ogling her from afar as Scott called out, "You're **right**, sir! **Wow**! She's a real living doll!" while Warren added, "A **redhead**! Look at that **face** . . . and the **rest** of her!" Jean had powerful telekinetic abilities but played only a minor part in their battle with Magneto, sending a missile off its course to detonate harmlessly in the sea. The boys drove the rest of the action while Jean tagged along behind them and shouted out encouragement.

Jean was an amalgam of Lee's worst tendencies with female characters. Like with Sue, the boys fought over her affections, though it was more of a love pentagon than a love triangle with everyone involved in the ongoing parade of jealousy. Like Janet, she caught the eye of a much older man when Professor X fell for her and had to reprimand himself: "I can never **tell** her! I have no right! Not while I'm the leader of the X-Men, and confined to this wheelchair!" Romance became even more central to Jean's narrative when she realized she had feelings for Scott but was conflicted over acting on them.

As Marvel Girl, Jean's heroics were hit and miss. She went out with the team on every adventure, but was plagued with issues. Overusing her powers caused her to faint, making her a liability during dangerous confrontations. She was prone to extreme fright as well. When they faced a *Tyrannosaurus rex* in one outing, Warren had to warn her not to panic because she was "almost numb with fear!" Meanwhile, the boys' abilities worked without any ramifications and they never ended up paralyzed in terror.

Willaert's *Kirby Without Words* argues that Lee undercut Jean just like he did Sue. In a sequence in *X-Men* #3, the team was captured and Kirby's art showed Jean using her telekinetic powers to remove her blindfold, nab a blade from a passing knife thrower's wagon, and cut her own bonds before freeing everyone else. It was a rare triumphant moment for Jean, one that immediately turned around when Lee added the dialogue. Instead of Jean taking the initiative, thought balloons had Professor X telepathically communicate with her and lead her through each step of the rescue. When an amazed Warren asked, "**Marvel Girl**! How did you manage to free yourself??" she replied, "We have **Professor X** to thank!" Lee never seemed keen to let a young woman take any credit when he could give it to an older, haughty mastermind instead.

Marvel's superhero line was groundbreaking in a great many ways. It represented the next evolution of the genre, moving away from zany yet simple tales with staid characters to bombastic, serialized story lines with more compellingly complex casts. Goodman, Lee, Kirby, and the rest of their fellow creators had changed the game entirely, laying the groundwork for a new, innovative superhero universe that would lead to decades of further comic books and adaptations.

X-Men #1, art by Jack Kirby, Marvel Comics, 1963. Marvel Girl trailed behind as Angel, Beast, Cyclops, and Iceman led the action.

These stories remain the foundation of the Marvel universe today. Unlike DC, where the entire line has been relaunched multiple times, Marvel has never done a full reboot. All these stories are still technically canon, influencing new stories even now. Subsequent issues have added to these original tales, but they've never been replaced. It's not surprising, then, that the skewed dynamics present in the early years of Marvel Comics continued for decades to come. This era established that the actual work of superheroics was a male domain, with masculinity rooted in arrogance and anger. Femininity was linked to weakness and fear, rendering female characters unsuited to save the world.

CHAPTER 4

Mania

Marvel's superheroes took off quickly in the 1960s with an ever-growing slate of comic books, along with Saturday morning cartoons for the Avengers, Fantastic Four, and Spider-Man by the middle of the decade. It was a meteoric rise for a publisher that had just jumped back into the genre on a lark. However, while Marvel's impact on pop culture was significant, the most influential superhero of the 1960s came from DC Comics. Somehow, inexplicably, Batman suddenly became one of the most popular characters in the entire world.

In started in 1964, when ABC wanted an action/adventure television program for an early evening time slot. One executive suggested they look at comic books, and Superman quickly emerged as their top choice. Wisely, too. From cartoon shorts, radio, and film serials in the 1940s to the *Adventures of Superman* TV show starring George Reeves in the 1950s, Superman had been a proven commodity for two decades running. Superman's rights were tied up in an upcoming Broadway musical, however, so the network went with Batman instead.

Batman didn't have the same pedigree as Superman. The character guest-starred on Superman's radio show occasionally in the 1940s, and apart from a couple of middling film serials he'd been relegated to the comics for most of his existence. The comics weren't doing well either. Sales were so low by 1964 that *Batman* and *Detective Comics* were on the verge of cancellation. DC's editorial director, Irwin Donenfeld, gave editor Julius Schwartz six months to improve sales, so Schwartz launched a "New Look" era for Batman that moved away from fantastical, zany narratives. The change stabilized the numbers enough to stave off cancellation, but the books were hardly bestsellers.

ABC offered the Batman show to William Dozier, a veteran producer who had no familiarity with comic books. Intrigued, he bought a handful of old Batman comics with stories that predated the character's "New Look," and the madcap antics sparked an idea. While ABC wanted a hip, modern adventure program, Dozier envisioned the show as a pop art piece. They'd lean into the comic book camp but play it all straight, approaching each wacky supervillain and their elaborate, harebrained schemes with the utmost seriousness. Kids would love the colorful chaos, while parents could laugh at the ironic performances.

The network reluctantly accepted the pitch, and production on *Batman* began in 1965. Dozier cast Adam West, known for TV westerns and a handful of film roles, as Bruce Wayne/Batman, and newcomer Burt Ward played his young ward Dick Grayson/Robin. The two-part pilot pitted the Dynamic Duo against Frank Gorshin as the Riddler, but the ABC executives were not impressed. Then their fall lineup flopped. Needing to fill a hole in their schedule, ABC was forced to run *Batman* despite their qualms, and the series debuted on January 12, 1966.

"Hi Diddle Diddle" aired on Wednesday, and opened with a mysterious riddle that stumped the police. They called in Batman and Robin, who raced from stately Wayne Manor to solve the clue and ended up tracking the Riddler to a discotheque. Batman was drugged and Robin kidnapped, and the episode ended with Robin strapped to a table as the Riddler gleefully wielded a scalpel. The closing narration encouraged viewers to tune in "Tomorrow night! Same time, same channel" for the exciting conclusion.

"Smack in the Middle" followed on Thursday, and revealed that the Riddler was actually making a mold of Robin's face for a mask so his assistant, Molly, could disguise herself as Robin. Her attempts to trick Batman proved futile, and led to her unfortunate demise. Batman ultimately rescued the real Robin and faced off against the Riddler in a brawl with large "KRUNCH! ZLONK! BAM!" sound effects that became a trademark for the series. The Riddler appeared to meet his end in an explosion, but no body was found.

This was the format for the first season, a setup and a cliff-hanger on Wednesday then an escape and a tussle on Thursday. Each week featured a special guest villain, including comic book mainstays like Catwoman, the Joker, and the Penguin, along with a few brand-new foes. The formula was consistent, with little variation apart from the mechanisms of the creatively complex traps each dastardly villain built to try and kill the Dynamic Duo.

The show's debut episode made one fact abundantly clear: Batman was not hip. Dozier admitted as much, calling the character a "very square, hard-nosed guy." He wasn't a dynamic action hero like his comic book counterpart, or angsty and angry like Marvel's heroes. Dozier was inspired by the comics, but not beholden to them and their trends. He viewed Batman through a sardonic Silver Age lens, and what emerged on-screen was something new and unique.

West had a firm grasp on Dozier's approach to Batman, and imbued the character with a corny earnestness that underscored his squareness. When

Batman tracked the Riddler to a new dance club, he remarked, "Odd, the new discotheque," and West pronounced "discotheque" like the word had never left his mouth before. Inside the club, he strode to the bar and ordered himself a "large, fresh orange juice," then danced awkwardly with one of the patrons, his moves jerky and janky. He was far and away the least cool person in the club, but he was also the most confident.

He was even keeled as well, perpetually calm and leading with thoughtful kindness. While Robin could be hotheaded, Batman tempered his rashness with gentle correction. He always had a lesson about good citizenship or law and order at the ready, but he was also quick to praise his sidekick, like when he enthused, "You've done it again, chum!" after Robin solved one of the Riddler's clues. Batman was able to manage Robin's emotions effectively because he was so in tune with his own. He even talked about his failures openly and honestly. After Molly's accidental death, Bruce looked back on the case and admitted to Dick, "I have only one regret in the whole affair, one thing that makes me heartsick. [. . .] If only I could've helped her somehow, weaned her from that tragic alliance with the underworld."

A key factor in Batman's distinctiveness was West's demeanor. He was serenely composed, and spoke his lines slowly and deliberately to illustrate his tranquility. Burt Ward thought that West's unhurried approach was a ploy to garner more screen time, and there may have been something to that. But regardless, the end effect was a calm confidence. The same was true with his appearance. Although Batman was barrel chested in the comics and George Reeves wore padding to beef up his muscular look in the *Adventures of Superman* a decade before, West was just a guy in some tights. He was in good shape, but hardly imposing. Physical intimidation wasn't his game.

All of this added up to a new take on superheroism. West's Batman was corny but compelling, strictly by the books yet compassionate and caring. He wore his heart on his sleeve, and led with warm sincerity. Instead of brawn, he relied on his wits and a utility belt full of tools, and met his frequent capture with a calm optimism. He was a clever nerd more than an action hero, an avuncular square against a bevy of flamboyant foes.

It was a unique combination, and an extremely successful one. *Batman* was the fifth most popular show in America in 1966 with fourteen million viewers per episode, and ABC quickly greenlit a second season. They also made a feature film for an immediate summer release to cash in on their surprise hit between seasons. A Batman craze ensued as Bat-mania swept the nation, with companies churning out scores of merchandise and memorabilia to meet the immense demand. Adam West appeared on the cover of *Life* magazine in his full Batman regalia while the Batusi, his awkward dance at the discotheque, sparked a fad at clubs across the nation.

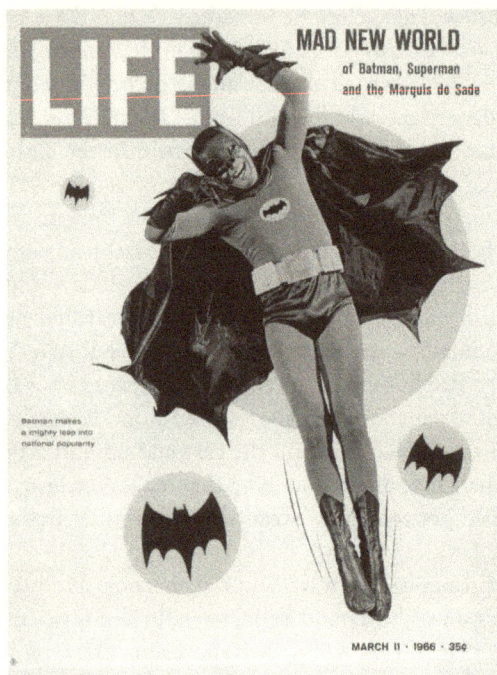

LIFE

MAD NEW WORLD
of Batman, Superman
and the Marquis de Sade

Batman makes
a mighty leap into
national popularity

MARCH 11 · 1966 · 35¢

Life magazine, 1966. Adam West at the height of the nation's Bat-mania.

Batman's first season ran for thirty-four episodes, and ABC bumped that up considerably to sixty episodes for the following season. But by the end of this second run, viewership had dropped precipitously. Whether it was oversaturation, boredom with the formula, or the novelty just wearing off, the Bat-bubble burst as quickly as it had grown. ABC ordered a third season for their 1967–1968 schedule but only commissioned twenty-six episodes. They also abandoned the dual-night format, switching to self-contained episodes once a week instead of the usual cliffhangers as they drastically slashed the budget.

Dozier's pitch for a third season had been no sure thing, but one major addition to the cast intrigued the ABC executives. Catwoman was a fan favorite, so Dozier had asked Schwartz to develop new female characters in the comics that he could use in the show. One in particular caught his eye, so for season three he decided to introduce Batgirl to their dwindling television audience.

Batgirl made her comic book debut earlier in the year in *Detective Comics* #359 with a story written by Gardner Fox and art by Carmine Infantino and Sid Greene. They ignored the existing Bat-Girl to create their own, and the cover showed a redhead in a black costume with a yellow logo as the text proclaimed, "Meet the *new* Batgirl!" The story soon revealed that she was Barbara Gordon, Commissioner Gordon's daughter and a bespectacled "plain Jane" librarian. She sewed herself a Batgirl costume for a masquerade ball, just for fun, but on the way to the event she saw the villain Killer Moth attacking Bruce Wayne on the side of the road and decided to intervene. Luckily she was a judo expert and equipped herself well, and she immediately fell in love with the thrill of crimefighting. She dedicated herself to the craft from then on, training extensively so she could work alongside the Dynamic Duo.

Batman and Robin weren't exactly thrilled to have her around. When she stumbled upon their trap to nab Killer Moth later in the issue, Robin griped, "Holy interference! She's ruining all our plans!" Batman quipped, "We can't let **Batgirl** fight our battles, now can we?" and refused to let her come with them to finish the job because "we can't worry ourselves about a girl." After she swooped in to save them, Batman begrudgingly acknowledged, "I'll welcome her aid, [. . .] when and where the occasion arises!" but this respect proved short lived. When Batgirl next appeared, Batman intentionally misled her about his secret identity, tricking her even though she'd expressed no interest in learning who was behind the cowl.

Subsequent outings showed that DC's writers didn't think too highly of Batgirl either as they relegated her to a run of clichéd stories. In one issue, Batgirl was plagued by vanity as her need to look pretty got in the way of her crimefighting, and she lamented that her "feminine weakness betrayed me so often." In another, Catwoman fought her to prove she deserved Batman's love. Wonder Woman then faced off against Batgirl in a different issue as they battled for Batman's affections. Everything worked out in the end, with Batgirl using her vanity to her advantage and the romances all a ruse, but the stories were generic reworkings of stale premises for female characters, centered on love and physical appearance.

The new Batgirl intrigued Dozier enough for him to add her to the program, and he cast Yvonne Craig in the role. A trained ballet dancer, Craig came to Hollywood a decade before looking for dance work, but she ended up acting and soon appeared on the big screen with icons like Bing Crosby and Elvis Presley. Her dance background gave her an acrobatic physicality that was ideal for Batgirl, and Dozier cast her even though she'd never seen an episode of the show.

Dozier maintained Batgirl's secret identity as librarian Barbara Gordon, though the season three premiere had an entirely new story. It began with the Penguin kidnapping Barbara in order to force her to marry him. The fowl fiend hoped he'd be immune from prosecution once he was related to the police commissioner, but Barbara wasn't having any part of it. She escaped out the window after he locked her in a bedroom, and returned as Batgirl just as the Dynamic Duo arrived. After the Penguin appeared to be defeated, Batgirl fled the scene, but then the Penguin woke up and gassed Batman and Robin. Batgirl followed the villain and his goons to their secret hideout, freed the Dynamic Duo from a death trap, and disappeared once more to take her place as the captive Barbara.

Before Batgirl, Batman's relationship with women on the program had been polite but patronizing. He was old fashioned when it came to gender dynamics and saw women as innocent beings who needed to be protected. Batman was aghast whenever a woman engaged in villainy, like when Zelda the Great kidnapped Dick's aunt Harriet and he exclaimed, "How could a woman stoop to such a trick?" Zelda later reformed and used her skills in magic to entertain children, which pleased him enormously. For Batman, women belonged in the domestic sphere, safe from the city's dark criminal underbelly.

Despite this chauvinistic bent, Batman departed from his comic book counterpart and welcomed Batgirl with enthusiasm when she first appeared. He and Robin were surprised initially, but after seeing her in action Batman remarked, "I don't know who you are, young lady, but you certainly know how to handle yourself well," and Robin chimed in, "Holy agility! I'll say!" After Batgirl was pivotal to solving a case in the following episode, Batman gave her all the credit when he said, "Well, that winds that up, fellow crimefighters, thanks to Batgirl," and when Barbara appeared at the end of the season's third episode to say, "Batman and Robin took care of things perfectly," Robin immediately added, "And don't forget Batgirl!" Batgirl worked independently of the Dynamic Duo, and Batman chose to respect her anonymity. The Dynamic Duo appreciated her assistance, acknowledged her contributions, and refused to pry into her private life.

Later in the season, Batman took a momentarily patronizing turn when he mused, "Perhaps crimefighting is better left to the men, Batgirl. Perhaps not. But this isn't exactly women's work." Batgirl was quick to disagree, and countered, "But I'm no ordinary woman, Batman." Instead of arguing further or getting upset, Batman immediately conceded the point and simply said, "Agreed," thus settling the matter.

The production embraced Batgirl as well. Despite the third season's limited budget, they outfitted Barbara with an apartment, a secret room for transforming into Batgirl, and a purple Bat-cycle. She even had her own catchy theme song when she appeared in the show with lyrics that asked, "Where did you come from? Where did you go? What is your scene, baby, we just gotta know!" The writers emphasized her competence as she built her own costume and gadgets, used her librarian skills for crimefighting research, and often solved cases before the Dynamic Duo. While she was captured regularly, that was a staple of the show. Batman and Robin were as well, and Batgirl rescued them as often as they rescued her.

Then, halfway through the third season, things began to change. Batgirl got captured more and more, nabbed early in the episode and set aside until she was freed at the end of the program. She participated less in the investigations as Batman and Robin came to the fore, and was left out of the regular third-act brawls. Her lessened role felt like a course correction, pulling back from introducing too strong a woman. Dozier was keen on the character, but the network aired *Batman* in their earliest slot and aimed the show at children. They wanted something noncontroversial, and such a liberated female character may have been a step too far for some executives.

When the season wrapped in March 1968, ABC decided not to renew the show, citing the still decreasing ratings. *Batman* almost found new life at NBC, where Robin would've been cut from the program and Batgirl promoted to a larger role, but ABC had already destroyed the sets and NBC didn't want to take on the expense of building new ones. The Bat-bubble had burst for good, leaving DC Comics editors with some big decisions about what to do with their now waning Caped Crusader.

The comics had embraced camp when the show was at its zenith, but now the goofy frivolity had become toxic for readers so Schwartz returned to the grittier "New Look" format. Writer Frank Robbins focused on street-level crime and detective work, without elaborate traps, brawls, or supervillains, especially those who'd been regulars on television. Artists Bob Brown and Irv Novick eschewed the simple, cartoonish style that had been standard for Batman for decades and moved toward a more realistic style that matched the tone of the books. Within a year of the program's cancellation, Schwartz and his team of creators had removed every last vestige of the show from the comics.

This rebranding was inevitable. While the collapse of the show played a significant role in the new direction, the entire superhero industry had changed by the end of the decade. Marvel's books had shifted the audience into an older bracket, with teen readers instead of young kids. Their stories were more mature, angsty, and authentic. Spider-Man was a web-slinging superhero, but his alter ego Peter Parker was bullied at school and struggled to balance his part-time job, romance, and home life. The Hulk appeared to be a big green monster at first glance, but his stories dealt with relevant topics like anger issues and ostracization. Marvel's serialized narratives drew readers in while DC's self-contained, wacky adventures grew increasingly irrelevant.

DC had to change, and a darker Batman was part of this process. The books literally became darker in 1969 when Dick Grayson went to college, removing Robin and his bright, colorful costume from the series. Batman was solo now, a shadowy specter of the night as befit his bat theme. The style of the stories shifted as well. Bruce left Wayne Manor behind for an apartment in downtown Gotham City, yet another way for DC to distance the character from the show, and he worked at the charitable Wayne Foundation by day while Batman haunted the streets of Gotham by night.

The shift in direction served its purpose, but it didn't yet feel entirely new. Robbins, Brown, and Novick were all industry veterans, steeped in the old way of doing things. As much as their work showed a stark evolution, it retained a degree of connection to the previous style that kept the writing a touch flat and the artwork stiff. To push things even further, Schwartz brought in two young talents, Denny O'Neil and Neil Adams. They were both relatively new to the industry, fresh off a surprising revitalization of *Green Lantern/Green Arrow* that dealt with modern topics like racism and drug addiction.

Schwartz let them tackle Batman with *Detective Comics* #395 in January 1970, and "The Secret of the Waiting Graves" sent Bruce Wayne to Mexico, where a series of attacks required Batman's attention. Soon he faced off against a mysterious, wealthy couple who cultivated flowers that made them immortal. Batman stopped their nefarious plans and burned their flowers, causing time to catch up with the duo and end their unnaturally long lives. The story was moody and sinister, tinged with the supernatural in a way that was genuinely eerie. O'Neil's writing amped up the tension, while Adams's dynamic page layouts and use of shadow were visually stunning. Batman had never been like this before. The difference between this outing and the issue previous was like night and day. O'Neil and Adams had changed the game entirely.

Reactions in the *Detective Comics* letter column were effusive. The issue was heralded as an instant classic, with fans enthusing, "What a perfect story! What flawless artwork! What total mood! [. . .] What an all-around masterpiece!" They praised O'Neil for his gripping, fast-paced script, while Adams's art was met with awe. For many, the issue put the final nail in the coffin of the Silver Age Batman and his television counterpart. One reader declared that the "super-goody-good *Caped Cornball* is *dead*," and another echoed his sentiments when he wrote, "At long last the annoying *Batjunk* is gone, and with it the commercialized, exploited, over-exposed *Batman* of yesterday."

The issue became a template for the following decade. Adams's stylized realism was adopted as the house style, not just for the Bat-books but for DC's entire line. Every artist did their best to imitate his distinctive, detailed technique and innovative panel layouts. Narratively, Batman expanded his scope beyond Gotham City, tracking down criminal organizations across the globe. His foes often had supernatural origins, like the menacing Ra's al Ghul, an immortal terrorist bent on remaking society who faced off against Batman in a lengthy, serialized saga.

One constant throughout this era was its consistently dark tone. Batman took on a grim countenance as the books became serious and heavy. He was a brooding hero now, fixated on his endless battle for justice against the many evils of the world. It was a stark change from the previous era, and even a step further than Marvel's line. As much as Marvel's books dealt with dark themes at times, there was always levity. Quips abounded, and there was usually a playful quality to even the darkest story. Not so with Batman, whose crusade dominated his life as he embraced the mantle of the Dark Knight.

The character's unhappiness was also tied to his romantic travails. Sending Robin off to university led to a new lease on life for Batman. He'd been a father figure previously, older and somewhat stolid in contrast with the vibrant

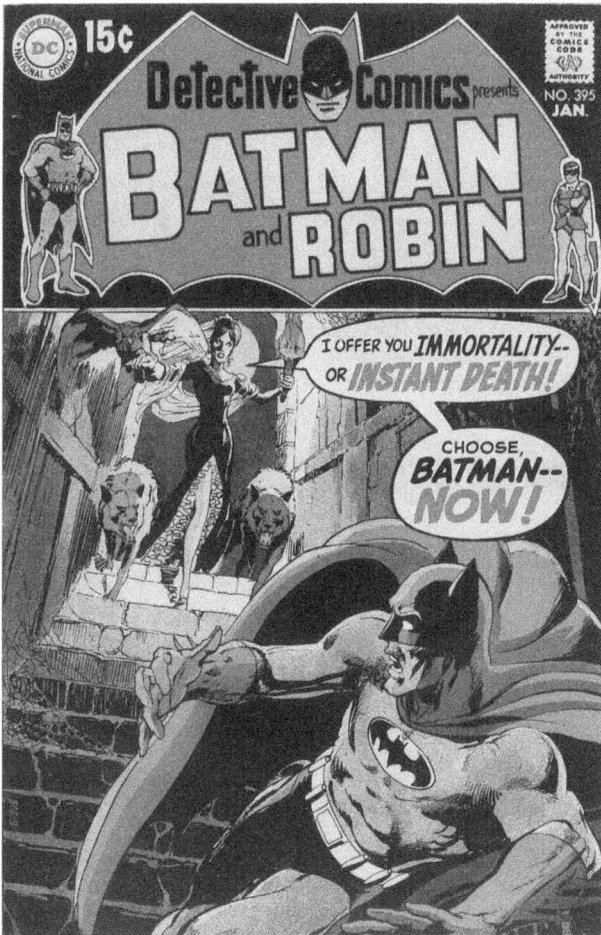

Detective Comics #395, art by Neal Adams, DC Comics, 1970. A turning point that marked Batman's evolution from the bright Caped Crusader to the ominous Dark Knight.

Robin, while Adam West was nearly forty years old when he put on the cowl. Neal Adams brought a new vitality to Batman, turning him into a younger, more muscular specimen. As Batman and Bruce Wayne, the character was often shirtless, posed to emphasize his powerful physique, and women flocked to him. While this era of superhero comics is known as the Bronze Age, for Batman it's more colloquially referred to as his "lothario period."

But the darkness loomed. Batman couldn't trust anyone and Bruce Wayne couldn't reveal his nocturnal escapades, leading to a series of short-term relationships. The romances burned hot and quickly fizzled as the limits of his mission superseded his own desires. Constant breakups only furthered Batman's brooding, and he grew ever more emotionally closed off. He was a solitary figure, with violent crimefighting as his sole reliable outlet.

These romantic failures also had skewed gender implications. Most female characters in Batman's comics were love interests, with little to do beyond that narrow role. Serialization made romance an ongoing plotline in many comics, but never the main story. Women were relegated to this small corner of the narrative, then discarded once the romance reached its inevitable end. It wasn't just Batman either. Even Superman got in on the lothario escapades, dating different women at the same time in his dual identities until each romance ran its course and new ones began.

Batman perfectly encapsulates the direction the superhero genre was heading as the 1970s began. Adam West's bright and congenial Batman, with his earnest enthusiasm and warm support for a new female colleague, was now a pariah. The new Batman was aloof and cold, a grim figure cloaked in shadow. Women were disposable, the world was dark and evil, and Batman met everyone with a perpetual scowl. The changes were spurred by a shifting audience, and the growing darkness slowly spread to the entire genre.

CHAPTER 5

Divergence

In the early 1940s, superhero comics were ubiquitous in schoolyards across America. Books like *Captain Marvel, Superman,* and *Wonder Woman* sold over a million copies per issue, and publishers estimated that each issue was read by approximately five different children. Comics were traded like currency, swapped constantly so that kids could keep up with all the high-flying adventures. Readership was evenly split along gender lines, with boys and girls equally engaged in the new genre. In short, superhero comics were everywhere and everybody read them.

Then the superhero boom collapsed and the uniform audience began to split, with boys migrating to crime books, science fiction, and westerns while girls shifted toward romance. It wasn't a complete division by any means. Some girls read crime books while some boys read romances, and a few genres maintained an even audience. Publishers with kids' comedy books, like Archie Comics and Dell Comics, appealed to all genders. But generally speaking, boys and girls were drifting apart in their comic book taste, and publishers and advertisers began to appeal directly to their dominant demographic.

When DC Comics revitalized their superhero line in the 1950s, they catered to this split. Their few remaining superhero titles had drifted toward male readership over the past decade, much like their western and science fiction books, so they aimed their new series accordingly. With primarily male leads and a strong science fiction angle, boys were the obvious target. Advertisements bore this out, with products aimed either at boys specifically or all genders, and none directed squarely at girls. DC's romance comics, meanwhile, were chock full of ads for young girls, ads that were entirely absent from the superhero line. The publisher divided advertising by genre, so despite a male lead in *Aquaman* and a female lead in *Wonder Woman,* the books had the same batch of ads each month, all male directed or gender neutral. Romance books had a separate, completely different package of female-directed ads. Editors clearly saw superhero reader-ship as a male domain, with a few female readers in the mix but not worth catering to.

While it's obvious that the audience for superhero comics has been male dominated from the Silver Age renaissance onward, we don't have hard data on this gender disparity or how the numbers have evolved over the decades. We do have letter columns, though. Soon after DC's superheroes returned, editors began to print a page of letters from readers in each issue. Marvel followed suit with their superhero line, and letter columns became a lively forum at both publishers, with many series expanding the feature to two pages to accommodate the wealth of submissions.

Each letter column provided a small snapshot of the readership each month, and tracking the gender breakdown of these fans over time can approximate a larger picture of each publisher's audience. It's not an exact science, of course. The letters sent in didn't necessarily capture the audience demographics, nor were editors concerned with the columns accurately reflecting what was submitted. Letters were chosen for a host of reasons. Praise was more likely to be printed than criticism, and letters that stirred up debate were more popular than bland commentary. Some editors were even known to fake letters, planting missives in support of their plotting decisions or to set up hints for future story lines. Despite these caveats, letter columns provide a substantial data set that offers a rough estimation of the audience for superhero comics and how this audience changed.

The chart below shows the percentage of letters written by male readers over three decades, 1960 through 1990, using the combined data of letter col-umns from three long-running DC series: *Batman, Justice League of America*, and *Superman*. The numbers suggest a major shift in the audience for superhero

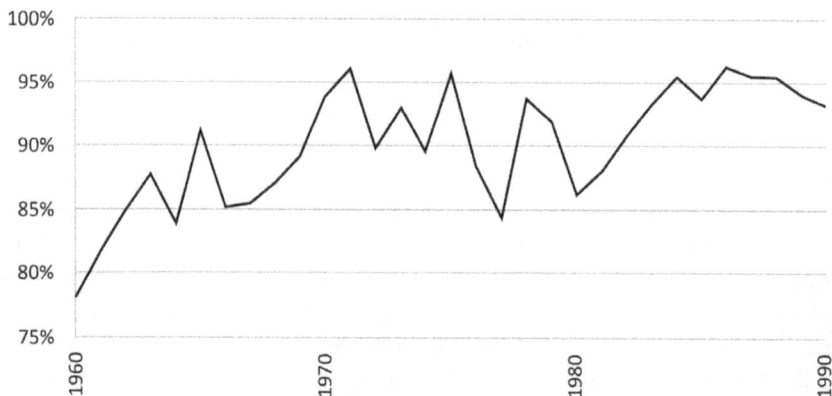

Letters written by male fans in DC Comics letter columns (from *Batman, Justice League of America*, and *Superman*), 1960-1990.

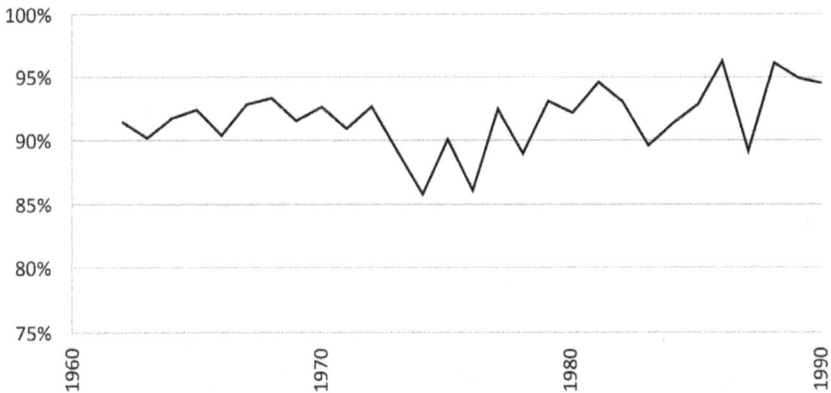

Letters written by male fans in Marvel Comics letter columns (from *Amazing Spider-Man, Avengers,* and *Fantastic Four*), 1962-1990.

comics in this era. The 1960s began as expected, with big numbers for male fans and percentages in the high 70s and mid-80s. By the decade's end, though, the numbers had grown even higher, all the way up into the 90s, where they stayed with some slight variations for the next twenty years. The 1960s were the turning point in this change, with vestiges of the old, somewhat more balanced audience quickly giving way to near-complete male dominance.

Batman, Justice League of America, and *Superman* all had male leads or predominantly male teams, and there was a marked difference between these books and female-led titles. The letter column in *Superman's Girl Friend Lois Lane* averaged only 56 percent letters from male readers in the 1960s, while *Wonder Woman* averaged 71 percent letters from male readers in the 1970s. Female-led books clearly brought in more female readers, but DC had little interest in courting this audience. Lois Lane and Wonder Woman were the only female headliners with sizable runs in this era.

The numbers for Marvel were even more divided. DC had stayed in the superhero game through the 1950s, cultivating a small but not insignificant female readership that carried over into the 1960s, however briefly. Marvel had no such continuity. The chart above shows the percentage of letters written by male readers from 1962, the first full year of letter column data from the new superhero line, through 1990, with data from three long-standing Marvel series: *Amazing Spider-Man, Avengers,* and *Fantastic Four.* Marvel started cold, building an entirely new audience from scratch, and it was male dominated from the get-go. The percentage of male readers in the letter columns began in the low 90s, dipped slightly in the 1970s when the publisher tried to actively court female readers for a brief time, then finished this span up in the mid-90s range. Marvel's superhero line was never meant for girls.

Girls knew it too. In a 1966 issue of *Fantastic Four*, Rosalyn Smith wrote in, "I have yet to see any representation of us females [. . .] on your letters page and, of course, the Bullpen. Is this because I am the only avid female fan of yours or are you prejudiced against the opposite sex?" Stan Lee replied, "Aww, you must be kiddin,' Roz—we've printed a zillion letters from our fascinatin' femme fans over the past five years! [. . .] Never, *never* let it be said that we're not maaaaaaaadly in favor of females! Okay, pussycat?" This was patently untrue. Only one out of every ten letters printed in *Fantastic Four* was from a female fan, and nearly a third of the letter columns published since the book debuted featured no women at all.

Marvel did have a solid base of female fans, just not for their superhero titles. Rom-com series *Millie the Model* boasted a whopping 97 percent female correspondents in the mid-1960s, but Goodman and Lee did little to try and interest them in the publisher's other titles. When Marvel did finally try a female-led superhero series in the 1970s, *Ms. Marvel*, male fans accounted for just 55 percent of the letters, but the publisher failed to hold on to the diverse audience. *Dazzler*, another female-led book, hit comic shops in the early 1980s, and 85 percent of the letters were from male fans, much more in line with the rest of their output.

For both publishers, the 1960s were key to establishing their superhero audience. Beyond gender, the demographics also shifted by age. When DC's letter columns began in the late 1950s, the audience was noticeably young. Letters were short notes, often addressed to Superman or Wonder Woman directly, and the editors replied to their fans in character. A decade later, letters were longer and more detailed, sent to the editors by name as readers delved into storytelling choices and continuity issues. Fans were much older now, many of them teens and even young adults.

This was largely due to Marvel, whose stories had cultivated a more mature audience. So mature, in fact, that a 1966 poll in *Esquire* magazine found that college students' top revolutionary icons included not just Bob Dylan and Che Guevara, but also the Hulk and Spider-Man. Marvel's innovative storytelling resonated with older readers, and many fans continued to follow the ongoing dramatics of their favorite characters into adulthood instead of growing out of the genre. By 1967, Marvel's sales had eclipsed DC's, buoyed by stories that engaged with the real world.

As the civil rights movement made news across the nation and led to groundbreaking social change, Lee and other Marvel creators actively worked to incorporate more Black characters into their comics. Black Panther, the leader of the fictional African nation of Wakanda, debuted in *Fantastic Four* #52 in 1966, while Sam Wilson was introduced as the publisher's first African American superhero, the Falcon, in *Captain America* #117 in 1969. The new additions came with some backlash from fans, so much so that Lee dedicated a 1968 installment of his monthly "Stan's Soap Box" column to taking a firm stand on the matter. He wrote, "Bigotry and racism are among the deadliest social ills plaguing the world today. [. . .] The only way to destroy them is to expose them—to reveal them for the insidious evils they really are."

Aiming to poach some of Marvel's booming audience, DC followed their lead in 1970 and addressed racism directly in *Green Lantern/Green Arrow* #76. In the issue, an elderly Black man spoke to Green Lantern and pointed out that the hero had helped people with blue skin, orange skin, and purple skin on different worlds. He then said, "Only there's **skins** you never bothered with . . . the **Black** skins! I want to know . . . **how come**?!" Ashamed, Green Lantern had no good response. The series introduced DC's first Black superhero the following year, when John Stewart was given the power ring and became a new Green Lantern.

Marvel addressed another timely topic in 1971, tackling drug use when Peter Parker's friend Harry Osborn took stimulant pills in *Amazing Spider-Man* #96. The web-slinging hero saved an addled addict from falling off a building earlier in the issue, but Harry's drug problem brought the matter closer to home. Lee had to buck the Comics Code Authority to print the issue, since the depiction of drug use was strictly forbidden despite the clear antidrug message. The story led the CCA to revamp its rules, and later in the year *Green Lantern/Green Arrow* dealt with a similar subject at DC when Green Arrow learned that his sidekick Speedy was addicted to heroin.

With both publishers engaged in pertinent topics that mattered to their more mature readership, it was only a matter of time before superheroes tackled the women's liberation movement. The fight for gender equality had built steam over the course of the 1960s, and by the early 1970s there was an ongoing national conversation on the issue as politicians debated the merits of the Equal Rights Amendment. Although Marvel had led the way on most other real-world matters, DC was the first superhero publisher to engage with women's lib directly and expose their new audience to the values of feminism.

Wonder Woman's initial foray into women's lib was an absolute failure, however. Her series had been one of DC's worst-selling titles for some time, and in 1968 the publisher decided to drastically alter the book. Writer Denny O'Neil and artist Mike Sekowsky took over from longtime writer and editor Robert Kanigher, and immediately changed everything. Diana gave up her costume and her superpowers to be with Steve Trevor and live as a normal woman, but then Steve was killed by the mysterious Dr. Cyber. Dedicating her life to finding his killer, Diana learned martial arts and traveled the globe to take down the assassin's nefarious criminal organization.

The choice to depower Wonder Woman at the height of the female power movement proved extremely ill timed. Even worse was the writing, which depicted Diana as a hysterical, emotional mess who flitted from one man to another, even as she sought to avenge her deceased boyfriend. The series' new direction caught the attention of feminist activist Gloria Steinem, who'd grown up reading *Wonder Woman* comics, and she lobbied the editors at DC to return the character to her roots.

They soon agreed, and Steinem celebrated by putting Wonder Woman on the cover of the first issue of *Ms.* magazine in 1972, launching the feminist publication with the headline "Wonder Woman for President." The magazine also printed an excerpt from her 1940s origin story inside. Wonder Woman was a feminist icon now, and Steinem was eager to see "the feminism and strength of the original Wonder Woman—my Wonder Woman—restored." She was especially pleased that Dorothy Woolfolk was going to edit *Wonder Woman* and bring female leadership to the series for the first time ever.

Woolfolk was already the editor of DC's only other female-led superhero book, *Superman's Girl Friend Lois Lane*, and had steered the character in an intentionally feminist direction. Lois quit her job at the *Daily Planet* to become a freelance reporter and cover the stories she cared about, and she broke up with Superman after decades of his fickle attentions, telling him, "I'm no longer the girl you come back to between missions! I can't live in your **shadow**—I've got things to do!"

Elsewhere at DC, Batgirl was making waves as well. She starred in a backup feature in *Detective Comics*, but found herself chafing under the limits of vigilante crimefighting. Frustrated with the broken justice system, she decided to set aside the cowl and run for Congress in order to make positive change. Barbara earned the nickname "Babs the Boot" when her dramatic antiestablishment speech asked, "Will **they** clean up the slums? Create new jobs . . . ? Stop dope-traffic . . . ? **I** say they **won't**! I say—**boot the rascals out—elect me**!" She ultimately won the seat, completing DC's bold feminist trifecta for their three most prominent women.

Then everything fell apart.

When Woolfolk pushed boundaries with her new direction for Lois Lane, fans pushed back. Or rather, male fans. Letters from female fans were generally complimentary, but the male response was not. One reader called Lois "a militant Women's Lib extremist," and another asked, "Why must every ish allude to Women's Lib? I can't tell you how boring the subject has become." The book received so many letters that DC added a new columnist to the series to address women's lib specifically. Known only as "Alexander the Great," the columnist dismissed Lois as an "obnoxious dame" and a "rude gal" who "must have a screw loose." He also stated outright, "Women should know their place. Lois never has known hers." Readers who criticized the book's new direction earned praise, while those who supported it were mocked. He also took aim at

Woolfolk directly, calling her a "crusader" and asking, "Who knows what evil lurks in the heart of Editor Woolfolk?" If the column was satire, it failed. Alexander's words echoed anti–women's lib rhetoric of the time almost exactly, and undercut the story's message with each outing. If it was sincerely antifeminist and anti-Woolfolk, it was cruel.

The latter may have been the case, because Woolfolk was fired from DC Comics seven issues after Lois's feminist revolution began, right before the new *Wonder Woman* was due to launch. She was replaced on both books by Robert Kanigher, just five years after he'd been summarily yanked from *Wonder Woman* for running the title into the ground. When the classic Wonder Woman returned in *Wonder Woman* #204, the story began with the assassination of "Dottie Cottonman, woman's magazine editor," a callous nod to Woolfolk's dismissal.

Lois soon returned to her previous status quo, while Wonder Woman's exciting new feminist direction never materialized. With Kanigher at the helm, the early issues consisted mainly of retreads of some of his old work. While female fans initially expressed optimism about Wonder Woman's return in the letter column, the watered-down take quickly led to a sharp decline in female correspondents. Meanwhile, despite the limited women's lib content, male fans still took issue with "Diana Prince's liberated personality," and warned, "Don't let her get bogged down in 'relevant'-type stories."

Superman's Girl Friend Lois Lane was canceled two years after Woolfolk got fired. Lois lived on in *Superman Family*, an anthology book that also included a feature set in an imaginary future where she was married to Superman. Batgirl's *Detective Comics* run ended as soon as she was elected to Congress, and she also returned a while later in an anthology book, *Batman Family*, with stories that largely focused on her burgeoning new romance with Robin. The publisher's embrace of women's lib at the start of the new decade was wiped away entirely, presumably because their readership was ambivalent, if not openly antagonistic, toward empowered female characters.

Marvel was slower to explore the feminist cause. The cover of *Avengers* #83 in 1970 introduced Valkyrie, standing over the unconscious bodies of the male Avengers as she exclaimed, "**All right**, girls—that finishes off these **male chauvinist pigs**! From now on, it's **Valkyrie** and her lady **Liberators**!" However, the story inside revealed that Valkyrie was the villain Enchantress in disguise, angry with men after she'd been jilted by her male companion. Putting feminist rhetoric in the mouth of a known villain for the purposes of petty revenge was hardly a promising start.

But Stan Lee, now publisher of Marvel Comics, wasn't finished. He tried to actively court female readers with three new series in 1972, featuring both female leads and female creators. Along with the medical drama *Night Nurse* and the jungle adventure *Shanna the She-Devil*, there was one superhero title in the line,

The Cat. Written by Linda Fite with art by Marie Severin and Wally Wood, the Cat was Greer Nelson, a young woman who gained superpowers from a medical experiment. When she learned that the scientist behind the experiment planned to control his subjects and use them as a private army, she donned the feline uniform meant for his soldiers and ended his evil scheme. The book failed to resonate with Marvel's core audience and was canceled after only four issues, along with the other two titles in the line.

Marvel waited until 1977 to address women's lib again, and this time they went big with a brand-new series, *Ms. Marvel.* She smashed through a wall on the debut issue's cover as the text exclaimed, "At last! A bold new super-heroine," and "This female fights back!" The story inside, written by Gerry Conway with art by John Buscema and Joe Sinnott, reintroduced Carol Danvers, an air force veteran and a former flame of the alien superhero Captain Marvel. She'd been a recurring character in his series, but now she was striking out on her own and leaving the military behind as the editor of *Woman Magazine,* an offshoot of the *Daily Bugle.* Carol also had superhuman abilities, powered by the DNA-altering effects of alien technology, and defended herself and her city from fiendish foes as Ms. Marvel.

The book was not subtle in its embrace of women's lib. In a letter to readers in the first issue, Conway explained that the series was about "the modern woman's quest for raised consciousness, for self-liberation, for identity." The name Ms. Marvel was very intentional. Unlike "Mrs." or "Miss," the honorific "Ms." was unrelated to marital status, and modern women had embraced it as a feminist statement, so much so that it became the name of Gloria Steinem's magazine. Carol was reimagined as a Steinemesque figure, with her own magazine and a zeal for gender equality. *Daily Bugle* editor J. Jonah Jameson was cast as her chauvinistic antagonist, suggesting that the magazine focus on "**new diets**, and **fashions**, and **recipes**," instead of "articles on **women's lib** [. . .] **yecch.**" Carol disagreed strongly, then rejected his low salary offer and argued her way up to more equitable pay.

Ms. Marvel's letter column made an obvious effort to highlight female fans, and two schools of thought on the new title soon emerged. Cynthia Walker, who proclaimed she was "Mrs., not Ms.," just wanted a fun series and argued that *Ms. Marvel* "should be action-oriented and not a soapbox for women's lib." At the other end of the spectrum, Mary-Catherine Gilmore took issue with the publisher as a whole and found the new book lacking because the creators and editors "are so indoctrinated by our society and dominated by your male egos that to have a female as a total equal to any male would be impossible." Marvel seemed to side with Cynthia over Mary-Catherine, and after nine issues the editors explained, "We've been trying to eliminate as much of the blatant, preaching feminism as we can; and instead, striving to

***Ms. Marvel* #1, art by John Romita and Dick Giordano, Marvel Comics, 1977. Carol Danvers took the lead as Marvel's first feminist hero in this short-lived series.**

let Ms. Marvel's—and Carol Danvers'—words and actions and feelings speak for themselves."

This came through in the stories. Carol's journalism took a back seat to the superhero antics, and the women's lib rhetoric faded from the book. Furthermore, the book was written and drawn entirely by men, and the art became increasingly skewed toward the male gaze. Ms. Marvel's costume was skimpy to begin with, a long-sleeved top with a sizable belly window that led to briefs, bare legs, and boots. Twenty issues in, the outfit was replaced with little more than a black bathing suit along with long gloves, tall boots, and a red sash. Her simple bob haircut was also changed to long, flowing locks.

None of these changes helped *Ms. Marvel* land a stable readership. The book switched to a bimonthly schedule after a year and a half, and was suddenly canceled shortly thereafter, ending with *Ms. Marvel* #23. More stories were finished and ready to print, but they weren't published for another thirteen years. When celebrating women's lib failed, the message was discarded. When shying away from women's lib failed as well, the character was discarded. The publisher's audience just wasn't keen on a female-led series.

Two similar titles also proved short lived. Marvel launched *Spider-Woman* in 1978 and *Savage She-Hulk* in 1980, both derivatives of established male superheroes created solely to establish a trademark on the names. *Savage She-Hulk* only lasted two years before it was canceled. *Spider-Woman* lasted twice as long, buoyed by having her own Saturday morning cartoon program, though the increased profile kept her afloat only slightly longer than her female peers.

In 1977, Lee dedicated a volume of Marvel's hardcover anthology collection series to the publisher's female characters, titled *The Superhero Women*. The characters chosen spotlighted mainstays like Black Widow, Sue Storm, and the Wasp, but it was slim pickings beyond them. Stories from two of Marvel's short-lived 1972 titles, *The Cat* and *Shanna the She-Devil*, made the book, along with the recently released first issue of *Ms. Marvel*, and a handful of lesser-known villains and supporting characters.

The collection opened with an introduction from Lee, who asked, "Do less females read comics because they seem to be aimed at a male audience, or are they aimed at a male audience because less females read them? If you're expecting an answer, forget it. I've spent years waiting for someone to tell me!" After this punt, Lee continued, "Many people have asked what Marvel's policy is in regard to women. Basically, we have no policy at all—just as we have no specific policy toward brunettes, or tap dancers, or podiatrists." Lee's words highlighted his clear lack of interest in understanding the sexist biases in his comics. He cast the gender divide as unknowable and himself as blameless, refusing to acknowledge that his male audience had been intentionally catered to for the past fifteen years.

With the utmost hubris, Lee wrote:

We have been, we are, and we shall continue to make the strongest possible effort to bestow the cultural blessings of superherodom upon male and female alike. Let chauvinism be eschewed. Let equality prevail. Let historians of the future look back upon this era and proudly declare, "'Twas Marvel that led the way!"

They did not. Throughout the 1960s, Marvel crafted a male-dominated audience that had no interest in empowered female characters, and DC did the same. Half-hearted efforts to engage with women failed swiftly, and the skewed nature of the genre's readership informed every decision at both publishers for the next several decades.

CHAPTER 6

Overpowered

With both DC Comics and Marvel largely ignoring women's lib and female characters throughout the 1970s, the publishers let their male leads take center stage. DC canceled their romance line and focused on their superhero titles, with lengthy story arcs that centered action and adventure, from Batman's global war on crime to new addition Jack Kirby's interstellar "Fourth World" epic. Long narratives were the norm at Marvel as well. Some focused on spectacle, like the Avengers' yearlong "Korvac Saga," which brought together scores of characters from across the Marvel universe to deal with a celestial threat. Others were more intimate, like when Captain America hung up the shield after uncovering a Watergate-esque scandal or an arc in *Iron Man* in which Tony Stark addressed his alcoholism.

Sagas defined this Bronze Age of superhero comic books, and while many are well remembered today, two in particular have gone down as definitive classics. At Marvel, the "Phoenix Saga" and subsequent "Dark Phoenix Saga" still rank high on lists of the best superhero stories of all time. So too does DC's "The Judas Contract," the culmination of a lengthy *New Teen Titans* arc that nearly led to the demise of the entire team. Interestingly, both of these well-regarded story lines featured surprisingly diverse casts for this era, unlike most of DC's and Marvel's output. They also highlight the evolution of superhero fandom and its relationship to gender, cementing and normalizing a dark new trend for the genre.

Lengthy story lines flourished in this era in part because of a switch from newsstand distribution to a direct market of specialty comic book shops. Newsstands were unreliable. Some comics didn't show up, books that did come were often late, and many had cracked spines and curled pages from bending over a spinner rack's low supports. The new generation of fans wanted their comics in a timely manner, and saw comics as collectibles that should be kept in good shape. Newsstands provided neither.

By this point, newsstands and their distributors weren't too fussed about comic books either. The long, complicated narratives were off-putting to young readers and casual fans, causing a decline in sales, while a poor economy and rising paper costs led to several price increases over the 1970s that drove down interest even further. Because of this, many newsstands and corner stores moved away from carrying comics at all.

Direct market comic book shops offered a useful alternative for dedicated fans. Their comics arrived not only on time, but typically earlier than their newsstand release date, and stores could order the specific books their customers wanted. Comic book shops quickly grew in popularity, so much so that Marvel released a new series exclusive to the direct market, *Dazzler*, in 1980. The book starred a mutant disco star, and the debut issue sold more than four hundred thousand copies—strong numbers for this era.

Dazzler was a wise choice. Mutants and their flagship series, *Uncanny X-Men*, were wildly popular thanks to a recent revamp of the title. In 1975, Marvel reinvigorated the franchise with *Giant Size X-Men* #1 as Professor X recruited a new team to save the imperiled original X-Men. Writer Len Wein and artist Dave Cockrum introduced heroes like the Russian metal man Colossus, the weather-wielding Storm, and the ferociously clawed Wolverine, and fans were intrigued with the new team.

Writer Chris Claremont took over for Wein with *X-Men* #94, beginning a landmark run for the series. What fans later dubbed the "Phoenix Saga" started six issues after, when Jean Grey sacrificed herself to save the team. She was exposed to deadly radiation from a solar flare as she piloted the X-Men's shuttle, and died when the shuttle crashed into the ocean. As the team searched frantically for her, she emerged from the water in a burst of light, reborn in a new green costume and imbued with celestial power as she announced, "I am fire! And life incarnate! Now and forever—I am **Phoenix!**"

Jean's new abilities proved impressive. She opened a gateway across space so the X-Men could intervene in a crisis in the Shi'ar Empire, prompting her boyfriend Cyclops to remark, "My . . . god. Jean used to be the **weakest** X-Man. Now she powers up an **inter-stellar transporter** without batting an **eyelash**." She then channeled her immense powers to fix the M'Kraan Crystal, also known as the "nexus of realities," the destruction of which would've obliterated the entire universe.

Cockrum left and was replaced by artist John Byrne, and the book was renamed *Uncanny X-Men* in 1978. The series quickly found an audience, one that was notably different from the rest of Marvel's books. Letter column data from elsewhere in the line showed over 90 percent male correspondents in the latter half of the 1970s, suggesting a substantial male audience. Meanwhile, the letters in *Uncanny X-Men* featured only 67 percent male correspondents over the same period. If we view the letter columns as broadly indicative of the readership, female fans accounted for roughly a third of the book's audience, massive for this time period.

And they weren't afraid to make their voices heard, especially when it came to the Phoenix. After Jean saved the universe, her power levels decreased sharply. Her abilities failed her when Warhawk, "no more than a **second-rate Colossus**," attacked the X-Men, and she couldn't save the team from Magneto, sparing only herself and Beast when the villain's Antarctic prison was destroyed. Brenda Robnett wrote in to express her frustration with the weakened Phoenix:

> I want a superheroine of **limitless** power. She could still be vulnerable, she could still be beaten. It would just take more ingenuity than sheer raw power to beat her. I don't want a Superman perfect hero. I'm not advocating that. I just want a heroine who is **special**. I thought Phoenix was going to be her. Apparently, I am wrong. [. . .] Why can't Marvel have at least **one** super heroine worthy of the name??? Women are not necessarily the "Weaker Sex." They are what **you** make them—at least in comic books.

Editor Roger Stern addressed the topic a few issues later as similar letters continued to pour in. He claimed that the decision wasn't based on gender and explained, "Phoenix's power was reduced because it was felt that having a cosmic X-Man would unbalance this team in exactly the same sense that Thor all-too-often unbalanced the Avengers," arguing that having someone with godlike powers made the rest of the team "pretty much superfluous."

Thor was an interesting comparison, in that his powers weren't reduced and he'd remained a recurring character in the constantly shifting Avengers lineup for the previous fifteen years. Meanwhile, Jean had her powers slashed drastically soon after they debuted and then, believing that the rest of the X-Men had died in the battle with Magneto, she was shuttled off to Scotland to mourn their passing for the next year. They weren't dead, just missing for a while, though they also believed that Jean had died. Scott got over her death quickly, admitting that after becoming the Phoenix "she wasn't the girl I'd **loved** anymore," and soon began dating Colleen Wing, a martial artist from the *Power Man and Iron Fist* corner of the Marvel universe.

But Claremont had big plans for Jean. While in Scotland, Jean met a mysterious man named Jason Wyngarde and began having visions that she was Lady Jean Grey, a Regency-era noblewoman being wooed by Wyngarde. The visions troubled Jean, and she thought she might be flashing back to a past life. She was not. Wyngarde was actually Mastermind, a mutant with the ability to create telepathic illusions, and he was working for the Hellfire Club, a cabal of fiendish mutants who wanted to control Jean and her Phoenix powers. Jean began to succumb to the visions, and not even a joyful reunion with the X-Men could break his hold on her. Before long, Jean was lost in his Regency world. She became the Black Queen of the Hellfire Club, and helped Wyngarde capture the X-Men.

The scheme then backfired on Mastermind. His entrapment of Jean not only unleashed the Phoenix, but also the destructive Dark Phoenix. She dispatched of him quickly before turning on everyone else, including the X-Men, as she declared, "**No longer** am I the woman you **knew**! I am fire! And **life incarnate**! Now and forever—**I am Phoenix**!" Now fully in control, the Dark Phoenix unleashed a swath of destruction across the galaxy, consuming an entire star in her unbridled hunger for more power.

Stern's Thor comparison rang increasingly hollow over the course of these issues as Jean fell into a story line no male character would have faced. Claremont and Byrne's execution of Mastermind's machinations was awash in fallen women tropes that cast this as a distinctly feminine arc from the start. Jean's Regency visions were reminiscent of romance novels, considered a naughty, taboo outlet for female sexuality in this era. Claremont's writing underscored the link as Jean, overcome with desire, thought to herself, "The emotions he stirs within me—so intense—must break away while I can!" The narration later added, "Every facet of her being is overwhelmed by a physical and emotional tidal wave, the like of which she has **never known**."

The Black Queen outfit further underscored the sexual nature of what Mastermind called his "psychic seduction." Normally reserved, Jean's Black Queen wardrobe consisted of a black leather bustier, laced in the front but still open enough to reveal more skin, along with a grand cape, black briefs, and tall leather boots. A whip completed the outfit and drove home the BDSM theme. When Jean confronted Mastermind after the Dark Phoenix took control, she accused him of "tailor[ing] your illusions to fit my most private fantasies—the repressed, dark side of my soul. You gave me what I secretly **wanted**, and used that to destroy me!"

Once freed, Dark Phoenix fought the X-Men and Storm pointedly observed, "There is no joy—no love—in Dark Phoenix. I sense pain, great sadness—and an awful, all-consuming **lust**." As Jean summoned lightning to blast her teammates, the narration read, "The awesome bolts of energy caress her body like a lover." The sexual connotation was clear, and it was explicitly connected with Jean's descent into madness.

The lust that fueled Dark Phoenix was contrasted with her love for Scott. His dalliance with Colleen was quickly forgotten when they reunited, and he rededicated himself to their relationship. After Professor X finally contained Dark Phoenix, the first thing Jean did when freed of her sexually charged hunger

Uncanny X-Men #135, art by John Byrne and Terry Austin, Marvel Comics, 1980. The Dark Phoenix, mad with power, shortly before her death.

was telepathically sense Scott's desire to marry her and agree to his implied proposal.

There's nothing inherently wrong with female lust or sexuality in any way. However, when a male writer and artist depict lust as the corruptive key to a female character's destructive downfall, in a mind control scenario no less, and present the love of a good man as her path to salvation, it's a trope as old as time. Linking female desire to madness conjures the tragic history of "hysterical" women who were institutionalized, sterilized, and ostracized for failing to comply with social norms, and the conclusion of the Dark Phoenix Saga did little to counter this association.

Uncanny X-Men #137 began with the Shi'ar Empire putting Jean on trial for Dark Phoenix's rampage. Her destroying a star had killed the planet that orbited it, along with its five billion inhabitants, and the empire demanded justice. The X-Men argued that it was Dark Phoenix, not Jean, who'd committed the crime, but the Shi'ar were unswayed and the team agreed to trial by combat.

Claremont's original plan was for a happy ending. The X-Men would win and Jean would return to the team, then defeat the Phoenix for good in the book's upcoming 150th issue, marry Scott, and go off to live happily ever after. But when Marvel editor in chief Jim Shooter saw the script for *Uncanny X-Men* #137, he wasn't pleased. He thought Jean was getting off too easy for destroying an inhabited planet, and demanded justice. Byrne agreed with Shooter. He later revealed that he "didn't like Phoenix since the word go," and had "agitated to get her out of the book." Roger Stern agreed as well, and suggested they kill off Jean. Claremont was reluctant to do so, but he ultimately acquiesced and rewrote the issue.

In the new ending, Dark Phoenix possessed Jean once again. She told Scott that she couldn't control the power, not every hour of every day, and that it would eventually break free to cause more death and destruction. A tear streamed down her cheek as she said, "It's better this way. Quick. Clean. **Final**," and she turned the power on herself, destroying the Phoenix and ending her own life.

April Curry responded to the issue in the letter column, and didn't hold back when she wrote, "How could you do such a thing?! [. . .] I bet if Phoenix had been a man, you guys would have wrote in the story that he was emotionally strong enough to control his power. However, since Jean was a woman, you guys killed her off!" It was hard to argue otherwise. The framing of the entire saga was a classic fallen woman narrative, right down to her being punished for her wanton sexuality. As much as Byrne, Shooter, and Stern pointed to justice and accountability, the underlying message was that Jean didn't deserve mercy or happiness, that she'd fallen too far to be redeemed.

There was also an intriguing juxtaposition between Jean and Scott. Jean's "relationship" with Wyngarde was a nonconsensual fabrication. She was loyal to

Scott, mourning him when she thought he died and taking him back when he returned. The Phoenix possessed her by force, not of her own volition, and she did everything she could to remain even keeled and contain the power. Even so, she was cast as a villain and punished. Meanwhile, Scott took up with Colleen Wing once he thought Jean was out of the picture, then began dating another redhead, Madelaine Pryor, after Jean died. He flew off the handle throughout both sagas, clashing with the team and exorcising his anger on the foes they encountered. And yet, he was the hero of the book, depicted as the valiant voice of reason. The standards for men and women were vastly different, and this trend continued at DC Comics.

New Teen Titans was DC's answer to *Uncanny X-Men*, an ongoing soap operatic series with young adults squabbling, falling in love, and fighting villains. The original *Teen Titans* had debuted in 1964 as a team-up book for young side-kicks with Aqualad, Kid Flash, Robin, and Wonder Girl, and ran for a decade. Although a revival a few years later failed to find an audience, DC brought back the team once again in 1980.

The publisher was in a rough spot at this point. All of the harsh economic circumstances that spurred the shift to the direct market had hit DC especially hard, and they'd recently canceled more than twenty titles in a culling known as the DC Implosion. With DC lagging far behind Marvel's continued success, writer Marv Wolfman and artist George Pérez borrowed their competitor's winning *Uncanny X-Men* formula with *New Teen Titans*, and gave DC their first bona fide hit of the new decade.

Robin, Kid Flash, and Wonder Girl returned to the team along with former Doom Patrol member Changeling and the new characters Cyborg, Raven, and Starfire. The ratio of male to female characters was almost even, a rare feat, though the readership failed to follow suit. Unlike *Uncanny X-Men*, letter columns in the early years of *New Teen Titans* featured 85 percent male correspondents, roughly in line with DC's broader numbers for this time, and Wolfman and Pérez crafted their female characters to appeal directly to this audience.

The archetypes were clear. Starfire was the sexy one, fierce and fiery with a small outfit that showed off her curvaceous figure. Wonder Girl was the classic beauty, elegant as a superhero as well as smart and artsy in her civilian identity. Raven was the goth, dark and moody and mysterious, covered up by her cloak until she suddenly wasn't, like when she was drawn nude while she was trapped in a hellish vision of her future. Wolfman and Pérez knew how to play to their readership well. Male fans ate it up, and their letters regularly mentioned which female character they were in love with.

With this dynamic in mind, *New Teen Titans* #26 introduced a new female character, Terra, a.k.a. Tara Markov. She debuted as a villain, using her abilities to control earth and rock as she attempted to destroy the Statue of Liberty.

Changeling intervened and stopped her, and although she escaped, he remained intrigued. He found her again two issues later, and learned she was forced to commit crimes by terrorists who were holding her parents hostage. The two connected, and he invited her to use her powers for good and join the Teen Titans.

Terra was a petite blonde, just shy of sixteen years old when she debuted, and her design was purposefully thought out. Wolfman later said, "We went out of our way to make her cute—but not too cute, with the buck teeth and everything." Pérez confirmed this intention: "I wanted her to be cute but not beautiful. She looked like a young girl. I gave her a substantial overbite, her eyes were wide, her body was slim, she wasn't particularly busty." The wayward waif was innocent and naïve, and readers soon embraced her.

The team was slower to do so. Terra's story never quite added up, and her youthful petulance put off the older members. She could have a bad attitude; but, to be fair, she also faced constant sexual harassment from Changeling, who propositioned her often and kept suggesting that "we could always head up to my room and **neck**." Over time, Terra continued to prove herself, and she pushed to become a full member of the team so she could know her new friends beyond their superhero identities. She eventually earned their approval, with code names dropped and true names revealed when she was welcomed into the fold.

That issue also included a more shocking reveal: Terra in a low-cut robe with nothing on underneath, smoking a postcoital cigarette in the home of the Teen Titans' archenemy, Deathstroke the Terminator. She'd been working with him the entire time, infiltrating the team to learn their secrets, and the plan had finally come to fruition. Wolfman and Pérez had been building to this moment for the past year, sculpting the character specifically to maximize the shock. Pérez later explained:

> I wanted her to look almost elven, so that when you see her for the first time wearing full make up and dressed in a provocative outfit where you know she's just been in bed with Deathstroke that it does jab you a bit. "Whoa, good God! This little girl is a slut!"

The culmination of this arc, "The Judas Contract," launched three issues later. Years before, the criminal organization H.I.V.E. hired Deathstroke's son to assassinate the Teen Titans, but he died in the attempt. Now, armed with the team's secret identities thanks to Terra, Deathstroke was able to capture all of the Teen Titans, fulfill his son's contract with H.I.V.E., and have his revenge. Terra was right by his side, and taunted Changeling, "Your pwetty widdle girlfriend isn't all true-blue an' pure? Mister, you don't know the **half** of it."

Then the plan fell apart when Deathstroke's second son, Jericho, helped Robin rescue the Teen Titans. Jericho could possess and control other people, and he took over his father's body to make him attack H.I.V.E. agents and

Terra. What appeared to be Deathstroke's betrayal sent Terra into a rage, and as she battled the now freed Teen Titans she cried, "But I—I thought he **cared** 'bout me, thought he **loved** me." She lashed out with uncontrolled ferocity, so lost in her powers that she ultimately brought down H.I.V.E.'s mountain headquarters on herself, ending her life.

The story put the blame for Terra's death squarely on her own shoulders. Deathstroke said, "That girl was loony **before** we met. [. . .] She was always **unstable**—she hates for no reason." One might expect that of a villain, but the heroes echoed his sentiments. Robin remarked, "I didn't want to believe—but she **is** crazy." Raven concurred, "The girl is **evil**. [. . .] Her soul is **corrupt**," while Wonder Girl simply said, "She was **insane**." The narration agreed, and

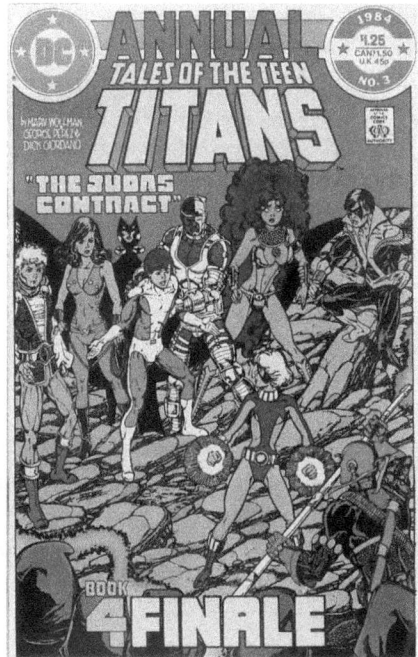

Tales of the Teen Titans Annual #3, **art by George Pérez, DC Comics, 1984. Terra bests the Teen Titans before another untimely death.**

as the rocks rained down on Terra the text read, "Due to the fault of no one but herself, she is **insane**. [. . .] She hates without cause, without reason."

Blaming Terra so fully also absolved Deathstroke of his involvement, both in the scheme with H.I.V.E. and, more damningly, in his relationship with Terra. Getting vengeance on the Teen Titans was his quest, and Terra had nothing to do with the team before he brought her into it. Moreover, while Terra turned sixteen in the course of her time with the Teen Titans, she was still at least fifteen when they met and, presumably, began their sexual relationship. This is statutory rape, and corruption of a minor besides. Without Deathstroke, Terra wouldn't have had the resources or inclination for such a grand scheme. He was behind it all, in grotesque fashion, and walked away from the situation unharmed, free to continue his villainous ways and grow to become a beloved antihero for decades to come, even starring in his own series on multiple occasions. Terra, meanwhile, remained dead.

The reactions from male fans in the letter column were a mix of sorrow and shock. One reader lamented, "It was difficult to see Terra die; I had such hopes that she could come to terms with her betrayal of the Titans and truly end up a Teen Titan in every sense of the word." Another added, "Traitor or not, Terra is still an intriguing and interesting character, and I still like her," sentiments echoed in another letter that read, "Though she deserved death and her power and madness made it impossible for her to survive, I still felt a pang of sorrow when she did die."

Wolfman had mixed emotions as well, and explained to fans that while killing Terra was the plan from the start, he and Pérez had to "make certain that we didn't, in the meantime, fall so much in love with our character that we decided to reverse her ultimate fate. It was hard, almost impossible, not to care for Tara." Years later, Brad Meltzer, a writer on DC books like *Identity Crisis* and *Justice League of America*, looked back on reading "The Judas Contract" as a teen and called Terra "the first girl to break my heart." Reflecting the sentiments of many fans, he recalled "my stomach sinking down to my testicles" upon the reveal of her affair with Deathstroke, and he continued, "Terra betrayed me. She deceived me. She shoved a knife in my belly and sliced upward all the way to my heart."

The "Dark Phoenix Saga" walked so "The Judas Contract" could run. *New Teen Titans* was inspired by the success of *Uncanny X-Men*, so much so that Wolfman and Pérez managed to kill their own highly powered, sexually transgressive female character. These two high-profile deaths by suicide in the span of four years spoke to an underlying issue within the genre. Creators in this era did not know how to handle powerful female characters, especially ones that slipped into villainy, and so they fell into gendered tropes. These stories taught the books' predominantly male fans that women couldn't handle such abilities and couldn't be trusted if they spurned a hero's love, that they didn't deserve redemption. Their deaths, while tragic, were presented and subsequently accepted as a fitting end.

Speaking of fans, each year the subscribers of *Comic Buyer's Guide* voted for the magazine's Fan Awards, recognizing the best in superhero publishing. Chris Claremont and John Byrne won Favorite Writer and Favorite Artist, respectively, multiple times in the early 1980s, while the 1984 award for Favorite Comic Book Story went to "The Judas Contract."

CHAPTER 7

Despair

Modern superhero fandom coalesced in the 1980s. Comic book shops continued to grow and create communities for dedicated readers, and DC Comics and Marvel catered further to this narrow audience. Teenage boys and young men were their target demographic, so publishers crafted their narratives accordingly. Along with the popularity of the lengthy sagas in *Uncanny X-Men* and *The New Teen Titans*, the decade also saw the rise of event books that brought disparate heroes together for world-changing adventures, like Marvel's *Secret Wars* and DC's *Crisis on Infinite Earths*. Both publishers released scores of books from a legion of writers and artists, but two creators emerged from the pack to become the defining voices of the decade.

While many stories from the 1980s are remembered fondly by fans, Frank Miller and Alan Moore created work that remains a fixture on the bestseller lists even today. Books like *The Dark Knight Returns* and *Watchmen* are perennial chart toppers, and continue to influence not just comic books but also major motion pictures and award-winning television. Their comics were creative, original, and undeniably brilliant at times, but they also left a complicated legacy. Sometimes intentionally, though often not, Miller and Moore's stories ushered in an even more grim and violent era for the genre.

Frank Miller was barely in his twenties when he moved to New York City to become a comic book artist in the late 1970s. He landed small gigs at Gold Key Comics and DC but didn't have much interest in superheroes, his work leaning more toward a retro crime noir vibe, until he was hired as a fill-in artist at Marvel for a short run on a Spider-Man book. The issues guest-starred Daredevil, and when a full-time spot opened up on the solo *Daredevil* title in 1979, Miller took over drawing the series.

Daredevil was Matt Murdock, a lawyer who'd been blinded by a radioactive substance as a child. The accident enhanced his remaining senses to superhuman levels, and he used his abilities to fight crime in the downtrodden Hell's Kitchen neighborhood of New York. Sales were poor when Miller started drawing the book and, facing cancellation, editorial decided to mix things up and let Miller write it as well. He reoriented the series, giving Daredevil martial arts skills and introducing a new foe in the Hand, a deadly ninja cult. Miller also continued the stories of existing villains like the assassin Bullseye and the crime boss Kingpin. Sales went up once Miller took over writing the series, and the book soon upped its schedule from bimonthly to monthly to meet the growing demand.

Miller's artwork moved away from the realism that dominated the genre. His style was expressionistic, and he wasn't afraid to push the envelope and skew his drawing to capture the emotion of the scene more than physical accuracy. For Miller, it was important that "the external reality represents the internal reality of the characters," and he did just that with his claustrophobic take on Hell's Kitchen, his animated characters, and his brutal fight scenes.

Although Miller wasn't particularly interested in realism artistically, he was dedicated to realism when it came to the violence in his comic books. Most superhero fights were pristine and bloodless, stylish yet lacking any repercussions. Miller hated "action where people don't get nosebleeds," and remedied this with artwork that showed the true pain and physical ramifications of violence. His combatants got bloody and bruised when they fought, often in visceral detail, and these effects lingered after the fact via bandages and slings until enough time had passed for them to heal. The realistic violence didn't sit well with some fans and critics, but Miller didn't care. He remarked, "I enjoy the fact that my work makes people uncomfortable, and I think it makes them uncomfortable because people are hypocrites. They want to enjoy violence but not see anybody get hurt by it." Most fans enjoyed his style, though, and *Daredevil* was a top seller for the remainder of his run.

Miller moved to DC for his next major project, the futuristic samurai tale *Ronin*. He pushed his artwork to even more expressionistic realms for the miniseries, and upped the violence considerably. There was more sexual content as well, and the editors at DC decided not to even submit the book to the Comics Code Authority for their seal of approval, knowing full well it would be rejected on multiple fronts.

He brought this sensibility back to Marvel when he returned for another run on *Daredevil*, this time with artist David Mazzucchelli. While he'd been hard on Matt Murdock the first time around, the new "Born Again" arc was an absolute cavalcade of misery for the character. The story began with the Kingpin learning Daredevil's secret identity and slowly dismantling his entire life. He ended up destroyed financially, personally, and even physically after a brutal confrontation with the Kingpin left him battered and broken. Utterly ruined, Matt had to build himself back up from nothing.

Daredevil's secret identity had been revealed by Karen Page, Matt's former secretary and girlfriend. She'd been written out of the series a decade earlier, leaving him behind to become an actress, but when "Born Again" began she was a strung-out wreck making pornographic films, and she traded his secret identity for drugs. It was a harsh turn for the character, but one typical of Miller's treatment of female characters. In his previous run, he'd revealed that Matt's new secretary, Becky Blake, was the victim of a violent sexual assault that left her paralyzed, and also introduced and then killed off Elektra, Matt's former girlfriend turned assassin. Now with "Born Again," Miller wrecked Karen Page's life and had her trading sex for passage back to America so she could try to warn Matt.

Looking back on Miller's body of work, pop culture critic Susana Polo wrote, "I have never read a Frank Miller book with an original female character who didn't fall into two categories: sex worker—or victim of a brutal beating or murder." His dedication to realistic violence frequently came at the expense of female characters, who suffered and often died in order to further the narratives of his male protagonists. Both his brutality and his narrow, harmful depiction of women continued in his most famous book, *The Dark Knight Returns*.

Created during the same period as "Born Again," this prestige miniseries, which consisted of four oversized issues, was written and drawn by Miller. *The Dark Knight Returns* was set in a future where an older Bruce Wayne, now retired from crimefighting, was compelled to don the cape and cowl again when punk gangs began to take over Gotham City. This Batman was ruthless, almost barbarous, as he fought to regain control of the city, pummeling his way through every foe with Miller's trademark carnal ferocity.

It was a new brand of darkness for the Caped Crusader. The Neal Adams–influenced 1970s era had been horror tinged, more foreboding in tone than previous incarnations but not graphically so. This had lessened over the years as well, especially once *Uncanny X-Men* and *The New Teen Titans* became hits. Batman was embroiled in lengthy, soap operatic drama throughout the early 1980s, and Miller wanted to return to the grit of the original 1930s Batman, before the character was sanitized.

There was a militaristic bent to this older Batman. He referred to Robin as a "good soldier," turned villains' guns against them, debuted a new Batmobile that was essentially a tank complete with missiles, and fashioned himself armor; by the end of the story he'd assembled his own army. Batman's war escalated with each issue. He stopped the bomb plot of the supposedly reformed Two-Face, defeated the gang plaguing Gotham and became their new leader, had a final confrontation with the Joker, and then, after essentially taking over the city, faced off against Superman when the American government sent him in to break Batman's hold on Gotham.

Throughout the book, Miller showed that being Batman was an addiction for Bruce Wayne, a drug that made him feel more virile and alive. He pushed himself to extremes chasing the high, as evidenced by him facing off against the superpowered Man of Steel. The end of the book also offered a degree of critique of Batman's violent fervor. He faked his own death, gave up his occupation of the city, and returned to the shadows, suggesting that he realized he'd gone too far and pushed past the limits of what Batman should be.

Miller's old tendencies remained, though. He returned to his poor treatment of female characters with his harsh approach to Selina Kyle. Retired from her life as Catwoman, Selina was now the madam of a prominent escort service, and was severely beaten by the Joker. Her battered body served its narrative purpose, with her vicious assault fueling Batman's last battle with the Clown Prince of Crime.

Also, while Miller's fuzzy critique of Batman's methods was interesting, it got lost in his fixation on graphic violence. He got carried away with the action, to the detriment of any larger point he was trying to make. Early in the story, two citizens were asked their opinion on Batman. One said his approach "makes me sick. We must treat the socially mis-oriented with rehabilitative methods. We must patiently realign [them]," while the other simply said, "Batman? Yeah, I think he's A-okay. He's kicking just the right butts—butts cops ain't kicking, that's for sure. Hope he goes after the homos next." Both men were depicted as shallow interviewees, one out of touch and the other clearly bigoted, and yet the story bore out one of their visions.

Rehabilitation failed spectacularly. Both Two-Face and the Joker were released from Arkham Asylum, seemingly cured with cutting-edge psychological treatment, and both went on murderous rampages immediately. Meanwhile, Batman kept kicking butts successfully, including the overtly queer-coded Joker. Throughout their ultimate confrontation, the Joker called Batman "darling" and "my sweet," and their fight ended in a carnival's Tunnel of Love. Miller later said of the scene, "The homophobic nightmare is very much part of the Batman/Joker mythos. It's always been there, I just spelled it out a little more plainly."

The butt-kicking enthusiast was proved correct, along with his bigotry. It's unlikely that this was intentional on Miller's part, given that the book is littered with panels of news segments, interviews, and talking heads. He probably didn't see the dichotomy of this particular pair as the lynchpin of the story. Nonetheless, violence did dominate the book, along with the fan reactions. While some came away with a more nuanced appreciation of the character, many more focused on how awesome it was when Batman beat up the gang leader and how it was even more awesome when Batman fought Superman. The latter battle has been revisited countless times since, the merits of each combatant's chances

Batman: The Dark Knight #2, art by Frank Miller and Lynn Varley, DC Comics, 1986. A more violent and grisly take on Batman.

debated ad nauseam across comic shops, message boards, and social media in the thirty-five years since the book debuted.

DC reunited Miller and Mazzucchelli two years later for "Year One," a new take on Batman's early years. The publisher had just rebooted their continuity with *Crisis on Infinite Earths* and, owing to the ongoing popularity of *The Dark Knight Returns*, wanted Miller to craft the character's definitive origin in the flagship *Batman* title. He set the stage for his grim vision of Batman's future, painting young Bruce as an addict much like his older self, using crimefighting as a coping mechanism for the loss of his parents. Batman was grim and violent, wholly dedicated to the mission that would ultimately consume the rest of his life. Also, in classic Miller fashion, Selina Kyle was a prostitute, cementing her future as a madam in canon. The approach that had been a shocking new direction for Batman and his world in *The Dark Knight Returns* became mainstream in "Year One."

When Frank Miller was busy with Daredevil and futuristic samurai in the early 1980s, Alan Moore made his debut in American comics with *The Saga of the Swamp Thing* at DC Comics. He was a staple in the British comics scene, known for now iconic work like *Marvelman* and *V for Vendetta*, and DC editor Len Wein hired him to revamp their floundering, generic horror comic. Moore took *The Saga of the Swamp Thing* in a new, experimental direction, digging into environmentalism and the supernatural as he built a vivid, mystical world around the character. Sales went up, and Moore soon landed more superhero work, including the iconic Superman tales "For the Man Who Has Everything" and "Whatever Happened to the Man of Tomorrow?"

Moore began toying with the idea of a superhero universe of his own where he could tell a more shocking, inventive story. DC had recently purchased the character rights to defunct publisher Charlton's superhero lineup, including heroes like Blue Beetle and the Question, and Moore thought they might be a good fit. DC's managing editor liked the proposal but, fearing Moore would kill off several of his new acquisitions, suggested that Moore come up with his own, original superheroes instead. He did just that, teaming up with artist Dave Gibbons to craft what would become the most-lauded superhero story of all time.

The first issue of *Watchmen* debuted in 1986 and was set in a world much like our own, apart from the impact of superheroes. They'd changed the course of history, leading America to a swift victory in Vietnam but also heightening Cold War tensions to such a degree that the world was on the brink of nuclear war. Superheroes had recently been outlawed, with only the curmudgeonly Rorschach still active, and he landed a new case when the book opened with the murder of Edward Blake, formerly known as the superhero the Comedian.

Rorschach's investigation drew in other retired heroes, including Doctor Manhattan, Nite Owl, and Ozymandias. Doctor Manhattan was inspired by Charlton's Captain Atom, Nite Owl by Blue Beetle, and Ozymandias by Thunderbolt, but Moore and Gibbons's versions of the characters grew far beyond Charlton's basic fare. Doctor Manhattan had almost godlike powers and evolved past a human concept of time, Nite Owl was a sad sack dealing with impotence, and Ozymandias was a megalomaniac businessman. Ozymandias was also Blake's murderer, killing him as part of his master plan to launch an interdimensional attack on New York City that would kill millions but unite the world against this unknown foe. The scheme worked as nations banded together and nuclear war was forgotten. Nite Owl and Doctor Manhattan decided to stay quiet about the plan to preserve the new peace, and when Rorschach vowed to expose the truth, Doctor Manhattan killed him.

Watchmen was a brilliant deconstruction of the superhero genre, eschewing the usual moral certitude for an ambiguous outcome that raised questions about the greater good and the limits of truth and justice. It was also artistically inventive, built on the solid formality of a nine-panel grid before proceeding to jump through time, space, and even stories within the story. Gibbons's art worked seamlessly with Moore's dense writing as the duo blasted through the boundaries of what superheroes could be and do. *Watchmen* shook up the genre, laying bare its formulas and showcasing the challenging, creative heights it could achieve.

The Dark Knight Returns and *Watchmen* were published in the same year, and had a similar influence. *Watchmen* was brutal and violent as well, often disconcertingly so, in its commitment to graphic realism. The subject matter was much darker than the usual superhero fare, and other creators wanted to follow suit. Both books also raised the stakes narratively. Between Batman battling Superman and a monster destroying New York City, a costumed villain robbing a bank paled in comparison. Comics had to go bigger and bolder, and creators proceeded to do so with grim destruction.

For Moore, his imitators were missing the point. *Watchmen* wasn't meant to be a template for everyone else to follow. The tone and style worked for this story, not for every story. Moreover, the violence and devastation were in service of a larger commentary on the genre, not just for spectacle. Other creators took away the flash and not the substance, to his annoyance.

Many fans misunderstood his intentions as well, especially when it came to Rorschach. There was no good guy in *Watchmen*. The moral ambiguity was the point. Yet fans embraced Rorschach wholeheartedly, championing him as the hero of the book. Rorschach was inspired by the Question, and Moore meant him to be a gruesome culmination of the right-wing, Randian views of Steve Ditko, the Question's creator. Moore called Rorschach a psychopath and said, "The entire world is just horror and shit to him, and he's the only moral person in it in his head. He's really frightening." Rorschach was wholly committed to his twisted view of justice. He was sullied by the "morally blank world" and the "accumulated filth of all their sex and murder," and "felt cleansed" whenever he killed a foe. Before *Watchmen* began, Moore predicted that fans would see Rorschach as a villain, and was shocked when the unwashed, mentally unwell murderer was cheered as a hero.

Watchmen, however innovative and genre redefining, also succumbed to the same pitfalls as *Daredevil* and *The Dark Knight Returns* when it came to women. There were only two major female characters in the book: Laurie Juspeczyk, a.k.a. Silk Spectre, and her mother Sally Jupiter, the Silk Spectre before her. Sally was a hero in the 1940s, and the bulk of her story line revolved around the Comedian raping and assaulting her. Laurie's story, meanwhile, centered on her romantic relationships with Doctor Manhattan and Nite Owl.

While the male characters had specific Charlton antecedents, Laurie did not. Moore admitted, "The Silk Spectre was just a female character because I needed to have a heroine in there," and he went on to explain, "The Silk Spectre, in that she's the girl of the group, sort of was the equivalent of Nightshade, but really, there's not much connection beyond that." She began the book as Doctor Manhattan's girlfriend, as well as his keeper to some extent, until she grew dissatisfied with the relationship and left him. Any potential self-actualization went by the wayside when she connected with Nite Owl a day later, a pairing that ultimately led to the curing of his impotence. Her role within *Watchmen* was always in relation to one of these two men, driving their behavior, which in turn drove the narrative rather than her ever driving the narrative herself.

Moore's limited use of female characters continued in another notable DC project two years later when he teamed with artist Brian Bolland for *Batman: The Killing Joke*. The story explored the duality between Batman and the Joker as the villain tried to push the hero to his limits by torturing his friends. It also gave the Joker an origin story, casting him as a failed stand-up comedian driven mad after the death of his wife and child. *The Killing Joke* was a hit in 1988, has remained a bestseller ever since, and has inspired multiple big-screen incarnations of the Joker.

The book began with the Joker kidnapping Commissioner Gordon, but not before he encountered his daughter Barbara. She answered the door at the commissioner's apartment and found the Joker, dressed in a Hawaiian shirt and a Panama hat. He shot her in her midsection, sending her flying backward through a glass coffee table as she fell to the floor. The Joker snarked, "She thinks she's a **coffee table edition**. Mind **you**, I can't say much for the volume's **condition**. I **mean**, there's a **hole** in the **jacket** and the **spine** appears to be damaged." The shooting left her paralyzed below the waist, but after two pages of Batman visiting her in the hospital, she didn't appear again in the book.

At least, not directly. As part of the Joker's psychological torture of Commissioner Gordon, he'd undressed and photographed Barbara immediately after he shot her, then showed Gordon the pictures in a twisted attempt to drive him mad. Bolland's snapshots were disturbing, showing Barbara bloodied and writhing in pain, though the printed panel was a second pass. The nudity was more explicit in his original artwork, fully exposing Barbara's bare torso, but the editors insisted he tone it down. After this scene, Barbara was mentioned once more in passing, and that was it. The focus was on Batman and the Joker, who ended the book sharing a demented laugh in the rain.

Barbara was still Batgirl when work on *The Killing Joke* began, and Moore and Bolland had to get permission to paralyze her. They asked editor Len Wein, who cavalierly replied, "Yeah, okay, cripple the bitch." DC embraced the change, and retired the character in *Batgirl Special* #1, a one-shot comic that came out the same month as *The Killing Joke*.

Despite its continued popularity, Moore doesn't care for *The Killing Joke*, calling it "clumsy [and] misjudged," and he feels that DC "should've reined me in, but they didn't." Bolland's not a huge fan either, and said of the book, "I must admit I had to grit my teeth a couple of times during the drawing of it." Very little of the book lives on in continuity. The Joker's origin story didn't really stick, and Gordon's torture has had no lasting impact on the character. Only the assault and paralysis of Barbara carried on.

Originally DC had no plans for Barbara, and the editors were happy to leave her to obscurity after the events of *The Killing Joke* until writers Kim Yale and John Ostrander brought her back a few years later as the computer genius Oracle in *Suicide Squad*. She went on to become the communications master for the Bat-family and the leader of an all-female team in the long-running series *Birds of Prey*. As one of the few superheroes in a wheelchair, Barbara became an inspiration to many in the disabled community, a wonderful turn of events after DC was ready to discard her entirely.

At the same time, her trauma in *The Killing Joke* has been replayed constantly over the past thirty years, referenced and redrawn in gruesome detail again and again. Creators have dealt with Barbara's posttraumatic stress in moving and compelling ways, but the fixation on this violent act against a female character is a disturbing trend. Multiple stories have established the assault as a fixed point that was key to the DC universe, a destined event that couldn't be altered by magic or time travel. When DC rebooted their line once more in 2011, Barbara regained the use of her legs and became Batgirl again, but *The Killing Joke* remained canon. She'd just recovered this time, and the Joker's hollow-eyed rictus grin as he shot her remained a constant flashback presence.

The legacy of Miller and Moore's work in the 1980s has been ruthless violence. While both men made remarkable, groundbreaking comics with depth beyond that, their appetite for brutality has had the biggest impact on the genre. Their proclivity for depicting sexual violence against women has been particularly influential, but harsh violence as a whole became the norm as their fellow creators brought the sensibilities of their work into the mainstream.

This bled into the fan community as well. Late in 1988, two years after *The Dark Knight Returns* and just months after *The Killing Joke*, the Joker captured the current Robin, Jason Todd, in the arc "A Death in the Family." The Joker beat Jason senseless with a crowbar and left him to die in an explosion in *Batman* #427, and the issue ended with a twist: readers could call into a 1-900 number and decide whether Jason lived or died. After over ten thousand votes, the verdict was in, and the following issue opened with Batman finding the lifeless body of his former partner.

CHAPTER 8

Caliber

The work of Frank Miller and Alan Moore normalized a new brand of graphic violence in superhero comics. Heroes had always punched out villains, but the tone changed from a swift sock on the jaw to more visceral beatings as mainline books tried to copy their style. This pursuit inevitably escalated, and soon punching wasn't enough. Between the desire to push the envelope further and the focus on realistic outcomes of violence, the brutality only increased. Instead of simple knockouts, now the villains were dying.

As a general rule, superheroes didn't kill. There was a more cavalier approach to death in the early years of the genre, especially in wartime environments, but by the time superheroes went mainstream in the early 1940s, killing was largely off the table. The Comics Code cemented this further in the 1950s, and even Miller and Moore still followed suit thirty years later. Daredevil and Batman stuck to a strict moral code, and while some of the superheroes in *Watchmen* did kill, they were hardly meant to be paragons of virtue. The conclusion of *Batman: The Killing Joke* emphasized the fact that heroes don't stoop to the level of villains, with Commissioner Gordon insisting that Batman bring the Joker in "by the **book**," because "we have to show him that our way **works!**" But by the late 1980s, many superheroes no longer followed this principle.

The poster child for this shift was Frank Castle, better known as the Punisher. He debuted in *Amazing Spider-Man* #129 in 1974, wearing an all-black outfit with a white skull emblazoned on his chest, and the cover of the book proclaimed, "He's **different**! He's **deadly**! He's the Punisher!" Inside the book, the villain Jackal hired him to kill Spider-Man, who was wanted at the time for the murder of Norman Osborn. The well-armed Punisher was a former Marine dedicated to "the complete **destruction** of the crimeworld in **New York**," and he explained, "I kill only those who **deserve** killing!" Spider-Man managed to convince him of his innocence by the end of the issue, and the Punisher went off in search of other targets.

Subsequent guest appearances fleshed out his backstory further. After a decorated if harsh military career in Vietnam, Frank returned home to civilian life with his wife and children only to have it end tragically when the family stumbled upon a mob execution while out on a picnic. His wife and children didn't survive the encounter, and Frank became the Punisher to avenge their deaths, using his military training to track down and eliminate New York City's most deadly criminals. The Punisher was an antihero, created to contrast with Marvel's more straitlaced leads, and he guest-starred in a handful of books over the next decade as heroes like Captain America, Daredevil, and Spider-Man challenged his lethal methods.

Then in 1986, the Punisher took center stage in his own miniseries. His actions had landed him in prison, but an offer from a wealthy group of "concerned citizens" to fight organized crime soon had him back out on the streets. The book had a lot of shooting and action, but surprisingly little in the way of actual death at the Punisher's hands. While some carnage was implied, it wasn't shown. In what would become a pattern, however, the Punisher slept with the only female character in the book and then, after learning she'd betrayed him, shot her Jeep off the road and left her to die rather than saving her.

The miniseries went over well with fans, and Marvel launched an ongoing *Punisher* title the following year written by Mike Baron with Klaus Janson drawing the book. Janson had inked Miller's *Daredevil* run, and the new series was going for a similarly gritty feel. The story didn't hold back on the violence, with the debut issue revealing the Punisher in a full-page spread with a rocket launcher strapped to his back. After using it, he jumped into the fray with his machine gun blaring to take out his remaining foes. The Punisher's narration made the death toll clear when he noted that he "left one breathing for conversation," though the sole survivor didn't make it through his interrogation.

While the Punisher had mainly been confined to New York in his past outings, the new series sent him around the globe in search of criminals to kill, often in disguise before he revealed his iconic logo and an array of weaponry. He infiltrated a drug operation in Bolivia, exposed white supremacists in the American Midwest, and gunned down Middle Eastern terrorists over the course of the book's early issues. Some story lines were ripped from the headlines, including an arc in which the Punisher took down a reverend based on Jim Jones and the infamous Jonestown cult.

The body count was high, though one issue made a point of showing the Punisher using a tranquilizer gun on guard dogs as he explained, "I hate to cause animals pain." This type of morbid humor was typical for the series, which drew inspiration from violent action movies of the 1980s. There was a lot of Arnold

The Punisher #2, art by Klaus Janson, Marvel Comics, 1987. The antihero gleefully gunned down his foes.

Schwarzenegger, Sylvester Stallone, and Jean-Claude Van Damme in the Punisher's DNA, and the character became so popular that he got an action movie of his own in 1989. Dolph Lundgren starred in the titular role as the Punisher took on the Yakuza, though release was limited by the film studio's financial issues.

Much like the action movies that inspired it, female roles in the Punisher comic book were extremely limited. Whenever Frank encountered a woman, he either slept with her, she died, or both. Sometimes his behavior was callous, like when a grief-stricken husband hired him to save his wife from the Jonestown-esque cult. He did save her, but first he had sex with the estranged wife thanks to the cult's free love policy. Other times the Punisher grew attached to someone, like when he considered a crimefighting partnership with a female Mossad agent, only to have her die during their first mission together.

This approach to female characters may have been one of the reasons why the letter column of *The Punisher* featured a whopping 99 percent male correspondents. While male fans accounted for the vast majority of letters at Marvel in this era, hovering at just over 90 percent, *The Punisher* pushed this discrepancy to extremes. The letters were enthusiastic as well. One fan commented, "Few comics today offer as much gritty realism and non-stop action as *The Punisher* does," while another cheered for "an American comic where people actually bleed!" The violence was particularly appreciated, with one reader calling it a "refreshing jolt, a definite buzz. This comic offers a much needed counterpoint to all of comicdom's other traditional-minded moralists." Many fans were on board with the Punisher's methods, and one letter about the cult arc suggested, "If there had been a real life Punisher a lot of wasted lives could have been saved in Jonestown."

The effusive praise reflected the book's success. It was such a bestseller that Marvel shifted it to twice monthly, and an assortment of spin-offs soon followed. *The Punisher War Journal* debuted in 1988, and featured quick, single-issue stories that reveled in the character's signature brand of violent mayhem. The weaponry was extensive, and each issue included an "equipment page" that featured detailed artwork of the guns and ammo used in the story. These meticulous pages spoke to a level of gun fetishism in Punisher fandom, a glorification of military weaponry. The pages proved so popular that Marvel collected them in their own series, *Punisher Armory*, which simply reprinted the pages along with a loose story to tie them all together.

More spin-offs followed. *Punisher War Zone* focused on long-form narratives that explored the character's trauma in more detail. *Punisher 2099* was a futuristic series set in a dystopian world with a new Punisher inspired by Frank's old journals. The various books were accompanied by special annual issues, additional miniseries and graphic novels, and even a *Punisher Magazine* that reprinted older stories in black and white.

The first issue of the magazine opened with a foreword from editor Carl Potts examining the Punisher phenomenon. He acknowledged that "some might say it's the blazing, fast-paced action that makes the Punisher popular," but he suggested, "the Punisher is more than an angry man with a gun." For Potts, the character was someone who'd been failed by traditional law and order time and again, "who has served and triumphed in a world of hard realities," and ultimately the stories provided "universal themes of guilt and responsibility for readers to identify with."

This thoughtful foreword was countered with an afterword from writer Mike Baron, who began, "The Punisher seems to have burbled up from some deep dark well of the American spirit. The voice of 'conservative' Americans who see the quality of life threatened by criminal behavior and the confused thinking of 'liberals.'" Baron went on to defend the Punisher's methods by arguing that "most Americans are overwhelmingly in favor of capital punishment, but the message can't seem to get by the special interest watchdog groups whose primary function is to make work for lawyers." He eventually concluded, "The police and the courts may constantly disappoint us, but the Punisher never does. So read and enjoy—and don't let the 'liberals' make you feel guilty."

The two pieces presented a stark dichotomy. Potts voiced what Marvel wished the Punisher was, a layered character with emotional and thematic depth. Baron laid bare what many fans saw in the Punisher, a vehicle for lethal violence that was a legitimate solution to society's ills. His rise coincided with a growing narrative in America that the best answer for a bad guy with a gun was a good guy with a gun. This connection was borne out years later when "Blue Lives Matter" rose in opposition to the "Black Lives Matter" movement sparked by decades of police brutality. The Punisher's skull logo became a symbol for "Blue Lives Matter" as its adherents unironically, and perhaps intentionally, embraced the wanton murderer and his violent ways, making clear the character's long-standing ties to ultraconservative gun rights values. Frank's unbridled anger and aggression were an apt match for the group and its dedication to the violent enforcement of police power.

By the early 1990s, the Punisher was arguably the most popular character in superhero comics. No one else headlined as many books, and his prominence led Marvel to explore the brutal potential of their other characters. One of the biggest beneficiaries of this new direction was Wolverine, who'd debuted as a clawed and costumed Canadian superhuman agent in *Incredible Hulk* #180 in 1974. He wasn't intended to be a major character, but *Incredible Hulk* writer Len Wein liked him enough to bring him back the following year as part of the publisher's X-Men reboot. He had a minor role initially until artist John Byrne joined *X-Men* and his affection for his fellow Canuck resulted in Wolverine's rise in prominence.

The origins of Wolverine, his retractable adamantium claws, and his healing powers remained a mystery for some time, but his fierce nature was evident early on. A 1984 solo miniseries by Chris Claremont and Frank Miller introduced the character's iconic line, "I'm the best there is at what I do. But what I do best isn't very nice," as he clawed his way through hordes of ninjas in Japan. The book also addressed his berserker rage, though the story made clear that he incapacitated the bulk of his opponents rather than killing them. The violence became more explicit in another miniseries two years later when he explained that the rage was "the part I can't control, the part that's truly crazy. It doesn't think. It doesn't feel pain. It kills. And once it's loose, it doesn't stop till I'm dead—or everyone else is."

Wolverine launched a self-titled solo book in 1988, again written by Claremont with art by John Buscema and Klaus Janson. The cover of the first issue encapsulated the tone of the series with Wolverine, shirt torn and his claws out, standing grimly atop a pile of dead bodies. Inside the book, Wolverine infiltrated the island hideout of Indonesian pirates to free the surviving passengers of a hijacked airliner. He was stealthy at first, snapping one guard's neck as he made his way to the survivors and then stabbing the guard watching them through the heart. Once they were secured, Wolverine made his presence known and launched into a berserker rage, slashing his way through a hundred pirates over the next five pages until they were all dead. Wolverine explained his approach in contrast with his day job in the X-Men, calling the team "good people. Idealists. Dreamers—forever looking for the best in others. With them, killing is a last resort. With me, it's second nature."

With that mission statement established, the series that followed focused on Wolverine doing missions too unsavory for the X-Men. He spent the bulk of the book's early years undercover in Madripoor, a corrupt Southeast Asian principality that was a haven for the Marvel universe's criminal elite, infiltrating their organizations then unleashing his violent fury. The series was a hit out of the gate, moving to a bimonthly schedule just months into its first year of publication, and Wolverine's profile rose considerably throughout the Marvel line. He's headlined at least one series ever since and remains one of Marvel's most popular characters today.

The Punisher's and Wolverine's rampant success led to more of the same at Marvel. Antiheroes like Cable, a gun-toting mutant from the future, and Ghost Rider, the flame-headed spirit of vengeance, headlined their own long-running books beginning in the early 1990s. They were joined by series of various lengths that included *Foolkiller* and his purification gun, the heavily armed *Silver Sable and the Wild Pack*, and comics with ominous names like *Darkhawk*, *Deathlok*, *Nightstalkers*, and *Motormouth & Killpower*.

Wolverine #1, art by John Buscema and Al Williamson, Marvel Comics, 1988. Wolverine atop a pile of corpses.

DC Comics followed suit, though with a twist. Instead of antiheroes, the publisher began to highlight their villains, adding new depths to the violent criminals. *Suicide Squad* featured a team of supervillain inmates on dangerous missions for the government, *Eclipso* starred the fiendish "face of vengeance," and *Deathstroke the Terminator* was a vehicle for the famed assassin and statutory rapist. In 1990, Keith Giffen reintroduced his character Lobo in a miniseries that intentionally parodied Marvel's violent antihero trend, depicting him as a homicidal maniac killing his way across the galaxy with a chained hook. The satire was lost entirely. Fans loved the new take on the character, leading to more miniseries and eventually an ongoing *Lobo* book that ran for over five years.

Compelling fight scenes were pivotal to the rise of these action-packed comic books, which led to an increased profile for the artists who drew them. At Marvel, their most popular books were drawn by a new generation of young artists. Neal Adams's brand of realism had remained the house style for the main titles at both DC and Marvel well into the 1980s, but these new artists employed an exaggerated realism that pushed the artwork further. Muscles were bigger and better defined, the heroes were more powerful, and this injection of brute physical strength into even the most average superhero helped sell the impact of the violent action.

Some of these young artists worked on Marvel's premier antiheroes. Jim Lee started on *Punisher: War Journal*, and then launched a much-hyped new *X-Men* series in 1991. Rob Liefeld drew a team of militant mutants led by Cable in *X-Force*, Whilce Portacio had runs on *The Punisher* and *Uncanny X-Men*, and Marc Silvestri spent a couple of years on *Wolverine*. Elsewhere with the publisher's more conventional heroes, Erik Larsen was a mainstay on *Amazing Spider-Man*, Todd McFarlane wrote and drew his own *Spider-Man* title, and Jim Valentino had a lengthy run on *Guardians of the Galaxy*.

Soon fans bought Marvel books more for the dynamic art than the writing. Despite driving the sales, however, the artists only received standard page rates with low royalties and earned little from the licensed merchandise that prominently featured their work. Wanting financial control over their creations, Larsen, Lee, Liefeld, McFarlane, Portacio, Silvestri, and Valentino launched their own publishing company, Image Comics, leaving their work-for-hire jobs en masse in 1992 to build their own superhero universes.

What resulted was a new array of antiheroes, variations on the existing formula made popular at Marvel but taken to extremes now that the artists were free of the publisher's remaining strictures. With everyone writing and drawing their own books, the result was an absolute spectacle of grisly violence and wall-to-wall fight scenes across the line, even from those who had done tamer work at Marvel.

Lee's *WildC.A.T.s* starred a superhero team embroiled in an alien war, the characters armed with all manner of weapons from futuristic artillery to traditional handguns to swords. In an early brawl, the sharpshooter Grifter made a point of noting, "Have to make 'em all **headshots** . . . only way to kill them for sure." Liefeld's *Youngblood* careened from one bloody shoot-out to another, his heroes sporting impractically enormous guns that tore apart their foes. Portacio's *Wetworks* featured a well-armed vampire-hunting black ops team in gold symbiotic armor, Silvestri's *Cyberforce* had burly leads with evocative names like Stryker and Ripclaw, and Larsen's *Savage Dragon* starred a superpowered police officer who dual-wielded machine guns in one issue before trading them for double chainsaws in another. Valentino's *Shadowhawk* was a vigilante who paralyzed and mutilated his foes to keep them off the streets, while McFarlane's *Spawn* had a gruesomely supernatural bent as the title character used his Hell-given powers to battle demons and criminals.

The Image founders were artists, not editors and certainly not businessmen, and the rollout of the new publisher was a mess, with issues shipping late and promised books delayed. Fans loved the books nonetheless, and stuck with them. Several Image titles became consistent bestsellers, and before long the publisher accounted for more than 10 percent of all direct market comic books sold each month, trailing only Marvel and DC. The appetite for brutal antiheroes was enormous, and the Image creators gave the fans what they wanted.

Initially, the move toward violence was isolated to small albeit wildly popular corners of DC's and Marvel's publishing line. Their long-standing heroes maybe punched a bit harder and got a little bloodier now, but the rampant brutality elsewhere didn't seep into their books. This was especially true at DC, where foundational characters like Superman and Batman were thought to be above the fray of fads and trends. Then sales started to drop, and continued to fall more with each passing month. The old stalwarts weren't staying afloat on reputation alone, and DC decided to make some bold moves to become relevant to readers again.

Superman was popular outside of comics. Christopher Reeve's *Superman* film franchise had been a smash a decade earlier, and the character was set to hit the small screen in ABC's *Lois & Clark: The New Adventures of Superman*. Both projects featured an affable Clark Kent and a warm, caring Superman. There was action, but the heart of the story was always Superman's relationships with others, particularly Lois Lane. It was a winning formula too. The Superman films made over half a billion dollars, while *Lois & Clark* ran for four seasons. The general public liked a kindhearted Man of Steel.

Comic book fans did not. DC had rebooted the bulk of their line in 1986, with John Byrne relaunching Superman to much acclaim, but interest had tapered off by the early 1990s. With readers flocking to the Punisher and

Wolverine, sales for the Superman line were falling and the writers decided on a drastic new plan to make readers appreciate the formerly beloved character they were now ignoring: they would kill off Superman.

They did so in typical early 1990s fashion with a massive brawl. The villain was Doomsday, a mysterious, gargantuan creature covered in spikes whose imposing aesthetic was inspired by Image Comics' penchant for ferocious, muscle-bound monsters. Superman stepped in to stop the rampaging beast, leading to a fight that spanned four issues and culminated in *Superman* #75 with the combatants beating each other to death. While Superman appeared to emerge triumphant at first, he succumbed to his wounds and died in Lois's arms in a special three-page foldout.

His death let DC engage in a bit of fun with a spate of replacement Supermen. The young Superboy was all cocky attitude, while Cyborg Superman and the Eradicator were violent vigilantes in the vein of Marvel's antiheroes. Although the original Superman inevitably returned, he maintained a grim visage for a short while, with a black costume and a silver logo. The death of Superman made news across the world and the comics sold well, especially *Superman* #75, but most of the buyers were lapsed fans returning or curious newcomers. Established fandom didn't bite, and the new buyers didn't stick around for long. The event was a successful stunt but did little to stem the genre's larger slide toward antiheroes.

DC editorial decided that the short-term gain was worth the effort and tried a similar stunt with Batman the following year. The Caped Crusader was on more solid ground than the Man of Steel with a popular film franchise on the go, a well-regarded cartoon series, and decent comic book sales thanks to the lingering effects of the character's late 1980s renaissance. Nonetheless, the trend toward brutal violence was taking over the industry, and Batman was next in line to suffer through it.

The event was called "Knightfall," and it began in 1993 with the introduction of the villain Bane, a superstrong, luchador-inspired character. Bane freed all the inmates in Arkham Asylum, and recapturing them all left Batman exhausted. When he finally faced off against Bane, the villain handled him with ease, pummeling Batman mercilessly before lifting him up and snapping his spine over his knee. Bane then threw Batman off a roof in downtown Gotham and left him for dead.

Batman managed to survive the encounter, but he was paralyzed and Bruce Wayne began a lengthy rehabilitation process. While he healed, Jean-Paul Valley, better known as the hero Azrael, took over as Batman with a new armored costume and a decidedly more aggressive approach to crimefighting. He grew increasingly violent as the months went on, alarming Robin with his ferocity and his growing arsenal of deadly weapons, then lost Bruce's trust when he intentionally let a villain die. The event ended with a fight between a newly mobile Bruce and Jean-Paul, with the latter ultimately conceding the mantle to his predecessor.

"Knightfall" again allowed DC to explore darker antiheroes in their comic book universe. They didn't last for long, but the books were popular and the publisher continued to intersperse violent story lines across the line, making the rounds through the entire original Justice League. Green Lantern went mad, becoming the destructive Parallax. Wonder Woman had to relinquish her title to an intense, vicious upstart Amazon with far less mercy for criminals. Aquaman lost his hand in a fight and replaced it with a sharp harpoon. Green Arrow died in an explosion. The sheer carnage of it all was considerable.

And readers ate it up. The definition of heroism had changed for the predominately male teens and young adults who now comprised the bulk of superhero comic book fandom. Saving the world with restrained strength and compassion was an antiquated notion, and the old values that had defined the genre were dismissed as corny. Now vengeance was seen as honorable, anger and violence heralded as an appropriate response to villainy. Raw, fierce machismo ruled the day, and while the popularity of antiheroes did eventually wane, the lingering influence of this era and its savage masculinity still remains strong across superhero media.

CHAPTER 9

Exaggeration

The art style of the Image founders spread across DC Comics and Marvel before the artists left to form their own publisher, and only grew more prevalent in mainstream superhero books as the 1990s continued. Exaggeratedly muscled heroes became the norm, but not without variation. Wolverine was compact but strong, a ferocious nuisance who could slice his way through hordes of opponents. The Flash was sleeker than most, aerodynamically chiseled for high speed. The Punisher was solidly built, sturdy enough to carry heavy weaponry and absorb the kick of a machine gun. Superman was a wall of muscle, his bulk indicative of his superhuman strength. And the Hulk was just enormous, a towering mass of seething brawn that bordered on the grotesque. Appearance reflected the character.

At least, it did for male characters. Wonder Woman was slender, with impossibly long legs, a small waist, and a sizable bust. Catwoman, now the lead in her own series, was slender, with impossibly long legs, a small waist, and a sizable bust. The gun-toting mercenary Silver Sable was slender, with impossibly long legs, a small waist, and a sizable bust. And the newly resurrected Elektra was slender, with impossibly long legs, a small waist, and a sizable bust.

There was little to no difference between each female character. The influx of muscles didn't reach the women of DC and Marvel, though exaggeration certainly did. Limbs were longer and more toned, and while waists shrunk considerably, the losses were balanced by growth in the chest and posterior. Costumes were tight, necklines plunged, and coming up with new and creative ways to show more skin became a common pastime for artists.

Differences in the depiction of male and female characters were nothing new for the genre. Such discrepancies dated back to the earliest days of superhero comics. Batman and Superman were fully clothed, with capes to boot, while Wonder Woman ran around in a star-spangled bathing suit and boots. Some

Golden Age heroines were designed specifically to emphasize their sexuality, like Black Canary with her low-cut top and fishnet stockings or the midriff-baring Namora. The cut of Phantom Lady's wispy top plunged almost to her navel, prompting Dr. Fredric Wertham to decry her corrupting influence years after she'd ceased to be a regular player in the genre.

Wertham and the Comics Code Authority led to chaste depictions of female characters during DC's renaissance in the late 1950s. Unobjectionable content was the publisher's primary aim, so new additions like Bat-Woman and Supergirl had costumes with thorough coverage and weren't drawn to emphasize their figures. Marvel pushed that slightly with the form-fitting outfits of shapely characters like Sue Storm, the Wasp, and Jean Grey, but it was nothing overtly scandalous.

Then, as the audience for superhero comics shifted firmly to male teens and young adults by the mid-1970s, the depiction of female characters began to change. Ms. Marvel's costume started out small and only shrunk further, while Elektra was sheathed in a skintight red wrapping that left little to the imagination. The shocking reveal of Terra's affair with Deathstroke in *New Teen Titans* was drawn to be intentionally titillating, but so too was Starfire's minuscule everyday outfit. Supergirl donned a low-cut shirt and short shorts, and Jean Grey ended up in bondage gear during the "Dark Phoenix Saga." Artists intentionally steered toward objectification, far more than they ever had before.

Still, there was some diversity of appearance. Case in point: She-Hulk. While Jennifer Walters matched the standard proportions of most female characters, when she turned into She-Hulk her body changed entirely. She was considerably taller and more muscular, a rampaging behemoth who showed why her series was called *Savage She-Hulk*. The character embodied raw brute force, a far cry from the more carefully coiffed and posed women elsewhere at DC and Marvel.

At the same time, however, she was treated much differently than her cousin, the Hulk. Bruce Banner grew to inhuman proportions that bordered on the monstrous when he became the Hulk, his face contorting into a frightening visage. She-Hulk maintained a feminine figure, still curvaceous in a conventionally attractive manner, just bigger and green. Her face didn't change much either. She was angrier, but her features didn't shift in any abnormal way. Moreover, when she transformed, her ripped clothing was strategically placed, baring her shapely legs and highlighting her cleavage. Some issues of *Savage She-Hulk* even featured special pinup pages with her posed like a model in a photo shoot. There were no such pinups in the pages of *Incredible Hulk*.

Savage She-Hulk ended in 1982, but she remained a regular part of the Marvel universe, joining the Avengers soon after her book was canceled and later becoming a member of the Fantastic Four. She-Hulk's guest appearances continued to emphasize her sexual appeal, including "The Naked Truth" in *Fantastic*

Four #275. The issue opened with a full-page spread of her sunbathing topless, inspired by a Kevin Nowlan pinup in *Marvel Fanfare* #18 of a similar scene. As the story continued, a photographer in a helicopter took a picture of her, so she raced after him and demolished his helicopter.

The writer and artist of "The Naked Truth," John Byrne, launched a new series for the character in 1989 with a less aggressive title, *Sensational She-Hulk*. By this point, Jennifer could no longer return to her human form. She was tall and green at all times, which could make life challenging, but she had the confidence and strength to deal with whatever came her way. Perhaps with "The Naked Truth" in mind, the opening issues of the book showed She-Hulk in a variety of small outfits, including one improbable scene where a barrage of alien weapon fire completely destroyed her oversized turtleneck sweater, leaving her in just her bra.

Sensational She-Hulk's letter column made clear that this was the sort of content readers wanted. One fan admitted, "I have had the biggest crush on the She-Hulk for such a long time now," and another concurred: "I know it's insane to be in love with a girl who's 4 1/2 inches taller than me, green, and able to bench press a neighborhood, but I don't care." Readers called her "beautiful," "gorgeous," and "sexy," with one writing, "I'm proud to say I'm addicted to your sensational greenness. The way you are drawn in your new series, how could any guy not be?" For the duration of the series, male fans comprised over 90 percent of the correspondence in the letter column, just slightly lower than the publisher's overall average in this era despite the book having a female lead.

Byrne leaned into this audience and their infatuation with She-Hulk during his initial run, and doubled down on it when he returned to the book a few years later. One cover parodied Demi Moore's famous *Vanity Fair* shoot in which she was nude and pregnant, showing She-Hulk in a tiny bikini holding a green beach ball to mimic the pose. Another had She-Hulk naked, just barely covering herself with the Comic Code Authority's "Seal of Approval." The cover text declared, "This is it! Because you demanded it!" and the book opened with five pages of She-Hulk jumping rope, seemingly nude as the blur of the rope strategically covered her private areas.

The treatment of She-Hulk was in no way subtle. There was the usual superhero action and adventure, but both the creators and regular readers understood that everyone was there to ogle the statuesque lead character and the storytelling catered to that. It's no wonder that years later David Goyer, the cowriter of Christopher Nolan's *Dark Knight* trilogy, cavalierly referred to She-Hulk as "a giant green porn star." That's how many fans viewed not just her, but female superheroes as a whole in this era. *Sensational She-Hulk* was not an outlier by any means.

Sensational She-Hulk #34, art by John Byrne, Marvel Comics, 1991. The green giantess re-created Demi Moore's classic *Vanity Fair* cover.

Many of the Image launch books included female leads, all with identically slender yet curvaceous bodies. *WildC.A.T.s* introduced Zealot, a sword-wielding warrior in a tiny red outfit, calling her "an avenging angel with a body worth killing for. [. . .] Sex and violence, all rolled together with a bad attitude." Void, in her skintight silver costume, had the exact same body shape, as did Voodoo, a telepathic, shape-shifting stripper. *Youngblood's* Riptide followed suit, along with *Cyberforce's* Cyblade and Velocity, and *Wetworks'* Mother-One and Pilgrim. The women were practically interchangeable, differentiated only by hair color and skin tone. That the publisher positioning itself as the innovative future of the superhero genre treated their female characters with such hypersexualized uniformity spoke volumes about the state of the industry in the early 1990s.

This bled into established characters at DC and Marvel as well. When artist Mike Deodato Jr. joined *Wonder Woman* in 1994, the character immediately conformed to the new standard body shape, and her costume adjusted to match. Her briefs rode up past her waist and her breasts perched high upon her chest, while her face adopted the sultry gaze that was now ubiquitous for all female characters. He brought a similar look to the Amazons, duplicating the body type and putting them in minuscule outfits. When Artemis won the mantle of Wonder Woman, Diana shifted to a new outfit composed of black leather shorts, an open leather jacket, and a small bikini top.

Elsewhere at DC, the new *Catwoman* series trod similar ground. Artist Jim Balent's Catwoman had the same body shape, albeit more well endowed, though she was covered from head to toe as her purple outfit, black boots, and black gloves left only parts of her face exposed. However, the costume was impossibly tight, basically a second skin. According to an assistant editor who worked on the series, Balent drew Catwoman nude and the colorist just colored her purple. The editor had to regularly erase nipples from Balent's penciled pages before sending them to the inker. Such sexualized artwork led to rumors that Balent was tracing pornography, an accusation also leveled at several other popular artists at the time with varying degrees of proof.

At Marvel, sometimes the publisher didn't even bother with the nuisance of storytelling. In 1991, they released *Marvel Illustrated: Swimsuit Issue*, a take on *Sports Illustrated's* annual swimsuit issue, and dedicated a twenty-two-page spread to pinups of their characters in beachwear. At the time, Marvel had far more male superheroes than female. In the same month the swimsuit issue was released, there was only one solo book with a female lead, *Sensational She-Hulk*. Men headlined more than twenty solo books, and comprised the majority of Marvel's team titles as well. And yet, women accounted for 60 percent of the characters drawn in the swimsuit issue. Half of the pages featured only women, with mixed groupings on several more, and just two pages had only men.

The characters were treated differently as well. All the female characters were in bathing suits, most of them quite revealing, and they were posed to show them off. The majority of the male characters were shown in swim trunks rather than briefs, with some even appearing in full superhero costume, and their posing leaned toward goofy beach fun rather than displaying their assets. Marvel released annual swimsuit issues in the years that followed with more equitable posing, but even then the fact remained that showing male characters wearing small outfits in revealing, intentionally sexualized poses was a novelty. For female characters, such depictions were par for the course.

This constant objectification didn't go over well with female fans who, while a small minority of the readership, made their voices heard. The letter column of *Catwoman* became a forum to debate Jim Balent's artwork and the exaggerated portrayals of female characters generally. Male fans praised Balent, heralding him time and again as one of the best in the business. Some female fans, however, had reservations. One female reader asked outright, "Why is Catwoman so busty?" and another pointed out, "Catwoman's chest looks completely out of proportion. For a person who relies on balance and agility like she does, you'd think those huge protrusions would interfere tremendously." When male readers and editors continued to defend Balent's work unreservedly, Laura McLellan provided some perspective when she wrote in:

> Please reconsider your stand on how Selina's body is drawn. Girls are surrounded by unrealistic images of women every day, and by filling comic books with women whose bodies are consistently out of proportion, you are simply encouraging young women to have poor self-images and unrealistic expectations about how they should look.

Her concerns went unheeded. A male reader expressed the majority opinion when he pointed out that male superheroes were also drawn in an exaggerated way and said, "Shirtless men with abnormal biceps are standard fare. I'm curious why Catwoman is being singled out as a sexist character in her current incarnation." The editorial response chimed in, "Well said," agreeing with his argument that superhero artwork was over the top across the board, and that its excesses affected characters of all genders equally.

But it didn't. With primarily heterosexual male writers, artists, and editors crafting superheroes for a predominately heterosexual male audience, two different approaches were at play. While male characters were drawn in an exaggerated way with massive muscles, this was a male power fantasy, a projection of masculine might. The artists' intent wasn't to make the characters sexually appealing. It was to show off their strength, to highlight how hard they could punch, how much they could lift, how fast they could run. There was a degree of wish fulfillment at play as well, as male creators and fans imagined who they might be if they were the last son of an alien planet or an orphaned billionaire.

Conversely, female superheroes were crafted specifically to be sexually appealing. They were a male sexual fantasy, drawn in proportions and poses that catered directly to the desires of the audience. Strength, ability, and personality were not a concern. Instead, there was a uniform concept of the idealized feminine form and every female character was made to fit it. Failing to do so meant disaster. For instance, when Jim Balent left *Catwoman* and the new artist moved away from Balent's embellished proportions, sales dropped immediately.

A power fantasy is about projection, rooted in imagining what you could do as the character. A sexual fantasy is about objectification, rooted in imagining what a character could do for you. In superhero comics, men were drawn to be powerful and women were drawn to be sexy, and those were two extremely different intentions. There was no equality there, and it's only recently that fans and creators have started to reckon with this skewed dynamic.

The hypersexualization of female superheroes was so widespread that in recent years, as fans and critics began to deconstruct it, specific lingo was developed to articulate its excesses. One common descriptor was "boob socks," a phenomenon in which a tight, supposedly spandex outfit conformed exactly to a character's breasts. In real life, spandex compresses and evens out curves. In comics, spandex maintained a globular structure, as if the costume was built with two pockets on the chest. Such costuming was ubiquitous in the 1990s; it's still not uncommon today. Balent's Catwoman was the poster child for it, but any female lead in any superhero comic book from that decade probably exhibited it to some degree.

Related but different was the "boob window," a hole in the costume that highlighted a character's décolletage. Power Girl was its most well-known employer, given her substantial chest and the sizable void in the costume that adorned it. Various writers tried to explain the outfit, with some calling it a useful distraction when battling male criminals and others tying it to an identity crisis because she couldn't decide on a logo. These weak justifications failed to disguise the true intention of the window: showing more of the character.

Windows were less common than socks, but there was more variety. At one point in the early 1990s, Sue Storm uncharacteristically changed her costume and had the number "4" cut out across her cleavage. Emma Frost took the idea to extremes in the early 2000s, crafting an "X" for X-Men across her bare torso with the negative space created by four triangular pieces of fabric at her neck, across her breasts, and along her waist. The Star Sapphires extended the window to their navels, the costumes barely peeking around their sides enough to cover the essentials. For the women, anyway. Male Star Sapphires were fully clothed.

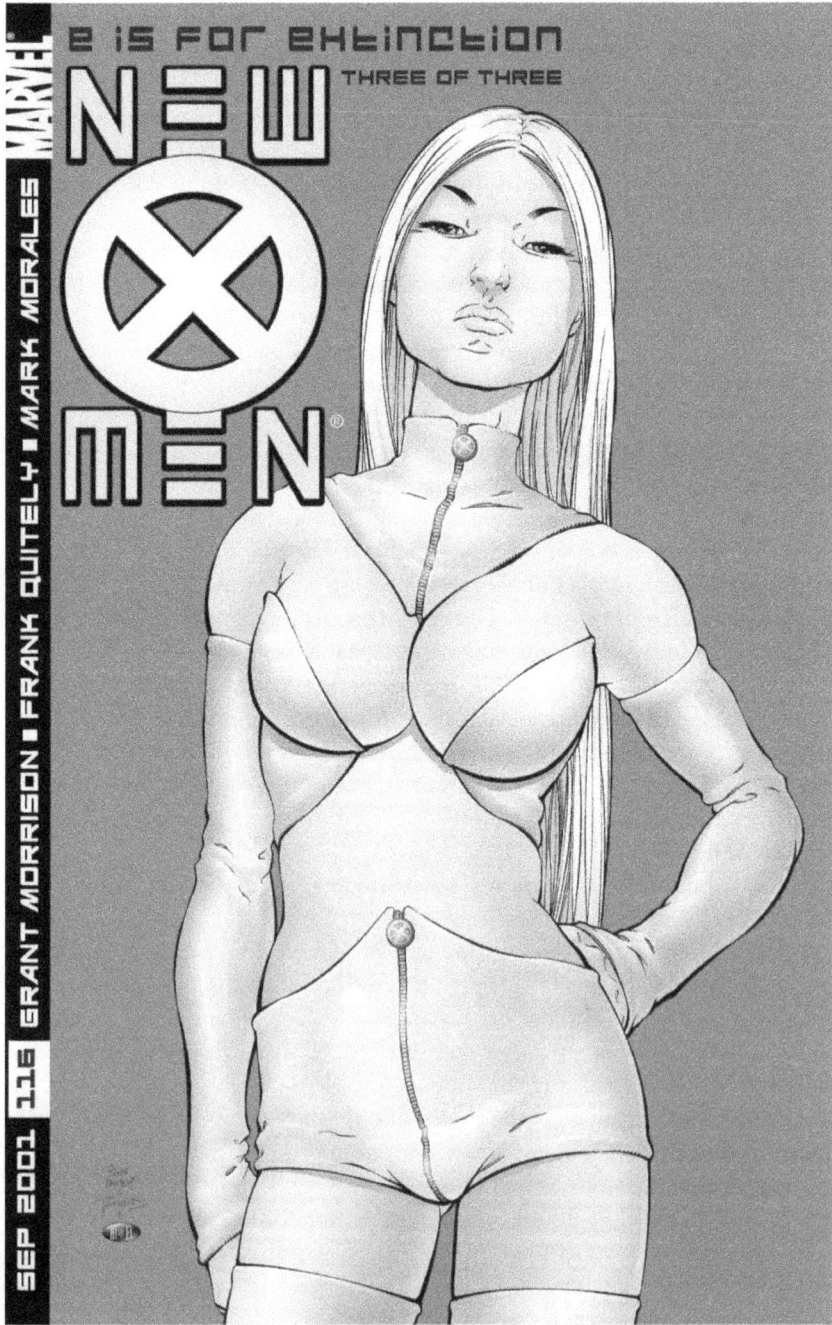

New X-Men #116, art by Frank Quitely, Tim Townsend, and Hi-Fi, Marvel Comics, 2001. Emma Frost with a negative space "X" design.

Starfire did the same as the female Star Sapphires, with the core of her entire upper body on display.

Starfire's costume somehow shrunk even further in 2011 when DC debuted their New 52 relaunch. Her collarbone was well covered, but her entire torso was exposed apart from two small, strategically placed pieces of fabric. The costume was met with much derision, but again writers tried to explain it away. Judd Winick had attempted to rationalize her previous look when he had Starfire opine, "Human prudishness still baffles me. I will never fully comprehend how a society that is so intensely preoccupied with sex is equally cowed by nudity," while her New 52 writer Scott Lobdell tied it to her alien species' embrace of sexual freedom. During Lobdell's explanation, Starfire was in a tiny bikini propositioning a coworker, and she was fully nude in a full-page spread during Winick's monologue.

The New 52 relaunch as a whole brought an array of hypersexualization. *Catwoman* #1 opened with Selina Kyle undressed, the panels focused on her chest and her lacy red bra, and didn't show the character's face until several pages into the issue. *Voodoo* #1 began with a similar fixation, with five straight pages of the lead character stripping in a club. Costumes for female characters were smaller and tighter throughout the line, including *Suicide Squad* swapping out Harley Quinn's full-body jester outfit for tiny shorts and a loosely laced cropped bustier.

Small outfits weren't just for superheroes either. Over the course of the 1990s, Lois Lane traded her trench coats and bulky sweaters for negligees, if even that. Her marriage to Clark Kent gave artists the opportunity for strategically covered postcoital nudity, which they took often. Everyday outfits shifted, too, her shirts becoming smaller and tighter while the trend toward low-rise pants led to panels in which Lois's thong was clearly visible above her waistline. Thongs that peeked up in such a manner were a bizarre preoccupation throughout the early 2000s, as if artists wanted readers to know exactly what sort of underwear female characters were wearing for fear they'd assume it was a less sexy brief. Even teenagers were subject to this, like when Michael Turner drew the return of Supergirl in *Superman/Batman* and made sure that her underwear rode up well above her jeans.

Turner was adept at another much-discussed term for critiquing comic book art: the "brokeback pose." This occurs when a character, almost always female, is drawn so that her rear end and her chest are visible at the same time, a position that in real life would require a degree of painful contortion. It was common on covers, where group shots often showed male characters simply facing forward while female characters wracked their spines to show off all their assets at once. Fight scenes were a major culprit as well, with women literally bending over backward to ensure their kicks and punches looked suitably sexy.

The cover of *Marvel Adventures Super Heroes* #17 in 2011 demonstrated this well as Black Widow and Hawkeye jumped down from a tall building. Hawkeye jumped normally, vertically positioned with his knees bent for a safe landing. Black Widow, meanwhile, was upside down, her chest facing forward with her waist twisted to show her behind as she did the splits in midair for no discernible reason. A year later, Tumblr user HoursAgo was struck by the discrepancy and redrew the cover, swapping the characters while maintaining the posing so Black Widow was falling sensibly and Hawkeye was on full display. The art was posted with the message, "for real though look me in the eye and tell me which is more likely for these two."

At the time, Hawkeye was the bumbling lead of a much-lauded solo series by Matt Fraction and David Aja, and the goofy pose certainly matched his persona more than the businesslike Black Widow. The post blew up, and *Nimona* artist ND Stevenson suggested, "how to fix every Strong Female Character pose in superhero comics: replace the character with Hawkeye doing the same thing." Stevenson drew a few examples, inserting Hawkeye in place of contorted artwork of Ms. Marvel and Psylocke. The idea caught on and led to the *Hawkeye Initiative*, a Tumblr page dedicated to fan art that exposed sexist double standards.

The *Hawkeye Initiative* was part of a defining moment in superhero fandom. Readers had been vocal in their critique of superhero artwork for a few years at this point, especially in the wake of the New 52 relaunch, with the growing audience of fans of marginalized genders leading the charge. The *Hawkeye Initiative* received a lot of press coverage, and the lighthearted but incisive pieces spurred more conversations about the unexamined gender biases that plagued the genre. These readers loved the characters, and celebrated the moments when they were treated well without being afraid to criticize publishers when they fell short. Calling out the male gaze was one of the first in a long list of issues the genre continues to wrestle with today.

One of the primary criticisms was the ubiquity of the genre's objectification. Laura Hudson, then editor of the *Comics Alliance* site, noted that DC's and Marvel's books "range from comics where women are sexualised to comics where they are really, really sexualised in offensive ways." Female characters were drawn to fit the same mold, in the same small outfits, for the same purpose. There was no diversity, no nuance, no range of form. This particular brand of "sexiness" wasn't even the problem. There was nothing wrong with being sexy. The trouble came from making every female character sexy, all the time, especially with men writing and drawing the bulk of the comics. That's just fetishism, and a growing segment of the audience was now demanding better.

The *Hawkeye Initiative* and other critiques of the genre faced backlash from many fans who, after being the targeted demographic for the past forty years, were happy with the way things were. Nonetheless, publishers started to listen and things began to change. Ms. Marvel became Captain Marvel, going back to her air force roots and trading her black bathing suit for a flight suit–inspired costume. Batgirl swapped her tight outfit for a leather jacket and sensible Doc Martens boots, and Spider-Woman hung up her spandex for a similar look. Realistic proportions were added to the mix as well. Squirrel Girl embraced her curves and was a beacon of body positivity, while Valiant Comics' *Faith* became the first superhero comic book with a plus-size female lead. A common denominator in all these changes was more female creators at every level, spurring new ideas from within the major publishers.

Change has been slow, with many ups and downs. Batgirl is in tight spandex again these days. So is Spider-Woman. New designs sometimes fall into old patterns, as if the enlightening discourse of the past decade had never happened. But little by little, the industry's approach to female characters is growing. DC and Marvel have shown that they have the ability to treat them like people, not objects, and a sizable core of the fandom continues to push them to do so. While the progress is minor, it's progress nonetheless.

CHAPTER 10

Breakdown

After decades of young men dominating superhero fandom as publishers catered directly to them, the 2000s saw a major shift in readership with a noticeable rise in female fans. The numbers swelled over the course of the decade, and by the 2010s young women were the fastest-growing demographic of comic book readers. In 2016, Marvel senior vice president David Gabriel said, "[Based on] analysis that Disney does on who is buying Marvel as a brand, and from talking to retailers and looking at our titles, we're probably up to at least 40 percent female, which eight years ago might have been 10 percent. And 15 years ago might have been nothing."

There were many avenues that led to this influx. Some female fans had always been there, sticking with the genre even when it showed no interest in their patronage. Others came to superheroes via the massive rise in superhero media. Movie franchises like the *X-Men* films, the *Dark Knight* trilogy, and the Marvel Cinematic Universe had a wide appeal, while cartoons like *Justice League: Unlimited* and *Teen Titans Go!* appealed to young fans of all genders and shows like *Smallville* proved popular with teens. The increased profile of other genres made the comic book medium more popular as well. Manga developed a substantial female fan base in North America, while comics like *Sandman*, *Fables*, and *Alias* served as gateways to DC and Marvel, where new readers became enthusiastic followers of female-centered titles like *Birds of Prey* and *Runaways*.

Although female readership was clearly on the rise as the new century began, publishers were slow to respond. They were flummoxed by the shift, even dismissive at times as the growing ranks of women readers shared both their love and their concerns about the genre and expressed hope for better representation. This poor response came in large part because nearly everyone in positions of power at DC and Marvel were men, as were the bulk of their workforce. Male creators had been writing and drawing stories for male readers for decades now,

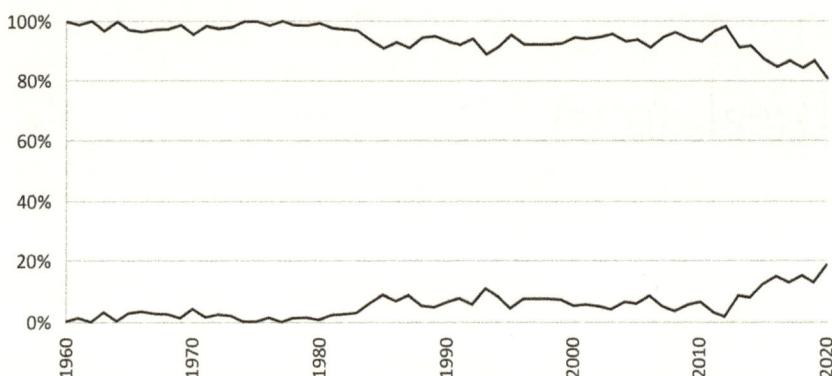

Male (top) and female (bottom) writers at DC Comics, 1960-2020.

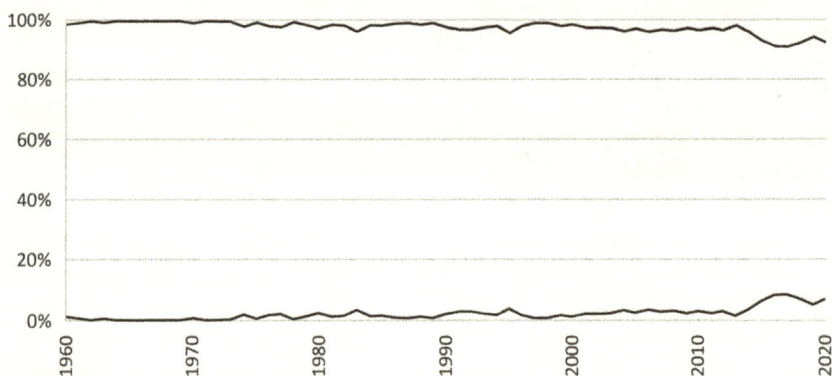

Male (top) and female (bottom) artists at DC Comics, 1960-2020.

and most had never known otherwise. It took some time for this dynamic to shift.

To illustrate the degree to which men have dominated the creation of superhero comics, we're going to look back at data from the past sixty years, starting with DC Comics. The charts above break down the percentage of male and female creators by year, first for writers and then for interior artists. This data was assembled by tabulating the credits from every issue published in two months from each year, January and August, and charting out the subsequent percentages.

DC's comic books from the 1960s and 1970s were an almost entirely male domain, with the percentages for female writers and artists barely peaking into the low single digits. The vast majority of these few female writers worked on romance comics, and their numbers dropped from low to practically nothing once DC ended their romance line in the mid-1970s. A significant portion of the art credits were from Ramona Fradon, the only woman to work regularly on DC's superhero titles across this span. She drew the "Aquaman" feature in *Adventures Comics* and cocreated Metamorpho in the 1960s, then had runs on *Plastic Man*, *Freedom Fighters*, and *Super Friends* in the following decade.

Kinney National bought DC in 1967 then put the company under the umbrella of Warner Communications in 1972, and the corporate bosses hired a new publisher from the world of magazines, Jenette Kahn, in 1976. Kahn was promoted to president five years later, but having a woman running the show didn't do much to change representation initially. Irene Vartanoff, an assistant editor at DC in the early 1980s, said of the publisher, "Although the company is headed by a woman, her advisors and lieutenants in the chain of command either overtly or unconsciously are chauvinistic, believing there is little merit in any comic with a female point of view. [. . .] The major effort required to win back the female market isn't an important current priority."

While men continued to monopolize the art scene in the 1980s, the number of female writers began to grow. However, many of these credits belonged to the wives of male writers who cowrote books with their husbands, including Dann Thomas and her husband Roy, Carla Conway and her husband Gerry, and Kim Yale and her husband John Ostrander. This fact is pointed out not to diminish their contributions, because these women were instrumental in many key story lines from this decade, but to illustrate DC's narrow pipeline for female talent. Beyond the wives of established creators, editors weren't looking hard elsewhere for women to work on their books. A handful of other women landed short gigs in this era, but they were few and far between.

In the late 1980s, Kahn oversaw the expansion of DC's mature readers line after the success of *Batman: The Dark Knight Returns* and *Watchmen*, and tasked editor Karen Berger with finding new talent and titles. Books like *Animal Man*, *Hellblazer*, and *Sandman* led the charge, and the mature readers line ended up collected under a separate imprint, Vertigo, in 1993. Vertigo's smaller line featured more female creators than DC's superhero titles, including artists Colleen Doran and Jill Thompson on *Sandman*, writer Nancy Collins on *Swamp Thing*, and writer Rachel Pollack on *Doom Patrol*.

There were women on the mainline books, though, albeit intermittently. Doran and Thompson drew a few issues of *Wonder Woman* while Mindy Newell cowrote the book for a brief time, and *Catwoman* had several female writers including Jo Duffy and Devin Grayson. The sole constant initially was Louise Simonson, who began a lengthy run writing *Superman: The Man of Steel* in 1991. Grayson launched *Batman: Gotham Knights* in 2000 and added *Nightwing* the following year, while writer Gail Simone took over *Birds of Prey* in 2003, revitalizing the flagging title and making it a haven for female fans.

Simone became a fixture at DC in the 2000s on books including *Action Comics*, *Secret Six*, *Wonder Woman*, and many more, but the publisher's creator split remained fairly constant for both writers and artists. Not a lot changed, even as DC began to recognize their growing female fan base and introduced new titles with female leads. Books like *Batgirl*, a relaunched *Catwoman*, *Detective Comics* starring Batwoman, *Manhunter*, and *Supergirl* all had long runs in this period, all written and drawn by men. In trying to appeal to this new audience, the publisher bizarrely insisted on doing so only through a male lens.

The stagnant numbers for female writers dipped to almost zero in 2012, coinciding with the debut of DC's line-wide reboot, the New 52. Across the publisher's fifty-two relaunched titles, only two had a female creator involved and both credits went to Gail Simone. She wrote *Batgirl* and cowrote *The Fury of Firestorm*, while men penned the rest of the line and drew every title. Only eight of the new titles had female lead characters, and the new *Justice League* was a return to the same old, with Wonder Woman as the sole woman on the team. At San Diego Comic-Con shortly before the line launched, copublisher Dan DiDio responded belligerently to questions about the lack of female creators and insisted, "We're just trying to hire the best people," implying that the best were men. The predominantly male panel attendees booed anyone who asked about the gender imbalance, egged on by DC's onstage representatives.

A lack of female creators in major publishing initiatives was the standard at DC in this era. Event books were an almost exclusively male domain, only one of their many weekly series featured a female creator in a prominent role, and special monthly themes and tie-ins centered male creators first and foremost. But over time, the publisher began to expand their ranks. The "#DCYou" rebranding in 2015 featured several new titles with diverse casts and creative teams, while the "Rebirth" soft relaunch in 2016 served as a course correction for the dark tone of the New 52 line and again featured more women writing and drawing the books.

Several titles became bastions for female creators in the 2010s. Babs Tarr drew a much-lauded run on *Batgirl*, and writers Hope Larson, Mairghread Scott, and Cecil Castellucci each penned the book. *Wonder Woman* featured writers like Meredith Finch, Shea Fontana, G. Willow Wilson, Mariko Tamaki, and Becky Cloonan along with artists that included Nicola Scott, Bilquis Evely, Mirka Andolfo, and Emanuela Lupacchino. *DC Comics Bombshells*, set in an alternate universe in which female superheroes fought in World War II, was written by Marguerite Bennett with art from Marguerite Sauvage, Laura Braga, Evely, Andolfo, Ming Doyle, Elsa Charretier, Aneke, Carmen Carnero, and more. As the charts show, by the end of the decade DC's numbers for female writers and artists were the highest they'd ever been, though both remained a significant minority, especially artists.

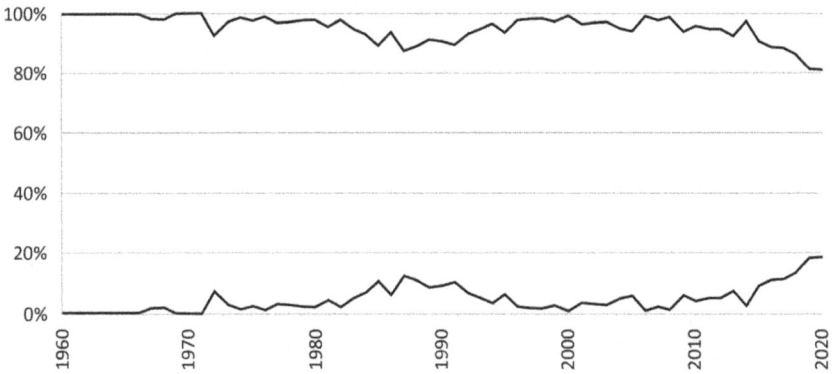

Male (top) and female (bottom) writers at Marvel Comics, 1960-2020.

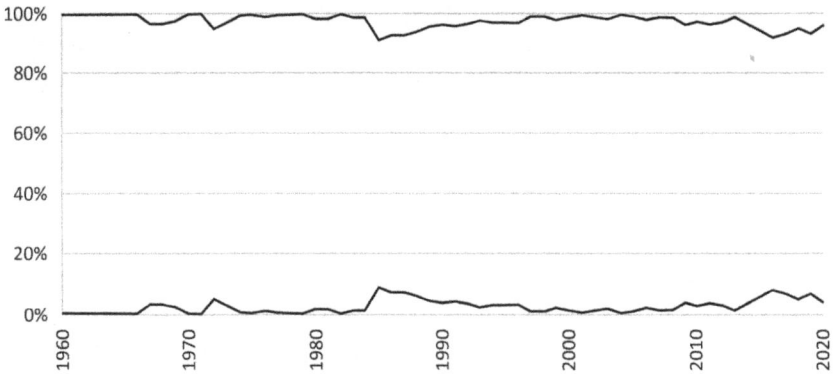

Male (top) and female (bottom) artists at Marvel Comics, 1960-2020.

What the charts don't show is DC's middle grade and young adult lines of graphic novels, which weren't counted alongside the publisher's single-issue output. Beginning in 2019, more than thirty graphic novels have been released or announced thus far, the bulk of which feature creators of marginalized genders in at least one prominent role, if not both. Writers come from mainstream superhero comics and young adult prose fiction, while many of the artists work outside of the traditional superhero comic style entirely. It's a fresh approach targeted at a broad swath of readers of all genders, much more so than DC's mainline titles. This pivot shows a willingness within the publisher to expand the parameters of superhero narratives for the first time in decades, opening new opportunities for fandom to grow and evolve.

Marvel had a similar arc to DC, though with different twists and turns along the way. The charts above track writers and artists at the publisher by gender, spanning sixty years of single issues using the same criteria as DC's tabulations.

They begin before Marvel even published their first superhero book, though shifting into a new genre did little to change the breakdown at the company.

For the first half of the 1960s, Marvel didn't have any women writing or drawing their comics. The bullpen was small at the time, with Stan Lee writing most of the comics and farming out only a few gigs to trusted associates. There weren't many artists on the payroll either, and most drew multiple issues each month. It was a tight operation, even as the publisher's foray into superhero comics began to take off.

All the credits for female writers and artists in the 1960s belonged to one woman, Marie Severin. She was a veteran of the industry who began working in production for EC Comics in 1949, coloring the artwork and proofreading the pages. In 1959, she moved to what was then Atlas Comics, still working in production as they became Marvel Comics and their superhero boom began. When *Esquire* magazine requested original artwork for an article on comics in 1966, Severin got the gig because Marvel's usual artists were all on tight deadlines. Impressed by her drawing skills, Lee assigned her to the "Doctor Strange" feature in *Strange Tales* the following year. From then on, she was a regular across the line, stepping in to draw stories when deadlines were tight and even writing a few on occasion.

In 1972, Marvel made their big push into women's lib with three female-led titles, and the numbers spiked accordingly. Linda Fite wrote *The Cat*, with Severin on art, while *Night Nurse* was written by Jean Thomas and *Shanna the She-Devil* was penned by Carole Seuling. Much like DC, Marvel editorial didn't look too far for their female creators. Fite worked at Marvel as a production assistant and was married to artist Herb Trimpe, Jean Thomas was married to Roy Thomas at the time, and Seuling was married to Phil Seuling, organizer of the local New York Comic Art Convention and a comic book distributor. Again, all three women were talented in their own right, but their hiring shows that Marvel wasn't going out of the way to find female talent.

After all three books failed to find an audience and were canceled, the numbers reverted to the previous status quo quickly. They didn't move later in the decade either, when the publisher launched *Ms. Marvel* and made a big deal about their female characters and fans in *The Superhero Women* hardcover. As *Ms. Marvel* writer Gerry Conway explained when the series launched, "Why is a man writing this book about a woman? [. . .] For one thing, for whatever reason (right or wrong), at the moment there are no thoroughly trained and qualified women writers working in the superhero comics field." It should be pointed out that in this era Marvel was literally hiring guys off the street. A good pitch in a letter could get a fellow a writing gig with Marvel, and Conway landed his first comics job at DC that way a few years earlier when he was only sixteen, hardly "thoroughly trained."

Both metrics for female creators picked up in the 1980s, along two major avenues. First, Marvel landed several licensed properties including *Care Bears*, *Fraggle Rock*, and *Muppet Babies*, and many of these children's titles featured women writing and drawing the stories. This was paired with a rise in women writing superheroes as well. Marvel's editorial ranks had grown over the years to include several women, and some of them shifted to writing. Jo Duffy began as an editor at Marvel in 1978, and wrote many issues across the publisher's line in the years that followed, including lengthy runs on *Power Man and Iron Fist* and *Star Wars*. Louise Simonson started as an editor in 1980, then moved to writing books like *Power Pack* and *X-Factor* before she left for DC. Ann Nocenti had a handful of writing credits before she became an editor in 1982 and continued writing throughout her editorial tenure, most notably a much-lauded run on *Daredevil*.

The 1990s saw these gains in female representation slowly dissipate as established women moved on from the publisher and weren't replaced. For the first half of the decade, the only constant presence for female creators was two licensed properties, *Barbie* and *Barbie Fashion*, which had multiple women working on each issue. When those books ended, Marvel again became an almost exclusively male domain.

This was connected to the publisher declaring bankruptcy in 1996. Old comics were worth money now, and Marvel aggressively stoked the speculation market in the early 1990s by releasing scores of books with multiple covers marketed as new collector's items. When they failed to grow in value because of the sheer glut of them, the bubble burst. Readers bought fewer books and revenues dropped precipitously industry-wide in a collapse that hit Marvel particularly hard. The publisher found a new owner and continued on, but with their lineup pared down considerably. Fewer books meant fewer jobs, and the gigs went primarily to established male creators as Marvel catered aggressively to what they perceived to be their die-hard male fan base.

As part of their road back from bankruptcy, Marvel established their Ultimate line in 2000 to update their classic characters in a new, modern setting. The line ran for fifteen years across seven hundred issues with titles like *Ultimate Spider-Man* and *Ultimate X-Men*, and in that span not a single issue was written by a woman. There were a couple of female artists over the years, most notably Sara Pichelli on the Spider-Man books, but women accounted for only 2 percent of the art credits over these fifteen years. It was a fallow decade for female artists across the board at Marvel, and most of the publisher's very few writing credits for women came from licensed properties like *Anita Blake* and *The Dark Tower*. Much like DC, the 2000s saw a rise in superhero books with female leads, but new titles like *Spider-Girl*, *Ms. Marvel*, and *She-Hulk* were written and drawn almost exclusively by men.

In the early 2010s, Marvel started to feature female creators in occasional specials. The books featured a wide array of talent, but few of these spots translated into long-term gigs initially. When the publisher responded to DC's New 52 in 2012 with their Marvel NOW! line of relaunches, there were no female creators attached to any of the new debut issues. However, one of the existing books that took on the Marvel NOW! branding was *Captain Marvel*, which featured Kelly Sue DeConnick writing Carol Danvers. The book was a hit, with dedicated fans who called themselves the Carol Corps, and it led to the spin-off *Ms. Marvel* written by G. Willow Wilson, with Pakistani American teen Kamala Khan gaining superpowers and defending Jersey City from evildoers.

The success of these titles marked a new era for Marvel. They invested in books with female leads from female creators, including Amy Reeder and Natacha Bustos on *Moon Girl and Devil Dinosaur*, Kate Leth and Brittney L. Williams on *Patsy Walker a.k.a. Hellcat*, Stacey Lee and Tana Ford on *Silk*, and Erica Henderson on *Unbeatable Squirrel Girl*. While the art numbers plateaued in the single digits, representation for female writers has continued to grow. In recent years, Kelly Thompson is a constant presence across the line while the 2019 relaunch of the X-Men titles has featured female and nonbinary writers like Vita Ayala, Tini Howard, and Leah Williams in prominent roles.

These small steps toward breaking up the male hegemony at DC and Marvel are new developments and, as the charts from both publishers demonstrate, a bump in female creator representation does not necessarily mean that growth will last. Superhero publishers are a fickle bunch. Nonetheless, although the art numbers remain low, one in every five comic books at DC and Marvel is written by a woman currently, the highest level in the history of the genre.

Women have gotten work in sizable numbers elsewhere in the industry as well. Since the earliest days of comic books, women were a presence behind the scenes in comics, inking pages in the 1940s and handling coloring and production in the 1950s, though the vast majority of those gigs went uncredited. By the late 1960s, credits for colorists became common, and over the next two decades women like Liz Berube, Nansi Hoolahan, Glynis Oliver, Adrienne Roy, Christie Scheele, Marie Severin, Lyn Varley, Tatjana Wood, and more became well known by regular readers.

Many of these colorists had aspirations to work on the "creative" side of comics drawing books, but were instead relegated to "production." One female creator said in the 1980s, "Sure—some women get all the work they can handle—usually in coloring. Creative jobs go to the boys," while an editor at the time called the production department "an economic ghetto full of female artists." When comics began to credit creators on the cover in the late 1980s, only writers and artists were listed, further underscoring the separation between "creative" and "production." This finally changed in 2014, after creators and fans campaigned for colorists to get equal billing on the cover in recognition of coloring as its own, vital art form. In recent years, women accounted for 15 percent of colorists at DC and 18 percent at Marvel, with artists like Jordie Bellaire, Tamra Bonvillain, Kelly Fitzpatrick, Laura Martin, Trish Mulvihill, Rachelle Rosenberg, and many more all well-respected fixtures in superhero comics today.

Despite these gains, the credits pages of most superhero comics remain a male-dominated affair, perhaps because of the demographics of one particular category. Most editors at DC and Marvel are men, making up 70 percent of DC's recent editorial credits and hitting 88 percent at Marvel. Not that men only hire men, but in most business structures the makeup of people at the top tends to be reflected elsewhere in the company. Interestingly, the numbers for assistant and associate editors are more even, with men landing just 57 percent of those credits at DC and an even lower 32 percent at Marvel. However, a stronger female presence in the category with "assistant" in the title is hardly ideal. While pivotal to making comics, most assistant/associate editors don't have a lot of sway at the publisher and aren't making hiring decisions.

How these hiring decisions are made also influences creator numbers. Neither DC nor Marvel has an open submission policy, meaning that there are few avenues for a creator to get an editor's attention. Networking is key, but most networking is done at comic book conventions, especially in hotel bars after the convention day is done in a practice commonly known as "Barcon." Many creators of marginalized genders do not find these alcohol-fueled events comfortable or safe, further limiting their ability to get a foot in the door. These barriers compound over time, leading to the current state of the industry in which editors rely on their own rolodex of preferred creators, a rolodex composed primarily of industry veterans and new creators who were able to jump through the necessary social hoops. In both instances, established and new, such creators are likely to be men. Editors have to go out of their way to find creators of marginalized genders, a task that has rarely been a priority in superhero comics, though this is slowly changing.

Another barrier, especially for artists, is a lack of high-profile jobs. While the writing numbers are creeping toward more equitable representation, artists lag behind in part because DC's and Marvel's most famous writers tend to work with only male artists. Editorial is responsible for some of these pairings, but prolific superstars like Brian Michael Bendis, Geoff Johns, and Scott Snyder have the power to choose their own collaborators and rarely use that influence to elevate artists of marginalized genders in their own work, especially for prolonged arcs. Men account for at least 97 percent of Bendis's, Johns's, and Snyder's artistic partners over the course of their expansive careers thus far as they've headlined some of DC's and Marvel's biggest series. The books that get the most attention and garner the highest sales are typically written and drawn by men, perpetuating the message that superhero comics are a male domain.

So too does limiting female creators to books with female leads, which has been the case for the bulk of the last decade's rise in representation. This division suggests that boy comics are for boys and girl comics are for girls, segregating the readership just like DC and Marvel did with their superhero and romance lines in the 1960s. Over the decades, men have written and drawn the full gamut of superheroes, male and female, and true inclusive hiring practices will only come to fruition when women can do the same. We're starting to see a shift on that front, albeit slowly. At Marvel, Becky Cloonan wrote *The Punisher* and Kelly Thompson wrote *Deadpool*, both for sizable runs, while Mariko Tamaki recently took the reins of *Detective Comics*, becoming the first ongoing writer on DC's namesake franchise.

The average consumer probably doesn't care too much about the gender of the creators who write and draw a particular comic book. They care if the writing is good, if the art is exciting, if the story grabs their attention. But when the vast majority of the credits across a publisher's entire line are only men, the signal is stark, intentionally or not. These numbers say, "for boys only." They say, "no girls allowed." If publishers truly believe that superheroes are for everyone, they need to be written and drawn by everyone. The industry is moving in this direction, but decades of male dominance and the expectations and assumptions that this brings are making for a glacial transition.

CHAPTER 11

Frozen

Content warning: This chapter discusses violence against women in the form of sexual assault, torture, rape, and death. The specifics are not described gratuitously, but many of these incidents were quite grisly in their original comic book form and are recounted here in a factual manner.

Before becoming one of the best-known writers of superhero comics in the 2000s, Gail Simone was a lifelong fan with an online column discussing the industry. Looking back on the history of the genre, Simone noticed some startling trends and sent a letter to various comics professionals that pointed out, "It occurred to me that it's not that healthy to be a female character in comics." Included with the letter was a list of female characters "who have been either depowered, raped, or cut up and stuck in the refrigerator," and she asked, "I'm curious to find out if this list seems somewhat disproportionate, and if so, what it means."

Simone's list sparked a lot of discussion, and was soon posted on its own site called *Women in Refrigerators*. The title referred to *Green Lantern* #54 from 1994, in which the eponymous hero returned home from a mission and went to visit his girlfriend, Alexandra DeWitt, only to find her murdered and stuffed into her refrigerator. It was a horrific act, and spurred Green Lantern into a violent battle with Alex's killer, Major Force. The villain was defeated and the hero ultimately learned valuable lessons about himself and his power ring, all at the expense of the callously discarded Alex.

She was one of more than a hundred different women listed on the site who were depowered, tortured, sexually assaulted, otherwise traumatized, or killed. In a genre without many female characters to begin with, the list was a shocking litany of mistreatment, and as fans began to connect the different narratives they noticed one clear through line. The bulk of these incidents involved women getting attacked in order to further the plot of a male hero, harmed to spur him into action. He would then battle through his anger and exorcise his grief, growing as a character through the experience, while the female character remained sidelined, often permanently. Sacrificing a female character for the development of a male character soon became known as "fridging."

We've encountered several fridgings already. Jean Grey's death led to years of drama for Cyclops. So too did Terra's death affect Changeling. Elektra and Karen Page were harmed to propel Daredevil's story, while Barbara Gordon was paralyzed to give heft to Batman's confrontation with the Joker. The intentionality of these fridgings varied. Some women were attacked specifically to affect the men's story, while other male characters just happened to benefit narratively from their demise. Either way, the men's stories carried on in new, dramatic ways and the women were left behind. Simone's list sparked a conversation about this trope that still continues today, but the reckoning has been limited.

This is partly because the trope is so ingrained in the superhero genre. Male characters have been the center of focus for decades, while female characters were rarely valued. Sacrificing one to further the other was accepted without a thought, and the practice dates back to the earliest days of modern fandom.

By 1973, the transition to a predominantly older, male readership was largely accomplished. DC and Marvel were telling darker stories now, with shocking twists and turns. One of these shocks involved Gwen Stacy, the blonde girl next door who'd been Peter Parker's on-again, off-again girlfriend for a decade. She was sweet and innocent, and Peter loved her very much. The trouble was, fans didn't. After vivacious redhead Mary Jane Watson joined the series, readers much preferred her over the more reserved Gwen.

So Gwen became expendable and was ultimately killed when Spider-Man faced off against the Green Goblin atop a tall bridge. Green Goblin threw Gwen off the bridge and Spider-Man shot a web to catch her, but when he pulled her up she was dead. The story is unclear whether it was the fall itself that killed her or if the web stopping her fall snapped her neck, and that ambiguity has plagued Peter for decades. In typical fridging fashion, he blamed himself for her death and that guilt still haunts him, adding deep pathos to the character. Her demise also opened up the door for new story possibilities, and Peter and Mary Jane later started dating and then wed, with many twists and turns along the way.

The next few decades went poorly for female comic book characters. Beyond Jean Grey, Elektra, Terra, Karen Page, and Barbara Gordon, dozens of other women met dark fates throughout the 1980s. Ms. Marvel was mind-controlled and raped in a story that was bizarrely casual about the entire situation. Spider-Woman perished in battle at the end of her own series. Supergirl died to inspire Superman in *Crisis on Infinite Earths* and was memorialized with an iconic cover of the weeping Man of Steel holding his dead cousin.

As the genre embraced darker tales for mature readers like *Watchmen* and *The Killing Joke*, imitators followed. One of the first was *Green Arrow: The Longbow Hunters* in 1987, a miniseries that sent the jovial Emerald Archer down a dark path as he investigated a drug lord. His girlfriend, Black Canary, was captured in the course of the story and brutally tortured. Green Arrow found her strung up by her arms, wearing nothing but the vestiges of a torn shirt, covered in cuts and bruises as blood dripped down her body. Some readers inferred that Black Canary was also raped based on her torturer's dialogue, her sexualized posing, and the fact that she subsequently learned she was unable to bear children. No such assault was shown on the page and writer/artist Mike Grell disagrees with this interpretation, saying it didn't happen, but that this was such a common interpretation speaks to both the tone and substance of the scene.

Finding Black Canary fired up Green Arrow. He attacked her captors, killing a foe for the first time in his career, and subsequently took down the drug lord and his organization. The miniseries proved popular, and led to a new era for Green Arrow with his own ongoing series. Black Canary was part of the book as the retired Dinah Lance, running the Sherwood Florist flower shop in Seattle. She'd lost her trademark "canary cry" as a result of her torture, and she rarely suited up to help her beau. Her powers eventually returned when she teamed up with Oracle in *Birds of Prey* more than a decade later.

The 1990s weren't great for female characters either. Beyond Alex DeWitt's fridging, a number of women were sidelined or killed in new, dark ways. At DC, Raven went mad and attacked her fellow Titans before disappearing into a different dimension for several years. There was another case of madness at Marvel, where Patsy Walker, a.k.a. Hellcat, was plagued by a demon and died by suicide. Mockingbird was killed after reconnecting with her ex-husband, Hawkeye. Colossus's sister, Illyana Rasputin, died of the mutant legacy virus. The numbers continued to pile up, leading to Simone's list in 1999; but, despite the conversation it sparked, the genre was slow to change.

Marvel was on the rise again in the early 2000s thanks to new lines with more mature content. Between the grittier *Marvel Knights* series, the bombastic alternate universe Ultimate imprint, and their 18+ MAX line, Marvel was heading into much darker territory with their superheroes. The bosses at DC felt like they needed to keep up, and soon centered entire events around fridgings.

One of these events was "War Games," which ran for three months across the Batman line in 2004. In the lead up to the event, Batman's third Robin, Tim Drake, decided to quit the job and was replaced by Stephanie Brown, who'd been fighting crime in Gotham City for years as Spoiler. She was a logical replacement for Tim, and eagerly accepted the role when Batman offered it to her, becoming the first female Robin in mainline continuity.

But Batman was a tough, cantankerous boss, and he fired her after a few months. Wanting to prove herself, Stephanie found his detailed plan to end the criminal underworld in Gotham and set out to implement it on her own. However, she missed one key piece and the plan fell apart as the city erupted into a full-on gang war.

In the midst of the chaos, Stephanie was captured by mob boss Black Mask, who tortured her to learn all he could about Batman. The torture had sexual connotations throughout. Black Mask taunted her, "You're pretty as a peach, but not exactly one of Batman's smarter minions, are you? Maybe he used you for your other, more obvious advantages, eh? Keep up morale? Keep the troops happy?" In a later issue, he called her "pretty-pretty," "sweetie," and "darling," telling her, "I treated you to a few hours of **wonderfully intimate** torture," and that he was sorry to have missed "that all-important cuddling in the afterglow." The art added to the sexualization of the scene, removing Stephanie's cloak to show her skintight costume and posing her to emphasize her figure.

Ultimately, Black Mask shot Stephanie when she tried to escape and Batman arrived too late to save her. She died in Dr. Leslie Thompkins's clinic, the go-to safe haven for Gotham's injured heroes, fulfilling what had been the plan from the very start. Stephanie had been promoted precisely for this moment, to make news as the first female Robin and thus increase her profile so that her death in "War Games" would have the maximum impact. It was a cynical ploy, one that sat poorly with some writers in the Batman line, but editorial held firm.

Stephanie was sacrificed for the grief of Batman and Tim Drake, now Robin once again by the end of the event. "War Games" ended with multiple graveside scenes as the male heroes mourned her loss. Her death was then used for more drama a year later in the "War Crimes" arc, which revealed Dr. Thompkins had killed Stephanie at the clinic to teach Batman a lesson about employing teen sidekicks. This led to the end of a friendship that dated back to Bruce's childhood, providing even more sorrow and character development for the Caped Crusader.

"War Games" hit just as female fandom was beginning to grow for the first time in decades. The audience was shifting, and Stephanie's death upset these new readers. At the very least, they thought she deserved a memorial in the Batcave, just like deceased Robin Jason Todd, but DC editorial refused. Executive editor Dan DiDio went so far as to say that "she was never really a Robin," angering many. It was one of several incidents in which DiDio interacted poorly with female fandom, as DC time and again failed to realize the obvious benefits of friendly engagement with their expanding audience.

While "War Games" was a big deal for the Batman books in 2004, DC had even bigger plans that year for their superhero line as a whole. Everything revolved around *Identity Crisis*, a miniseries by writer Brad Meltzer and artists

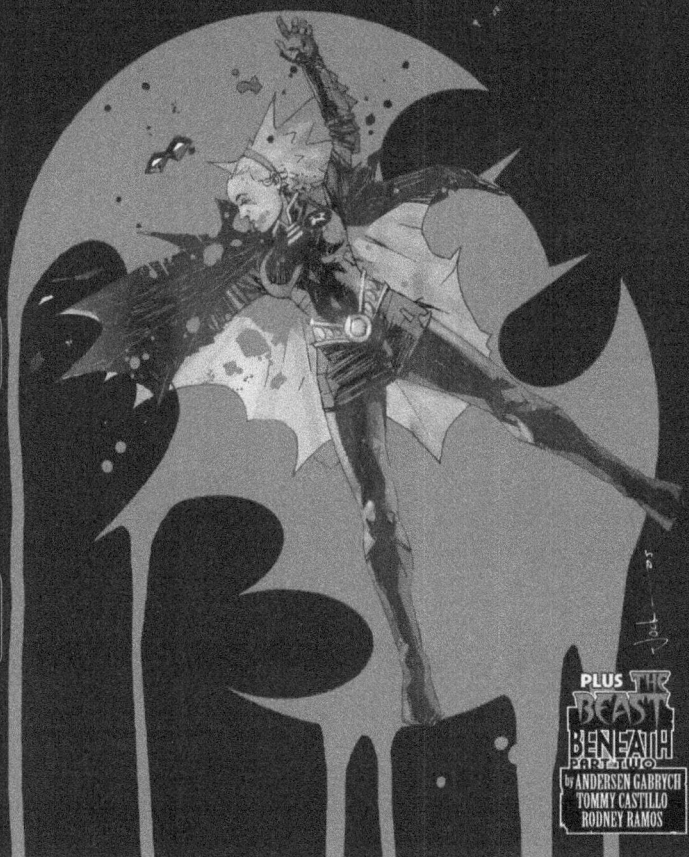

Detective Comics #809, art by Jock, DC Comics, 2005. Stephanie Brown was promoted then killed for shock value.

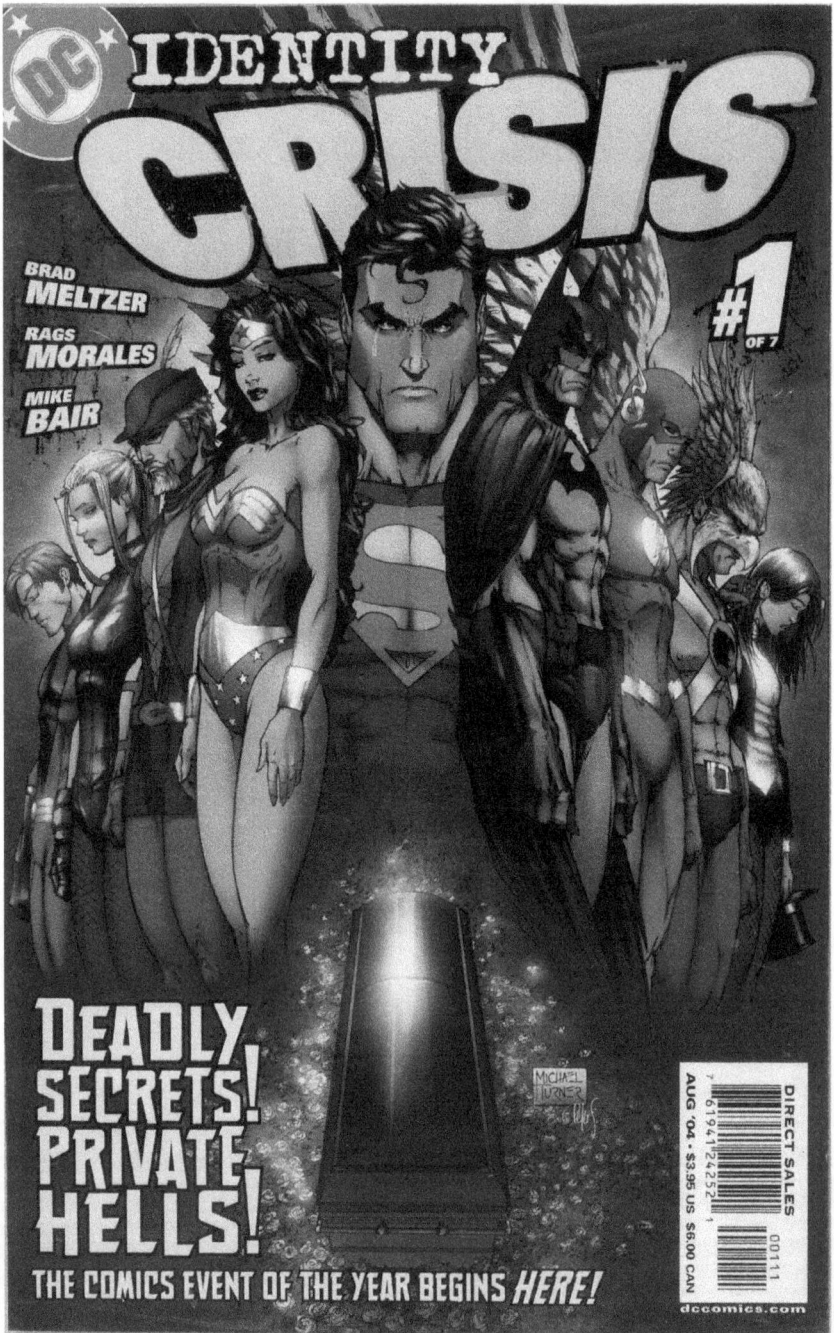

Identity Crisis #1, art by Michael Turner and Peter Steigerwald, DC Comics, 2004. Sue Dibny's rape and death led to emotional angst, mostly for male characters.

Rag Morales and Mike Bair that promised "Deadly secrets!" and "Private hells!" as the cover of the first issue declared that "the comics event of the year begins **here!**" The cover art showed the Justice League gathered around a coffin, a single tear rolling down the cheek of a stoic Superman. Something bad was about to happen.

The first issue started cheerily enough, with heroes preparing for the Elongated Man's annual surprise birthday party. His wife Sue tried to trick her beloved Ralph every year, but he always saw it coming and played along. Ralph and Sue had been regulars in the Justice League in the 1970s and 1980s, but had fallen out of use since then. *Identity Crisis* brought them back, allowing Ralph to recount their life together while out on patrol as Sue prepared the party. Then an unexpected guest arrived, attacked Sue, and burned her body. Instead of returning home to a joyous party, Ralph found only his deceased wife and his birthday surprise, a positive pregnancy test.

It was a grisly scene, and intentionally so. Sue was chosen specifically for her kindly, innocent reputation, to make her death all the more shocking. She was also considered disposable, given that the Dibnys had been on the bench for a while. Putting the friendly couple at the center of a brutal murder was the exact statement DC wanted to make with their dark turn, showing that no one was safe in their universe, and they weren't done.

At the end of the first issue, Ralph and some of his fellow Justice Leaguers gathered to go after Dr. Light. Flashbacks in the second issue recounted a scene years before when Sue was alone on the Justice League satellite and Dr. Light hacked the transport system, broke into the satellite, and raped Sue. The artwork showed Sue's pained face during the incident, and Dr. Light re-created the scene with his light manipulation when the Justice League returned and caught him. Sue's rape was the true centerpiece of the story for DC, her murder simply opening the door for this even more shocking revelation. An assistant editor later recalled the "gleeful" reaction at the DC offices when the artwork arrived, as a staffer excitedly ran to his boss's office and proclaimed, "The rape pages are in!"

Dr. Light promised to find Sue and rape her again, prompting the team to use Zatanna's magical powers and fundamentally change his personality. *Identity Crisis* revealed that Zatanna regularly wiped villains' memories, especially when they discovered heroes' secret identities, but changing someone's personality was a new step. The rest of the series was dedicated to the present-day ramifications of other heroes learning about the Justice League's mindwipes, along with a string of fight scenes as the team fought through various villains trying to get to Dr. Light. It was a miasma of drama, all kicked off by sacrificing Sue.

Ralph and the team were wrong about Sue's killer. It was actually Jean Loring, the ex-wife of the Atom, who wanted to scare the superhero community in hopes of reuniting with her former husband. She swore that she only meant to hurt Sue, not kill her, but the attack had gotten out of hand and she had to burn the body to cover her tracks. At this point, however, it was clear that Jean had lost her mind before the plan was even hatched. Even after her crimes were revealed, she kept insisting, "I've brought us together. Just like . . . just like . . . just like it used to be." Hearing her justifications, the Atom could only respond, "Oh, god—you're insane," and Jean was locked away in Arkham Asylum for treatment.

Identity Crisis started and ended with fridgings, embracing the sexist trope twice over. Sue remained dead, while Jean was later possessed by Eclipso, a malevolent divine being, and went on to perform more villainy. The series centered male grief, giving Sue only a few lines of dialogue before her death and never showing her dealing with her assault. Instead, the angst of male heroes like Ralph, Green Arrow, the Flash, and others was the focus throughout. Loring got a lengthy monologue to explain herself, at least, but her dark turn was reminiscent of the genre's prevalent "mad woman" tropes previously seen with characters like Phoenix, Terra, and Raven.

Marvel had their own "mad woman" event the following year with *House of M*. While not a fridging per se, the book nonetheless demonstrated a lack of lessons learned from the women in refrigerators discourse by using Scarlet Witch's lengthy history of trauma to turn her into the main villain. Her father was Magneto, a mutant terrorist, and she'd lost her marriage to Vision as well as their two children in a series of convoluted supernatural events. Scarlet Witch was mind-controlled often, like during the "Avengers Disassembled" story line that led into *House of M* and resulted in the death of Hawkeye. Fearing her inability to control her powers, several Avengers and X-Men suggested that the only safe response was to kill her.

In reaction to this, Scarlet Witch warped reality, creating a new world where everyone could be happy and safe. Some heroes remembered the old world, though, and fought to return to it. The conclusion of the series revealed that her brother, Quicksilver, had told her to change reality, but Scarlet Witch still bore the bulk of the blame. When confronted by the heroes, she feared for her life once more and, blaming anti-mutant sentiment, uttered the words, "No more mutants," wiping out the abilities of all but a handful of mutants across the Marvel universe.

Scarlet Witch has been a pariah ever since, distrusted by the Avengers and hated by the X-Men, all of them ignoring the trauma and mind control behind her actions. Quicksilver came out fine, joining various superhero teams over the years and even teaching at Avengers Academy. Even Magneto has done well since, despite his violent past, and is currently part of the ruling council of the mutant nation Krakoa. Meanwhile, Scarlet Witch remains an outcast, not fridged necessarily but trotted out primarily to be a villain in more mind control narratives. A solo series in 2016 gave her a voice but also underscored her exile status in the superhero community.

While *House of M* was a trope-filled quagmire, Marvel had a unique chance to atone for the mistreatment of their female characters with their Ultimate universe. Created in 2000, the Ultimate line existed within its own continuity, wholly separate from the main line, and reimagined all of Marvel's iconic characters in a new, different, modern setting. No one was beholden to past story lines, with a fresh start for everyone.

Marvel failed to take advantage of this opportunity. Gwen Stacy was a staple in *Ultimate Spider-Man* but, just like her original counterpart, she died tragically, killed by Carnage this time rather than Green Goblin. A clone of Gwen Stacy later became part of the series, with everyone in the book cavalierly deciding she was just as good as the original. Scarlet Witch was a mainstay in *Ultimates*, though her arc centered on her incestuous relationship with her brother and she was killed off at the beginning of the book's third cycle.

Janet van Dyne had a tough run since her days as a founding member of the Avengers in the 1960s, and was the victim of domestic assault when Hank Pym turned violent in the main Marvel universe in the 1980s, leading to their divorce. *Ultimates* replicated this story in an even more extreme manner, with Hank assaulting Janet and then spraying her with caustic insect repellent when she shrunk down into her Wasp form. Janet was then killed in *Ultimatum* and eaten by the Blob in one of the grisliest scenes in superhero comics history. In the end, the Ultimate universe just led to further fridgings for Marvel's female heroes.

The women in refrigerators list led to the discussion of another phenomenon, dead men defrosting, in which male characters who died tended to come back to life, quickly and often just as good as before, if not even better. Death rarely stuck in the superhero genre, especially by the early 2000s. The characters were too valuable, and anyone of note didn't stay gone for long. After Martian Manhunter died in the *Final Crisis* event, Superman said at his funeral, "We'll all miss him. And pray for resurrection," telegraphing what every reader knew was eventually coming.

At DC, Superman came back to life after his infamous demise, with no ill effects and little in the way of lingering trauma. Batman returned after "Knightfall" as strong as he was before, then died and came back to life following the "Batman RIP" arc, again no worse for wear. Aquaman, the Flash, Green Lantern, and Martian Manhunter were all killed and later resurrected, and found new monthly series waiting for them when they returned. Green Arrow died and came back as well, younger and healthier than he was before, his memories erased to before the tragic events of *Green Arrow: The Longbow Hunters*. Black Canary, however, still bore all her memories of her trauma.

Most of Marvel's male heroes have also died and come back. From Captain America to Hawkeye to Iron Man to Thor to Wolverine, death was inevitable and impermanent. Few fans shed a tear at the passing of a male hero, knowing that their death marked only the beginning of a countdown to their return. The hero they knew and loved would be back soon, fully restored.

This wasn't the case for female characters. Civilians rarely came back at all, and comic book history is littered with the deaths of myriad forgotten girlfriends. Female superheroes were more likely to return, but it wasn't a given and the trauma of their passing usually followed them. For characters like Elektra and Phoenix, who had resurrection wired into their story arcs, while dying didn't stick for long, their rebirths brought along the shadow of waiting for them to perish again. The characters were defined by their deaths as much as, if not more so than, their lives.

Other female characters returned in new forms. After Supergirl died in *Crisis on Infinite Earths*, a new Supergirl debuted in the early 1990s but she wasn't Kara Zor-El. She was Matrix, a synthetic shape-shifter who took the form of Supergirl. While Kara later returned in 2004, she was a reboot of Supergirl, not the resurrected version of the original character. Gwen Stacy returned as well in 2014, but this wasn't a resurrection either. Known as Spider-Gwen, she came from an alternate universe where Gwen was bitten by a radioactive spider and became a superhero instead of Peter Parker.

Sometimes original heroines did return, though. Stephanie Brown came back in 2009 to take on the mantle of Batgirl in a series that ran for two years and developed a strong fan base. Then DC rebooted their entire line in 2011 and Barbara Gordon became Batgirl once again. Stephanie was nowhere to be found, blacklisted at DC for several years to such a degree that top creators weren't allowed to use her and an appearance in an alternate universe title was scrapped after it was announced. She finally returned as Spoiler in 2014 and has remained a background player in the DC universe largely thanks to Bat-writer James Tynion IV being a fan of the character.

Such is the uncertain existence of female characters. Top-tier heroes will always come back. Batman, Captain America, Superman, Wolverine—they're never going to stay sidelined, but there are very few female heroes in this top tier. Wonder Woman is the only one with a consistent publication history. Every other woman depends on the whims of creators and editorial, doubly so if they've been benched or killed, and need a patron to champion their return. Spider-Woman returned to prominence in the early 2000s because writer Brian Michael Bendis was a fan. Renee Montoya has remained a player at DC for the past fifteen years primarily because of writer Greg Rucka's affection for her. Most male heroes will return, sooner or later. Most female characters exist in perpetual limbo.

Twenty years after the list debuted, women in refrigerators remains an ongoing topic of conversation today precisely because very little has changed. Fridgings are still common, women continue to stay sidelined, and some creators remain ignorant of the trope entirely. When *Deadpool 2* sparked accusations of fridging after the hero's girlfriend, Vanessa, was killed off to kick-start the film's plot, the screenwriters responded, "It didn't really even occur to us. We didn't know what fridging was. [. . .] And maybe that's a sexist thing. I don't know. And maybe some women will have an issue with that. I don't know." Deadpool, incidentally, is practically unkillable. Vanessa, on the other hand, was based on the mutant Copycat, who was fridged in the comics as well.

CHAPTER 12

Barriers

In 2014, cartoonist ND Stevenson posted a comic strip about visiting comic book shops. A published creator with many friends in the industry, Stevenson ventured into shops to find the work of pals and colleagues, and was often met with customer service that was indifferent at best and downright insulting at worst. Some retailers didn't bother to offer assistance, and those who did often turned to mockery, dismissing Stevenson's interest in non-superhero comics as invalid. Highly sexualized images of female characters sent the message, "This is what we think of you," while the complex, convoluted nature of superhero lines proved inaccessible. Ultimately, having been ignored and insulted, the strip concluded, "I don't go to comic shops anymore. I'm tired of all this."

The comic struck a chord. While Stevenson pointed out that not every shop was scornful or rude, it was a frequent experience that many others identified with, especially women and fans from marginalized genders. They weren't comfortable in comic book shops, in large part because little to no effort was made to welcome them. From the staff to the artwork to the comics themselves, not much was approachable or inviting. In many cases, the atmosphere was actively hostile.

Shows like *The Big Bang Theory* and *The Simpsons* have caricaturized comic book shops as inhospitable to newcomers, with disdainful employees who treat potential customers rudely, even cruelly. This caricature isn't far off base. Although there are many friendly, inclusive shops out there, a considerable number fit this rancorous mold to some degree. For several decades, as superhero publishers aggressively pursued male readers, comic book shops reflected this audience base. They were a predominantly male domain that catered to the most hard core of enthusiasts, creating the inaccurate notion that these were the only "real" fans. Anyone outside of this narrow group was an outsider, a phony rather than a true fan. There are innumerable accounts of condescending salesclerks interrogating women to prove their geek credibility with trivia questions, insisting that if they were a real fan they could name every Robin or provide a thorough account of Spider-Man's life. Men tended to receive the benefit of the doubt, but women were inherently suspect.

The insular nature of these comic book shops was representative of certain segments of the superhero fan community from the 1980s on. For many fans, their passion for superheroes brought them a lot of grief. They were labeled nerds, bullied, and ostracized, and they turned to comics for escapism. Much like the young men who created the superhero genre in the 1930s, they found solace in a world where the bad guys were always defeated. The comfort they found in comics drew them in further, and their knowledge grew to encyclopedic levels as they devoured decades of lore across multiple universes. When these fans found each other, the result was a safe space where they could be as nerdy as they wanted to be, and they were wary of outsiders for fear of further bullying.

At the same time, the comics that offered them refuge didn't always serve them well. Particularly with the rise of antiheroes in the 1990s, kindness was no longer a virtue. Anger was, along with cynicism. Simultaneously, the hypersexualization of female characters taught readers to view women as objects more than people. All the while, almost every advertisement, every letter column, every credits page told them that their beloved hobby was an exclusively male domain. This is important to point out not to excuse or justify any bad behavior, but to understand the larger environment in which fandom suddenly changed in the 2000s.

For decades, young male nerds had superheroes to themselves. Occasionally something would break through, like Christopher Reeve's Superman or Michael Keaton's Batman, but by and large the genre was theirs. Then superheroes went mainstream. The *X-Men* film franchise was a hit. So too was Sam Raimi's *Spider-Man* series, and Christopher Nolan's *Dark Knight* trilogy. Then the Marvel Cinematic Universe built on both of these successes and took the genre to new heights of popularity. Everybody liked superheroes now. Everybody had a Batman T-shirt, and they bought them from Walmart, not special ordered from the back of a comic book. These new fans loved the characters, and many ventured to comic shops and comic book conventions as a result. Moreover, a lot of these new fans were young women. It caused some upheaval, to say the least.

Some longtime fans were happy to see fandom grow, to see others appreciate the characters they'd always championed. It was still a tricky transition when it came to female fans, however, even from those with the best of intentions. The genre had been dominated by men for so long that it was difficult to fathom it otherwise. Even the words "geek" and "fan" were gendered terms at this point, assumed to be masculine because of this close association. Women who liked superheroes were called "geek girls" and "fangirls," underscoring their othered status from the start, and they faced gatekeeping on all sides.

"Gatekeeping" occurs when someone limits who has access to a community or an identity, making themselves the arbiter of someone else's intentions. Many well-meaning male fans questioned young women's fandom in small ways, thus engaging in unconscious gatekeeping. They assumed a woman's X-Men paraphernalia belonged to her boyfriend, or complimented her by telling her she knew a lot about Wolverine "for a girl." These actions often came from surprise rather than malice, but either way they signaled that the women didn't belong. Over time, inclusive male fans have learned about the ills of gatekeeping and are now far more welcoming as they strive to help fandom grow.

But some fans did not embrace this change. Their gatekeeping was intentional, even antagonistic, a way to keep new people out of their beloved spaces. They felt threatened by those who failed to meet their criteria of what a "real" fan was, and actively sought to exclude "imposters" from the community. More often than not, these so-called imposters were women. Over time, gatekeeping became as integral to their fandom as a love of the superhero genre.

Dr. Drea Letamendi, a clinical psychologist and superhero enthusiast, explained three key reasons why some fans reacted so strongly to perceived imposters. First was "the false notion of limited resources." Superhero fandom was strongly associated with collections, from comic books to action figures to all manner of memorabilia. Many of these items were limited properties. A Superman statue was restricted to just a few hundred units; a special comic book cover was a one-in-fifty variant. Because fans were conditioned to think of the tangible aspects of fandom as limited, the same sort of thinking bled into the intangible aspects. Gatekeepers saw fandom itself as a limited resource and didn't want to share it with others who didn't truly care about it as much as they did.

This tied into Dr. Letamendi's second point: "the misinterpreted sense of ownership." All the comics, all the toys, all the time fans devoted to superheroes could create the sense that the fandom belonged to them. This in turn made them think they had the ability "to decide who else is *in* or *out*." But they didn't. Superheroes belong to corporations like Warner Bros. and Disney. Concrete items like comic books belong to fans. A fan community, however, was its own evolving, esoteric organism that no one person or group had any real control over.

Finally, the crux of the matter was "resentment of the changing culture." On one level, gatekeepers who were bullied for liking superheroes begrudged the ease of being a fan today. Superheroes were cool now, and none of these new fans had to suffer for their fandom. On another level, gatekeepers wanted everything to be how it was back in the day when they felt like they were in charge. As fandom broadened and the genre expanded, longtime fans could feel out of place. The art styles and writing they enjoyed appeared less common, and things like extensive collections and encyclopedic knowledge were no longer as valued. Fandom seemed to be moving beyond them, which led to animosity.

This aggressive gatekeeping reached new heights in the early 2010s with the notion of the "fake geek girl." Tara Tiger Brown, a lifelong geek dating back to the days before the subculture went mainstream, introduced the term in a *Forbes* article titled "Dear Fake Geek Girls: Please Go Away." She took issue with how the term "geek," a moniker supposedly earned by devotion to a hobby, was now being used as a marketing gimmick, and had particular ire for "pretentious females who have labeled themselves as a 'geek girl'" because they "figured out that guys will pay a lot of attention to them if they proclaim they are reading comics or playing video games."

Brown's notion of the fake geek girl caught on in certain corners of fandom. On CNN's *Geek Out* blog, Joe Peacock noted that there was "a growing chorus of frustration in the geek community with—and there's no other way to put this—pretty girls pretending to be geeks for attention." He insisted he was glad to see fandom expand, but called out the "hollow egos" of "girls who have no interest or history" in geek culture. These "attention addicts" were "poachers" and a "pox," imposters who supposedly preyed on men. Peacock negated the possibility of casual fans by demanding that women had to be properly steeped in nerd culture to be counted as a real fan.

Much of the fake geek girl ire was directed at female cosplayers who dressed up in detailed superhero costumes at comic book conventions. Cosplay was a big part of this new generation of fandom, a rapidly growing subculture that encouraged creativity and empowerment. But for gatekeepers, the right to wear these costumes had to be earned.

In a 2012 Facebook post, superhero artist Tony Harris took aim at cosplayers, stating that he was "so sick and tired of the whole COSPLAY-Chiks." While "a few" were cool because they "love and read Comics," the rest were "pathetic" with "this really awful need for attention." Harris explained, "THE REASON WHY ALL THAT, sickens us: BECAUSE YOU DON'T KNOW SHIT ABOUT COMICS, BEYOND WHATEVER GOOGLE IMAGE SEARCH YOU DID TO GET REF ON THE MOST MAINSTREAM CHARACTER WITH THE MOST REVEALING COSTUME EVER." He concluded by calling these women "Lying, Liar Face," and told them, "Yer not Comics."

Many cosplayers faced Harrisesque demands to prove their fandom. They were interrogated with trivia questions about the history of the character they were dressed as, assumed to be imposters and grilled accordingly. They were also sexually harassed by aggressive convention attendees, subjected to catcalls, groping, and attempts at upskirt camera shots. This poor treatment echoed the disdain with which their critics addressed them. Peacock called them "6 of 9" because they were only a "6" in the real world in terms of attractiveness, but became a "9" in fandom circles. He also suggested that their harassment was deserved, calling them "gross" and telling them "don't be shocked" if they get vile messages from male fans. Harris had a similar approach to body shaming and wrote, "Some of us are aware that you are ever so average on an everyday basis." He said these women were "CON-HOT," insulting their bodies as either too skinny or too big, and argued they only got attention because they "are willing to become almost completely Naked in public." Both Peacock and Harris insisted these women would never deign to talk to male nerds outside of conventions, and only wanted to prey on them for attention.

Cosplayers were simply wearing the costumes artists like Harris designed and drew, but the transition from page to real life caused a disconnect. Comic books objectified female characters, teaching readers that they existed for their consumption and pleasure. When gatekeeping fans were faced with heroines in real life, they viewed them through the same lens. If she was found wanting, she was cruelly dismissed. If she was enticing, she must be a predator using her sexual wiles against them. They failed to see cosplayers as actual people, or to recognize the fun and empowerment that women enjoyed when they took on a superhero guise. By assuming that cosplayers were dressing up for them, they missed the truth of the matter, that cosplayers were actually dressing up for themselves.

The preoccupation with fake geek girls was just misogyny masquerading as concern. It wasn't really about protecting fellow fans from predators or imposters. Instead, it was about an inability to see women as anything other than sexual objects, or to appreciate that their approach to fandom could be different and still valid. While anger over supposed fake geek girls and this constant policing of female fans has yet to fully go away, the community as a whole has moved in a positive direction, especially in regard to cosplay. Many conventions now post guidelines for how to treat cosplayers with respect that state, "Cosplay is not consent," and cosplayers are recognized as a vibrant, integral part of fandom.

While portions of the fan community were busy gatekeeping the genre, publishers weren't doing a lot to help matters. Superhero comics were rife with inherent barriers, from byzantine backstories for each character to decades of convoluted continuity to the constant renumbering and reorganizing of series, and neither DC nor Marvel took significant steps to make their lines more accessible. Combined with a deep-rooted penchant for sexism, publishers proved to be effective gatekeepers as well.

The New 52 relaunch's poor treatment of female characters and near complete lack of female creators in 2011 made the intended audience quite clear, as DC tried to shore up their established fan base rather than expand their audience. In 2012, the new Marvel NOW! series failed to match the New 52's paltry sole female creator with male creators on every book, and only one of the new titles had female characters as headliners. The rest of the line was composed of male-led or team books, again underscoring who the new initiative was meant for.

DC tried a course correction with their "Rebirth" line in 2016, with far more female creators involved and titles that didn't hypersexualize their female characters. Still, the publisher stumbled. While explaining the intent of "Rebirth," DC's chief creative officer Geoff Johns said, "If you have, like me, long boxes of DC Comics, you will be *very* happy. If you've never read a DC comic before, you won't be too lost. This is definitely for comic book readers more than it is for casual readers [. . .] but that doesn't mean it's exclusive of them." Having long boxes of comics meant someone had been collecting for some time, which meant that their fandom likely dated back to the days when the community was dominated by male readers. This dog whistle, combined with Johns's dismissal of "casual readers," again sent the message that their long-term, base audience was still of paramount importance.

Even when publishers were trying to appeal directly to new readers, they still made major missteps that turned them away. Marvel announced books for several female characters in 2014, including action comedy fun for all ages in *The Unbeatable Squirrel Girl*, a female God of Thunder in *Thor*, and a new ongoing title for Spider-Woman. All the announcements garnered positive buzz, until Marvel revealed a variant cover for the first issue of *Spider-Woman* by famed Italian erotic artist Milo Manara. The cover showed Jessica Drew in an impossibly skintight costume, crawling on all fours with her back arched and her rear raised in an homage to one of Manara's previous covers for the pornographic magazine *Penthouse Comix*.

It went over poorly. At *The Mary Sue*, Jill Pantozzi wrote, "I honestly don't know what anyone involved was thinking," and pointed out that for female fans, "what the variant cover actually says is 'Run away. Run far, far away and don't ever come back.'" Her sentiments were echoed across much of fandom, and even *Spider-Woman* writer Dennis Hopeless clarified that he had no say over the cover and promised, "You have my word that our story treats Jess with the utmost respect." And yet, many within Marvel doubled down. Executive editor Tom Brevoort said that fans shouldn't have been surprised by Manara's depiction of Spider-Woman because "his body of work indicates what sort of thing he's going to do," while *Amazing Spider-Man* writer Dan Slott called the matter a "false controversy" because "Manara has been drawing this way for 30+ years. Did you expect something different?" Both men failed to tackle the issue of why Marvel would hire Manara for this book in the first place.

The cover garnered attention outside of the comic book community, with articles on major websites like the *Hollywood Reporter* and *Vox* covering the matter. Ultimately, Marvel editor in chief Axel Alonso apologized "for the mixed messaging that this variant caused," but still published the cover and continued to work with Manara on variant covers for other books. The *Spider-Woman* cover has been parodied repeatedly since then, and in 2020, Manara's original artwork for the cover sold at auction for $37,500.

DC garnered their own variant cover controversy in 2015 when an announced variant for *Batgirl* #41 by Rafael Albuquerque harkened back to Barbara's trauma from *Batman: The Killing Joke*. The cover showed the Joker in his iconic Hawaiian garb, grinning menacingly as he held Batgirl close with a gun in one hand and the other pointing at her bloody smile. Barbara looked terrified, her eyes wide and welling up with tears as her tense, clenched mouth belied the bloody grin painted across her face. It was an evocative image, but one that contrasted strongly with the lighthearted tone of the series. This iteration of Barbara was fun and vibrant, unburdened after decades of being plagued by the events of *The Killing Joke*, and the variant cast Barbara as a frightened victim haunted by the dark history of a story reviled by most modern Batgirl fans.

Both readers and the creators were displeased with the variant, and *Batgirl* cowriter Cameron Stewart made clear, "The cover was not seen or approved by anyone on Team Batgirl and was completely at odds with what we are doing with the comic." After seeing the fan response, Albuquerque realized "it touched a very important nerve" so he asked DC not to publish the cover and explained, "My intention was never to hurt or upset anyone through my art." DC agreed, and issued a statement that vaguely stated, "Threats of violence and harassment are wrong and have no place in comics or society," suggesting that outraged fans on both sides of the issue had gotten out of hand online. Stewart later clarified that only those objecting to the cover had been threatened.

Batgirl wrote *The Killing Joke* out of continuity eight issues later, with Stewart, cowriter Brendan Fletcher, and artist Babs Tarr making the events of the book a false memory implanted in Barbara's mind by a villain. This change didn't last for long, however. *Heroes in Crisis* referenced the shot that paralyzed Barbara by having her pull up her skintight costume and show her scars, the "Joker War" event referenced *The Killing Joke* repeatedly, and Geoff Johns and Jason Fabok's *Three Jokers* showed Barbara flashing back to the Joker's assault while nude in the shower.

With publishers and vocal segments of fandom barring the gates in myriad ways, the new generation of fans began to develop their own communities. Many inclusive-minded retailers held ladies' nights without male staff, special after-hours events where female fans and fans from marginalized genders who were understandably wary of comic shops could peruse the store without fear of judgment or interrogation. Online, sites like *SYFY Fangrrls*, *The Mary Sue*, and *Women Write about Comics* centered female fans, while pages like *Black Girl Nerds*, *Geeks Out!*, and many, many more amplified the voices of people of color and the queer community. Many of these groups intersect at inclusive events like Geek Girl Con, an annual weekend-long convention in Seattle that explicitly states, "ALL ages, gender identities, sexual orientations, sizes, abilities, ethnicities, nationalities, races, creeds, religions, familial statuses, physical and mental abilities, education levels, fandoms, etc., are welcome."

Communities also developed on social media among fans of particular characters, most notably the "Carol Corps" who embraced the new *Captain Marvel*. Kelly Sue DeConnick and Dexter Soy revamped Carol Danvers as Captain Marvel for an ongoing series in 2012, leaving the "Ms." moniker behind, and Jamie McKelvie's flight suit–inspired costume design became an instant cosplay favorite. The new take on Carol was brash and bold, and fans loved the character's defiant heroism. DeConnick later said of Captain Marvel's appeal, "Carol falls down all the time, but she always gets back up—we say that about Captain America as well, but Captain America gets back up because it's the right thing to do. Carol gets back up because 'Fuck you.'"

The term "Carol Corps" was coined by DeConnick, who stepped up to promote *Captain Marvel* when the publisher didn't do much to support the book aside from the usual in-house comics advertising. DeConnick provided merchandise and made new fans feel welcome with badges and dog tags to reflect Carol's military background, and even commissioned a knitting pattern for Carol's lucky hat that she shared online for free. Between an unabashedly powerful, adventurous heroine and a creator who went out of her way to foster community, many fans connected with Captain Marvel because they felt seen for the first time. A superhero was finally catering to their interests, and it felt good.

Captain Marvel's success led to more female characters taking the lead at Marvel and DC. Comic book conventions began to host panels to spotlight female creators and characters, including the regular "Women of Marvel" panel. While the panels were open to everyone, "Women of Marvel" often served as a sort of group therapy for fans who found acceptance for the first time. DeConnick offered sage advice for new fans, telling one tearful young woman who'd been harassed by a comic shop bully, "No one gets to make you feel less than. No one gets to make you feel that they can decide what you can like. Nobody." She was also as defiant a presence as the character she reinvented, declaring at one panel, "I am willing to make other people uncomfortable, so my daughter won't have to," as attendees cheered.

Marvel introduced the spin-off series *Ms. Marvel* two years later, starring Kamala Khan, a Pakistani American teen with shape-shifting powers. Written by G. Willow Wilson with art from Adrian Alphona, the new book proved to be a massive bestseller, just not through the usual means. The monthly issues were middle of the pack in comic book shop sales reports but hit the top of the list in

Captain Marvel #1, art by Ed McGuinness, Dexter Vines, and Javier Rodriguez, Marvel Comics, 2012. Captain Marvel, with her flight suit–inspired costume, became a gateway for new fans.

digital sales. Collections of the series sold like gangbusters at general bookstores and online retailers as well, with several volumes hitting the *New York Times* bestseller list as they racked up combined sales of over half a million units.

Ms. Marvel's popularity outside of comic book shops was indicative of the fractured state of modern fandom. Many readers still avoid shops, opting for digital comics and paperback collections over traditional monthly paper comics. Ventures like DC's young adult graphic novel line recognize this split, and while the books are available in comic shops they're far more likely to be purchased elsewhere. Although the publisher connecting directly with this new generation of fans is admirable, it may also reinforce the fandom split if paired with the abdication of outreach in their mainline superhero books. Presenting empowered female characters in YA graphic novels and then objectifying those same characters in monthly floppies does nothing to bridge the divide. In order for fandom as a whole to come together, the superhero industry will need to move beyond toxic, gatekeeping fans and provide something for everyone across multiple lines and formats.

CHAPTER 13

Pride

The pernicious sexism and toxic masculinity that pervaded all levels of the superhero genre had negative ramifications for female fans, creators, and characters, and the same was true for queer representation. Not that the rest of American popular culture was swift to embrace queer narratives either; the nation was and remains rife with homophobia, and expanding representation has been an uphill climb. But it was especially slow for the superhero genre, which lagged behind its counterparts even as more inclusive views of sexuality began to grow in the 2000s.

Part of this was due to the specter of Dr. Fredric Wertham, whose anti-homosexuality views were baked into the fabric of the Comics Code Authority and superhero publishing as a whole. Although DC and Marvel long ago abandoned the pretense that superhero comics were for kids, who could thus be swayed by the "morbid ideals" in their comics, both publishers nonetheless clung to the fear of queer-related scandal for decades after the audience shift was complete. However, Wertham wasn't the sole culprit.

In a recent report, the American Psychological Association linked toxic masculinity to homophobia and stated that "disruptive behaviors such as bullying [and] homosexual taunting" were a common outcome. As we've seen, toxic masculinity was firmly entrenched in the superhero genre, especially in terms of violent machismo and heterosexual objectification, and anything outside of this narrow conception of heroic manliness was devalued and viewed as a weakness. Given this, it's not terribly surprising that queer representation has been an up-and-down battle throughout the industry as both publishers and fans proved resistant to social change.

The original Comics Code's firm stance against "sex perversion" was interpreted as a ban on depictions of homosexual characters, and few appeared in the decades that followed. Every so often a heavily stereotyped effeminate gentleman or a flamboyant villain could be interpreted as gay, but there was nothing confirming a character's queerness until 1980 with "A Very Personal Hell" in *Hulk* #23. The infamous issue opened with Bruce Banner on the run thanks to the Hulk's destructive tendencies, lying low in a New York City YMCA where he was accosted by two men in the showers who threatened to rape him until he managed to escape.

This inauspicious start to Marvel's queer representation was written by Jim Shooter, the publisher's editor in chief, and he allegedly instituted a policy barring queer characters at Marvel from then on after the issue sparked a strong negative reaction. Creators who wanted to include gay characters could only hint at their leanings. John Byrne intended *Alpha Flight*'s Northstar to be gay, but for the entire 1980s he was just an angry young man who wasn't at all interested in dating women. Captain America's old friend Arnie Roth was very fond of his longtime "roommate" Michael and desperately enlisted Cap's help when Michael was kidnapped, although they were just friends, regardless of their tearful embrace upon his rescue. Chris Claremont danced around multiple lesbian relationships in his lengthy *Uncanny X-Men* run, including a powerful connection between Storm and Yukio and references to Mystique and Destiny's past life together, but it was all subtext and no text.

DC introduced their first gay character in 1988 with Extraño, a Peruvian magician who was a member of the New Guardians, though "openly" gay is debatable. While the word "gay" never appeared in his comics, he was awash in stereotypes and the implication was quite clear. Extraño was colorful and flamboyant, with a pronounced lisp and a love of jewelry, and his dialogue was laden with double entendres. Northstar became Marvel's first openly gay hero in 1992, finally announcing, "I am gay!" in *Alpha Flight* #106 as he battled the homophobic villain Major Mapleleaf. His declaration came after thirteen years of being trapped in the closet, but following this issue his sexuality was barely mentioned again for the next two decades.

After Extraño and Northstar, most of the queer characters at DC and Marvel in the 1990s and early 2000s were civilians as both publishers seemed reticent to add more queer heroes. Green Lantern Kyle Rayner was a cartoonist in his daily life, and his assistant Terry Berg was gay. So too were Kyle's neighbors Lee and Li, Supergirl's friend Andy Jones, Catwoman's longtime pal Holly Robinson, Metropolis police captain Maggie Sawyer, and Gotham cop Renee Montoya.

Many of these characters faced tragic circumstances, with Renee estranged from her conservative Catholic family and Terry nearly beaten to death in a hate crime. Arnie's "roommate" Michael died in a later kidnapping, and Destiny was killed off as well. Extraño contracted AIDS from a white supremacist vampire known as Hemo-Goblin, while Northstar was stabbed to death by a mind-controlled Wolverine. At one point, Marvel introduced a new gay superhero,

Freedom Ring, with editor in chief Joe Quesada celebrating him as emblematic of the fact that "we've had more gay and lesbian characters appearing in Marvel comics than ever before," but Freedom Ring was killed off the following month in a battle with the Iron Maniac.

The few queer superheroes who survived rarely engaged in romantic relationships, with one exception, Apollo and Midnighter. At Wildstorm, an imprint of DC, the duo were a hyperviolent analogue of Superman and Batman who revealed their romance in *The Authority* in 1999. It was a chaste relationship, however, limited to occasional flirtation and a hug or a kiss on the cheek. A proper kiss was planned, but DC publisher Paul Levitz vetoed the artwork and cut it from the comic because he thought the character's gay relationship made fun of Superman and Batman. Apollo and Midnighter did kiss when they got married in 2002, in the final issue of *The Authority*.

Marvel was similarly cagey with their gay characters. The 2003 revamp of the western *Rawhide Kid* made news when the publisher revealed the titular character was gay, but the miniseries engaged in little but innuendo. While frontier townspeople all noted that the Rawhide Kid was "a sharp dresser," his attempts at flirtation went over the heads of every man he encountered. The Rawhide Kid himself was a cringeworthy caricature, a preening, gossipy hotshot who criticized women's outfits and exasperatedly described characters he didn't like as, "Ugh, **niiiiightmare**." Marvel released the book under their 18+ MAX imprint and put a "Parental Advisory: Explicit Content" warning on the cover of each issue solely because the Rawhide Kid was gay, which led to some controversy. There was no explicit content whatsoever in the book, and Joe Quesada faced questions over why the mere existence of a queer character needed such a warning.

After the *Rawhide Kid* debacle, Marvel approached their next queer characters with more tact. *Young Avengers* was a new teen superhero book from writer Allan Heinberg and artist Jim Cheung with a diverse cast of characters, and editorial was fully supportive when Heinberg decided that two members, Hulkling and Wiccan, would be gay. Hulkling was Teddy Altman, a half Skrull/half Kree with shape-shifting abilities and superstrength. Wiccan was Billy Kaplan, whose magical powers were mysteriously linked to the Scarlet Witch. Early issues of the series slowly revealed that the two were a couple, leading to a lot of discussion in the book's letter column.

After the first issue hinted at Hulkling and Wiccan's relationship, several readers expressed support. One fan wrote, "More on that, I say," and another agreed, explaining that he was "tired of seeing heterosexual relationships all the time." Queer readers were especially excited, with one hoping, "For once, I'd like to see a Marvel book treat us queers as normal instead of some 'event of the season.'" Another expressed, "If something like that existed when I was 15 [. . .] it would have helped me understand my sexuality a lot sooner and made me more comfortable with myself." Heinberg, who is gay himself, replied that he "couldn't agree with you more about the need for more positive (or at least more diverse and accurate) representation of gays and lesbians in the mainstream media."

But not everyone was on board. One longtime Marvel fan began his letter by stating, "Now, I'm not some anti-gay bigot," before arguing, "I do think a superhero comic is not the platform for exploring 'sexual identities,' especially for characters that are teenagers. [. . .] Comics were never meant to be an outlet for changing society's view or forcing sensitive issues to be discussed among the readership." The following issue's letter column was full of missives strongly disagreeing, and while the fan did later reply politely with a somewhat more nuanced take, he stood by his original points.

Others were more harsh. One aggrieved reader declared, "Due to the **very** one-sided discussion [. . .] I will be dropping the book from my pull list. I do not like the comics I read to be the platform for someone's social/political bias." This complaint was echoed by another former fan who groused, "We are constantly inundated with the homosexual lifestyle through all forms of media and entertainment. I will not support a comic book that is supposed to be uplifting and entertaining that promotes homosexuality as a lifestyle choice." One reader offered a unique perspective when he said he'd continue to buy the book even though he made clear, "I am anti-homosexuality," explaining that, "While liberals may consider Hulkling and Wiccan to be the rightful representation of a minority, I see their homosexuality as a character flaw, which lends their characters depth."

Despite such backlash, the fan response to *Young Avengers* was more positive than negative. The book garnered good press as well, and even won the GLAAD Media Award for Outstanding Comic Book in 2006 for its portrayal of Hulkling and Wiccan. However, Marvel has done little with the characters since. *Young Avengers* ended after twelve issues, and in the fifteen years that followed the team has returned only for brief miniseries and a second fifteen-issue run in 2013. Hulkling and Wiccan have popped up across the Marvel line occasionally for quick guest spots and cameos, but they're not core characters by any means and have faded into the background for extended periods of time. Marvel has not made them a priority.

In 2005, writer Devin Grayson and artist Dustin Nguyen began redeveloping Batwoman as Kate Kane, a wealthy Gotham socialite and a lesbian who would become DC's first openly gay character. Thanks to the legacy of Fredric Wertham, the publisher didn't have a great track record when it came to the Bat-family and queerness, and had even ordered an art gallery to take down intimately posed paintings of Batman and Robin by artist Mark Chamberlain earlier in the same year. But despite this corporate legal wrangling, plans for a new solo *Batwoman* series were underway.

Batwoman's lesbian leanings were announced in a *New York Times* article in 2006. She was described as a "buxom lipstick lesbian," coded language that suggested DC editorial was worried their heterosexual male fan base would be upset by the news. Promising that she'd be curvaceous and attractively feminine felt like a ploy to assuage their concerns. The announcement made waves beyond the fan community, however, getting global attention as news outlets the world over discussed the novelty of a lesbian crimefighter in Gotham.

This strong reaction, both positive and negative, made DC reconsider the character's rollout. The *Batwoman* series was abandoned, even though three issues were already written and Grayson, a queer woman, had put months into developing the character. Instead, Batwoman debuted in the pages of *52*, DC's new weekly comic book, with writer Greg Rucka handling the character and introducing her as Renee Montoya's ex-girlfriend. Renee was a major character in *52*, but the new Batwoman didn't play much of a role in the book apart from a handful of brief cameos.

DC promised that a *Batwoman* series was on the horizon, but it was slow to come to fruition. Whether it was a fear of backlash or wanting to take the time to do things right, it took over three years for Batwoman to land a headlining role, and she finally took over *Detective Comics* in 2009. Rucka and artist J. H. Williams III fleshed out her backstory, revealing that Kate was an award-winning cadet at West Point Military Academy before she was outed as a lesbian and expelled because of the military's "don't ask, don't tell" policy. She used her military training to her advantage as Batwoman, battling her long-lost sister Beth who'd returned to Gotham as the villainous Alice.

The *Detective Comics* run lasted for ten issues, resulting in critical acclaim and a GLAAD Award in 2010, and then the book reverted back to Batman stories. A *Batwoman* series was again promised, but was delayed until the New 52 reboot in late 2011. By this point, Rucka had left DC and Williams cowrote the book with W. Haden Blackman. Williams and Blackman then ended up quitting the book after two years due to constant editorial interference, and the last straw was DC not allowing Kate to marry her girlfriend, Maggie Sawyer. She'd already proposed and a wedding was the next logical step, but DC's recent reboot had undone every superhero marriage and the editors claimed they didn't want to create any new ones. The series lasted another year before it was canceled, and a relaunched series two years later ran for eighteen issues. Kate has been an occasional guest star in the Batman line since then, but is not a major player.

DC's treatment of Batwoman was indicative of the publisher's approach to queer characters generally. There's been a constant reticence, paired with a tendency to walk back big developments. In 2015, writer Genevieve Valentine and artist Garry Brown revealed that Catwoman was bisexual, but the character's

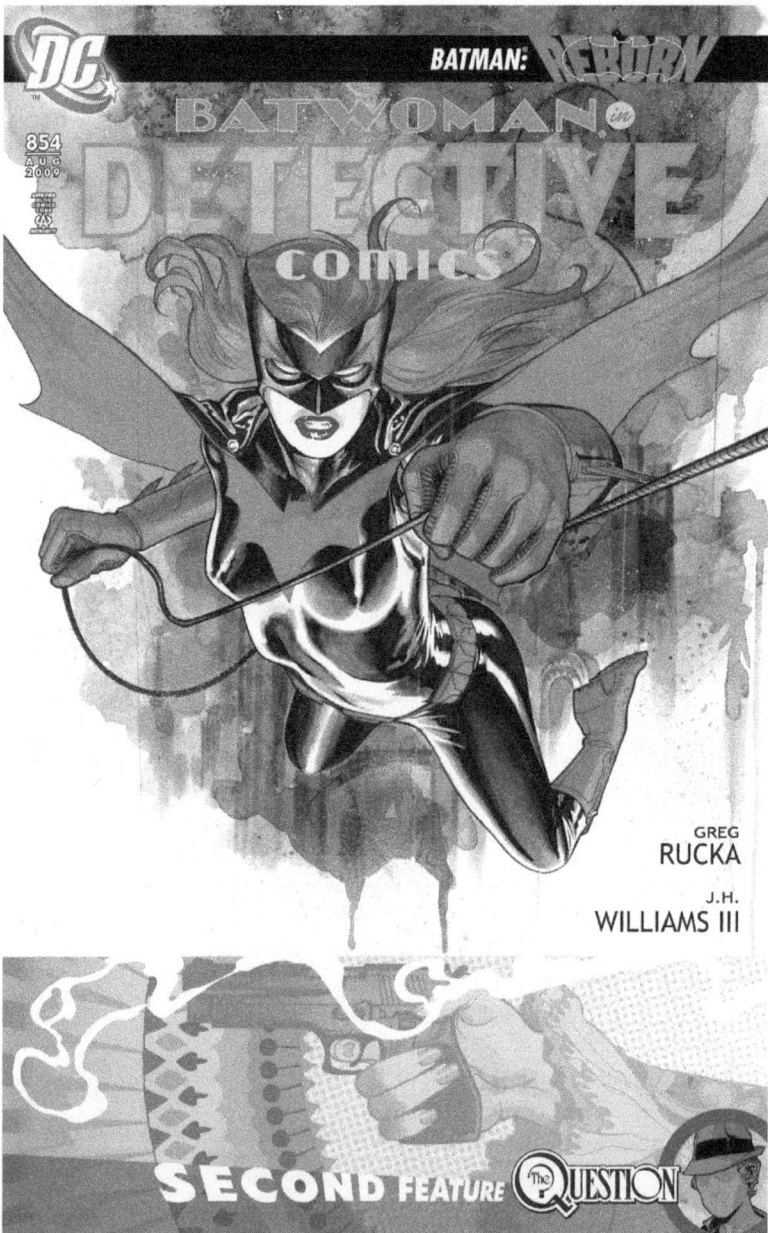

Detective Comics #854, art by J. H. Williams III, DC Comics, 2009.
Batwoman finally headlines her own series, albeit briefly.

first queer relationship lasted until Valentine left the book six issues later and her bisexuality has barely been mentioned since as she's been embroiled in a complicated romantic pairing with Batman for the last five years. Greg Rucka and artist Nicola Scott made Wonder Woman canonically bisexual in 2016, confirming a past relationship with her fellow Amazon Kasia, but she's been involved with Steve Trevor ever since and her queerness has yet to be explored in any depth.

Harley Quinn has been another roller coaster of representation. After escaping her toxic relationship with the Joker, Harley found solace with Poison Ivy, and the two women eventually became a couple. Then, with the *Birds of Prey* film on the horizon in 2020, DC pulled back. Poison Ivy had less of a role in the ongoing *Harley Quinn* comics, and the duo's miniseries ended with them separated. A collectible statue of the pair was originally called the DC Designer Series' "first official statue featuring a same-sex couple," but DC's own PR for the item described Harley and Ivy as "the epitome of what it means to be a loyal best friend" before extolling the statue as a "reminder that to love someone can mean many things."

Marvel has been similarly inconsistent with their queer heroes over the years. Northstar was resurrected and eventually married his boyfriend in a special issue of *Astonishing X-Men* in 2012, but the character hasn't been seen much since. Hercules was shown in a relationship with Wolverine in an alternate universe in *X-Treme X-Men* in 2013, but when Hercules launched his own series two years later, Marvel's editor in chief Axel Alonso emphasized that the pairing "took place in a unique alternate universe" and insisted Hercules was straight. Wolverine's son Daken is canonically bisexual, however, though his appearances across the Marvel line have been intermittent at best. Deadpool is pansexual, but that aspect of his character is often treated as a joke and he's only had on-page relationships with women.

In 2015, original X-Men member Bobby Drake, a.k.a. Iceman, came out—sort of. In a complicated bit of superhero fun, the original teen X-Men had traveled to the present day, where they interacted with their adult selves. *All-New X-Men* #40 revealed that teen Bobby was gay when teen Jean Grey called him out for objectifying women because, thanks to her mind-reading abilities, she knew it was all an act and saw Bobby's true inclinations. Bobby was upset at first but the conversation ended with hugs, and his adult counterpart came out to him soon after.

The issue faced criticism on an unusual front, not from the habitual homophobes but rather from inclusive fans who took issue with Bobby's forced outing and the way the story ignored the possibility that Bobby could be bisexual. Many suggested that writer Brian Michael Bendis, a middle-aged straight man, may not have been the ideal choice for handling a teen coming-out story, however well intentioned. Marvel appeared to take these criticisms to heart, and hired

Sina Grace, an openly gay writer, to pen a subsequent *Iceman* miniseries. But editorial warned Grace against making the book "too gay," failed to provide support when he faced a barrage of online harassment, and even tried to rein him in when he garnered high-level press for the book on his own that Marvel had failed to pursue. Ultimately, *Iceman* lasted for sixteen issues and Grace hasn't worked with Marvel since, while Bobby has returned to a secondary role in team books.

With gay, lesbian, and bisexual characters facing constant setbacks at DC and Marvel, it's perhaps unsurprising that representation for transgender characters was even more fraught. Historically, there was some gender fluidity in superhero comics thanks to various superpowers and fantastical technology. Characters switching bodies was common, and those swaps sometimes crossed genders. Other characters were shape-shifters, and moved between genders. But in terms of actual transgender people, representation was minimal. In one somewhat less fantastical example from 1992, the *Legion of Super-Heroes'* Shvaughn Erin was assigned male at birth and took the medication Profem to become biologically female, though the thirtieth-century setting marked a degree of separation between her and real-world experiences. The mutant Jessie Drake became Marvel's first transgender character in 1994, though she was a side character in a brief two-part story and didn't appear in a comic again for twenty-seven years. Meanwhile, Vertigo comics like *Doom Patrol*, *Invisibles*, and *Sandman* had transgender characters, but they weren't part of mainline continuity.

In 2011, Gail Simone introduced Alysia Yeoh as Barbara Gordon's new roommate in the first issue of the relaunched *Batgirl*, and two years later the book revealed that Alysia was, according to Simone, the "first non-fantasy-based, non-mature title trans character in a mainstream superhero book that we were aware of." The qualifiers were manifold, but key. Alysia was a normal, human transgender woman, without any superhero machinations, in a canonical superhero title, a landmark development for the genre. Simone had been at the forefront of increased representation for marginalized identities of all sorts at DC for some time, and consulted with trans writers and friends while crafting the character to ensure that Alysia's story was authentic and avoided stereotypes and tokenism. Her coming-out scene was heartfelt, with Barbara offering her love and support, and she remained a major player in the book moving forward.

But not as major as Simone hoped. She planned for Alysia to develop her own vigilante identity, Mouse, with a costume cobbled together from thrift shop offerings, and she was going to train with Black Canary and patrol the streets with a baseball bat. This would have led to an arc where Barbara got injured and Alysia took over as Batgirl for her while she recovered, which would have made Alysia the first nonfantastical transgender superhero. However, Simone's pitch was "soundly rejected" by DC editorial. They said they didn't want anyone else in a Batsuit, and "the idea was turned down flat."

Like DC's refusal to allow Batwoman to get married, keeping Alysia out of a Batsuit seemed to have rationale that had nothing to do with either woman's LGBTQ+ identity. At the same time, though, this rationale was selectively applied. Shortly after Simone left *Batgirl*, Commissioner Gordon took over as Batman, with his own fancy mechanical Batsuit. Then DC brought back their pre–New 52 Superman and Lois, restoring their marriage. The publisher's rules weren't hard and fast. Alysia got to be a Batgirl in the 1940s-set *DC Comics Bombshells* in 2015, at least.

Alysia was the first of several transgender characters to debut in the 2010s, including Koi Boi in *Unbeatable Squirrel Girl*, Sera in *Angela: Asgard's Assassin*, and Tong in *FF*. Comics soon saw the gender-fluid Porcelain in *Secret Six* and the nonbinary Lee Serano in *Supergirl* as well. Many of these characters were short lived and no longer regularly appear, but the ranks continue to grow. The most prominent transgender character in the world of superheroes actually premiered outside of comics with Nia Nal, a.k.a. Dreamer, on the CW's *Supergirl* television show. She was an entirely new character, created to be an ancestor of the Legion of Super-Heroes' Nura Nal, and trans activist and actor Nicole Maines took on the role in 2018. Maines remained a key member of the cast until *Supergirl* ended in 2021, and ensured that Nia would live on when she cowrote a story to introduce Dreamer into DC's comic universe in the publisher's *DC Pride* anthology that same year.

The CW's superhero shows have been a bastion of queer representation, but that hasn't been the case for most live-action superhero adaptations, with straightwashing a common occurrence. The *X-Men* franchise sidestepped Mystique's queer history across both incarnations of the character. Valkyrie's bisexuality didn't make the cut in *Thor: Ragnarok*, while Loki's gender fluidity has been referenced but not fully explored in the Marvel Cinematic Universe. *Black Panther* filmed a scene with some flirting between two of the female Dora Milaje warriors, one of whom was canonically lesbian in the comics, but it didn't make the final cut. Until *Eternals* in 2021, the only confirmed queer person in an MCU film was an unnamed character at Captain America's grief counseling group in *Avengers: Endgame*. The lack of queer representation on-screen led many fans to create their own, like the widespread "shipping" of Steve Rogers and Bucky Barnes, with entire internet communities devoted to fan fiction and artwork imaging the pair as a romantic couple.

DC has been accused of straightwashing as well. Across her four cinematic appearances thus far, Wonder Woman's queerness has gone unaddressed, even though star Gal Gadot said of the character, "She's a woman who loves people for who they are. She can be bisexual. She loves people for their hearts." *Suicide Squad* avoided Harley Quinn's bisexuality, though that's since been remedied with *Birds of Prey*. John Constantine has been straightwashed twice over, first in the 2005 Keanu Reeves film and then again in NBC's 2014 TV series starring Matt Ryan. It was only when Ryan revived the character on the CW's *Legends of Tomorrow* that Constantine was allowed to be his true bisexual self for the first time.

Most of the CW's superhero shows featured queer characters in notable roles, though certain segments of fandom were less than supportive. This was especially true when the network announced a *Batwoman* show, their first series with a queer lead. Many supposed fans were outraged that the CW "made Batwoman gay now," seemingly ignorant of the fact that Kate Kane had been a lesbian for twelve years when the network announced the show in 2018. When the show premiered, it was review bombed online, with irate nerds tanking its ratings on sites like IMDb and Rotten Tomatoes, all because it was headlined by a lesbian character. Despite this, *Batwoman* performed well enough to land a renewal that will ensure it runs for at least three seasons.

The superhero industry's reticence toward queer characters is slowly improving, but considerable roadblocks remain. While both DC and Marvel have expanded representation over the past decade, even releasing special comics each year for Pride Month, management is still tentative and some fans are vocally resistant. The superhero genre is heavily rooted in nostalgia, so new characters are a hard sell anyway, regardless of their sexuality. Many fans like the old characters to be the way they've always been, and thus don't want straight characters to suddenly come out as queer. The recent revelations that young heroes Tim Drake and Jonathan Kent are bisexual are met with a mixed response, with some celebrating the news while others bemoaned changing established characters. This resistance warrants interrogation, especially in terms of where nostalgia ends and homophobia begins. The overlap between the two has held the genre back from meaningful representation, and nostalgia's firm grasp has impacted other marginalized groups as well.

CHAPTER 14

Supremacy

Hal Jordan, the Silver Age Green Lantern, was killed off in 1996. He was an aging relic from an era when almost every hero was a generic white man, and his replacements were more diverse. In the comics, a half-Mexican artist named Kyle Rayner became the new Green Lantern and headlined a book that garnered steady sales after years of declining numbers for Hal's adventures. On television, Cartoon Network's *Justice League* animated series enlisted John Stewart, one of DC's first Black heroes, and established him as the quintessential Green Lantern for a new generation of young fans.

Then in 2004, DC Comics decided to bring Hal Jordan back. Sales for *Green Lantern* were slipping, and no one ever stays dead in superhero comics for long, especially white men. A newly young and vibrant Hal was resurrected in the six-issue *Green Lantern: Rebirth*, and became the de facto Green Lantern for the DC universe moving forward. He headlined a new solo *Green Lantern* series and rejoined the high-profile Justice League while Kyle and John were shuttled to secondary team books and became background players across the line.

Green Lantern: Rebirth was such a hit that DC editorial decided to bring back another dead Silver Age hero, Barry Allen a.k.a. the Flash, in 2009. Barry had died in 1985 during *Crisis on Infinite Earths* and his nephew, Wally West, took over as the Flash for the next two decades. Like his uncle, Wally was yet another white male hero, but his girlfriend and later wife Linda Park was Korean American, and their children, Jai and Iris, had speedster abilities and fought crime alongside their father. *The Flash: Rebirth* marked the beginning of the end of this multiracial superhero family. Barry became the primary Flash once again, and the New 52 reboot in 2011 kept Barry in the role and erased Wally's marriage, children, and life history.

Wally was reinvented for the New 52 as a biracial teenager, and appeared as Kid Flash in both *The Flash* and *Teen Titans* for a few years. Some fans clamored for the original Wally to return, however, and DC proved happy to oblige. In 2016, the publisher released *DC Universe: Rebirth*, a special one-shot that brought back the classic Wally. He's been featured prominently in several major titles since, while the new Wally has faded into the background.

Each of these resurrections sidelined characters of color in favor of their white counterparts, not a rare turn of events in superhero comics. But here, the writer behind each change was Geoff Johns, first as a freelancer and later as the chief creative officer and president of DC Comics as his high-profile-event books helped him rise through the ranks of the company. Pointing out this connection isn't meant to vilify Johns, but to see him as emblematic of the mindset of one of the major superhero publishers. In many ways, Geoff Johns is the ultimate fanboy. He grew up on the comics of the 1970s and 1980s, and has a deep love for the characters who influenced him when he was young. When he began writing comics, nostalgia was key to his work and he returned to many of these characters. His stories resonated too. A sizable portion of fandom shared his nostalgic view of the genre, and their support for his work propelled him to the top of DC's management.

Nostalgia, however, comes with baggage. Male dominance and white dominance have gone hand in hand across the history of the superhero genre. Just as male heroes have been coded as the norm, so too have white heroes been the default for decades. Bringing back old characters often means bringing back white characters, usually at the expense of what little diversity the genre has cultivated over the years. Gains for characters of color have been minimal and fleeting, with many fans and creators preferring callbacks to the old days over broadening representation. A lack of diversity behind the scenes has only exacerbated these issues, and even with recent changes the industry still struggles with its portrayal of people of color today.

Racism was a constant in the early years of the superhero genre, with caricatured villains and stereotyped allies as standard fare. These crass portrayals gave way to invisibility in the 1950s, so much so that actually showing people of color in the background of panels in the following decade marked significant progress for the genre. DC's Silver Age renaissance and Marvel's reentry into superhero comics were startling white, but by the early 1970s both publishers had introduced heroes of color like Black Panther, the Falcon, and John Stewart's Green Lantern.

More followed, including Blade, Luke Cage, Misty Knight, Colleen Wing, Shang-Chi, and Storm at Marvel and Black Lightning, Bumblebee, Cyborg, and Dawnstar at DC. Some headlined their own series, though most were secondary characters, and they were among the first to go when cuts had to be made. *Black Lightning* ran for eleven issues before getting caught up in the DC Implosion in 1978, and this wave of cancellations also ended plans for *The Vixen*, a new series that would have been DC's first comic with a Black female lead. The majority of these characters were also created, written, and drawn exclusively by white creators who, while often well intentioned, brought their own limited experiences and perspectives on race to the comics.

This changed with the debut of Milestone Comics, an independent imprint of DC Comics founded by Black creators Denys Cowan, Michael Davis, Derek T. Dingle, and Dwayne McDuffie. Debut titles *Blood Syndicate*, *Hardware*, *Icon*, and *Static* hit shops in 1993 and introduced a new universe of diverse heroes centered on the fictional Dakota City. Sales were strong initially, and the books even crossed over with the DC universe in the "Worlds Collide" event, but the comic book market hit a serious slump in the mid-1990s. While Milestone closed their comic division in 1997, the line's impact was significant. The comics showed that Black heroes and creators belonged in the superhero genre, Static lived on in the popular *Static Shock* cartoon that ran for four seasons in the early 2000s, and Milestone has been revived multiple times over the past two decades.

Milestone's Shadow Cabinet even appeared in *Justice League of America* in 2008, marking a rare influx of diversity on DC's flagship team. Historically, there were more aliens than people of color in the Justice League, most of them white presenting to boot. When the team finally added its first Latinx and Black characters with Vibe and Vixen, respectively, in the mid-1980s, it was just months before *Crisis on Infinite Earths* reset the universe and canceled the series. At Marvel, the Avengers were similarly unbalanced, with androids outnumbering heroes of color for the bulk of the team's existence. While the half-Vietnamese Mantis did join the team in the mid-1970s, her time as an Avenger was short lived.

"Short lived" was a common outcome for characters of color at DC and Marvel. From Mantis in *Avengers* to Black Lightning's solo series to Milestone, attempts to diversify the line rarely lasted for long. Characters were introduced and then faded away, often into obscurity though some survived as backlist team members. Meanwhile, the same white heroes continued to headline the bulk of superhero comics, year in and year out.

This trend continued in recent years, across a variety of ethnicities and nationalities. Lebanese American Simon Baz became a Green Lantern in 2012 and later joined the Justice League, but his profile diminished after a few years and he's since been sidelined. Egyptian American Khalid Nassour became the new Doctor Fate in 2015, launching his own solo series, but has been a secondary character in team books since the series ended. One of the genre's few Indian heroes, the technopathic mutant Trinary, took on a key role in *X-Men Red* in 2018, but became a background player after the series ended, and has yet to even be given a proper, non-superheroic name.

Indigenous characters have faced similar treatment. Most have been relegated to small roles on team books, including the Legion of Super-Heroes' Dawnstar, the X-Men's Dani Moonstar, and the *Super Friends* cartoon's cringingly stereotypical Apache Chief. Recent efforts to highlight indigenous superheroes have proven brief. At DC, *Justice League United* introduced the Cree hero Equinox with much publicity and fanfare, but the book didn't last and she's barely been seen since its cancellation. Marvel brought back the Cheyenne hero Red Wolf in a special miniseries in 2015 with covers and consulting from Native American artist Jeffrey Veregge, but he hasn't lasted either.

East Asian heroes have had a more prominent role at both DC and Marvel, though their treatment has been mixed at best. Asian characters began to appear in superhero comics during the kung fu craze of the 1960s and 1970s, often as mentors for white heroes. I Ching taught martial arts to Diana Prince during *Wonder Woman*'s mod era, while O-Sensei turned young Richard Dragon into a kung fu fighter. White characters mastering martial arts and even besting their peers and mentors was the norm, though some Asian superheroes emerged from this era, most notably Shang-Chi and Colleen Wing at Marvel. While Shang-Chi had his own series for several years, though, Colleen was a secondary character behind another headlining white martial artist, Iron Fist.

The origins of Iron Fist highlighted another trend in the genre whereby white characters became mystical masters of hidden East Asian orders. Iron Fist was Danny Rand, who as a boy traveled with his parents to find the secret city of K'un-L'un. Danny was the only one to survive the trek, and he was taken in by the masters of K'un-L'un, became their star pupil, and ultimately took the power of the Iron Fist by defeating the dragon Shou-Lau. Doctor Strange followed a similar path, learning his skills in the mystic arts from the Ancient One in Kamar-Taj, another secret East Asian city, before using this knowledge to become the Sorcerer Supreme.

All these stories are rife with Orientalism and appropriation, with predominantly white creators crafting narrow depictions of an entire region, all for the benefit of white heroes. The genre's East Asian characters have yet to escape the confines of the kung fu craze, with most closely connected to the mystic or martial arts. For every Jubilee or Ryan Choi who manages to escape these stereotypes, there are scores of supernaturally powered and/or katana-wielding and/or acrobatically combative East Asians.

While these characters often taught white heroes, in one bizarre case an East Asian character actually *was* a white hero. In the late 1980s, the mind of Betsy Braddock, an upper-class British mutant known as Psylocke, was placed in the body of Kwannon, a brain-dead Japanese assassin, where she remained for the next thirty years, utilizing Kwannon's martial arts abilities. Psylocke was also one of Marvel's most prominent Asian characters in this span, an uncomfortable situation for many fans until the two were finally separated in 2018 and both Betsy and Kwannon began to explore their own stories.

Psylocke was also hypersexualized while in Kwannon's body, even more so than her fellow female characters in a tight, high-cut outfit that's been described as a "sexy-ninja" costume. The fetishization of Asian women was a constant throughout superhero comics of this era, with characterizations ranging from passive yet sexy to kick ass yet sexy as artists reveled in stereotypical, objectifying tropes. Appropriation was common as well, and as recently as 2021, a variant cover for a new *Joker* series drawn by artist J. Scott Campbell showed Punchline, the villain's girlfriend, dressed in a skimpy kimono and geisha makeup standing dutifully at the side of the reclining Clown Prince of Crime.

Meanwhile, East Asian characters regularly comprised hordes of foes just waiting to be dispatched by a superhero, with villains flanked by a mass of nameless ninjas who existed only to be defeated. From Daredevil versus the Hand to Wolverine fighting his way through Madripoor to Batman battling the League of Assassins, the strewn bodies of Asian combatants, unconscious or dead, was a common sight. Characters like Iron Man and the Punisher have origins rooted in the Vietnam War, and as time has marched on and made those origins unworkable, Marvel invented the fictional Sian Cong War, unmoored in history, to replace it. By doing so, the publisher chose to villainize and kill even more Asian characters, adding to this cavalcade of death and defeat.

Marvel's cavalier approach to representation is a top-down affair today. The creators behind the publisher's poor depictions of East Asian characters and culture were predominantly white, but few went so far as Marvel's current editor in chief, C. B. Cebulski. Soon after his promotion was announced in 2017, news broke that when he was a lower-tier editor a decade earlier he'd secretly penned several stories as "Akira Yoshida." Marvel was exploring manga-style series at the time and wanted to hire Japanese creators, so Cebulski pretended to be one, even going so far as to create an elaborate backstory for Yoshida and doing interviews for him. Cebulski denied rumors about his pseudonym for years before confirming them after he became editor in chief. Many fans were outraged at the blatant appropriation, but Cebulski has remained in the role.

Representation for Latinx characters has been similarly fraught. For several decades, most were villains, often limited to roles as gang members in superhero-patrolled cities. New heroes have emerged, but have rarely stayed in the spotlight for long. At Marvel, the new Ghost Rider, Robbie Reyes, and the new Nova, Sam Alexander, each had their own title before moving to secondary roles in team books. At DC, the latest Blue Beetle, Jaime Reyes, pops in and out, while the first Latina Green Lantern, Jessica Cruz, was paired with Simon Baz for their own *Green Lanterns* title but has been shuttled off to team duty since the book was canceled. Other characters have had Latinx heritage revealed only for it to be quickly forgotten and rarely mentioned again, like Catwoman and Lois Lane. New characters continue to emerge, however. The Brazilian Yara Flor is DC's newest Wonder Girl, while Afro Puerto Rican Miles Morales is a star across Marvel media as Spider-Man.

Miles has been a huge success for Marvel. A native New Yorker like his predecessor, the new teen hero's mixed heritage represents the diversity of the city. He first debuted in the Ultimate universe in 2011, emerging as the new Spider-Man after Peter Parker's death. When the Ultimate universe ended in 2018, Miles was one of the few to survive its demise, and has continued on in the main Marvel universe with his own solo title along with various team affiliations. He's a hit outside of comics too, starring in the much-lauded *Into the Spider-Verse* animated film and his own popular video game, *Marvel's Spider-Man: Miles Morales*.

Early reactions to Miles replacing Peter in the Ultimate universe were met with strong reactions from certain corners of fandom, however. Many fans vowed to cancel their subscriptions, decrying the change as "disgraceful" and lamenting, "Affirmative action in comics . . . for shame." These predominantly white, male fans viewed the change as a personal attack, with one commenting, "straight white male bashing is the flavor of the day, I guess," and another sarcastically stating, "This is a brilliant strategy because I just realized I can't complain about it cause it'll make me sound racist!"

One former fan upset over Miles got at the heart of the matter when he responded, "It really seems as if the media and the politicians want to stamp out white people at all costs." We've already seen how toxic masculinity in superhero comics led to sexism and homophobia, with straight males held up as paragons of heroism above all else, and when those heroes are all white, toxic masculinity and racism go hand and hand to diminish heroes of color. Sociologist Michael Kimmel has linked toxic masculinity to a recent rise in white supremacy and explained, "These guys believe something has been taken from them that they were entitled to." A similar entitlement can be seen in fan reactions to Miles becoming Spider-Man. Even within the confines of a fictional, alternate universe, some fans were outraged that the white hero they were used to was replaced not just by a new hero, but a hero of color, and this anger continued.

In 2014, Steve Rogers lost his superpowers and aged up considerably, so Sam Wilson took over the role of Captain America in his own *All-New Captain America* series. Some fans were intrigued by the change, but others took issue with a Black man as Captain America and called the move "disgustingly cynical." A common refrain was that increasing diversity shouldn't come at the expense of existing characters, that heroes of color should develop their own identities instead. This argument ignored the fact that new characters rarely broke through in the nostalgia-based superhero market, and the phrasing of such objections were telling. One fan responded, "Make a new character, don't pervert an existing one," while another said, "[Don't] take characters that we grew up with and change their race or culture. It's incredibly disrespectful." The racist undertones became more pronounced in other responses, with some railing against "a concerted effort nowadays to get rid of all white male super heroes in comics in the name of inclusion," while another fan moaned, "the actual comic book readers are suffering because publishers are trying to bring you in at the expense of us."

The same sentiments returned two years later when, in the wake of Tony Stark's death, teen genius Riri Williams became the lead character in *Invincible Iron Man* as the superarmored hero Ironheart. Some fans were especially aggrieved to have a Black teen girl replace Tony, saying that this trend of diverse heroes "feels like racism toward white people," and arguing that "forced diversity is almost as bad as racism in my opinion." One fan said the quiet part out loud when he noted, "Comics have always been marketed towards white men. Nothing wrong with that."

This white anger emerges every time a hero of color takes center stage, despite the fact that white heroes always come back. Peter Parker remains the de facto Spider-Man in the Marvel universe. Steve Rogers regained his powers. Tony Stark came back from the dead. Yet the slightest change in the all-white hegemony sent certain segments of fandom into a tailspin. Marvel vice president of sales David Gabriel confirmed as much, relaying that some retailers told him, "Any character that was diverse, any character that was new, our female characters, anything that was not a core Marvel character, people were turning their nose up against."

Meanwhile, the predominantly white creators behind all these changes didn't do a terribly good job at crafting authentic portrayals of race. Miles's creator Brian Michael Bendis was criticized by fans of color for making the character ambivalent about race issues. Writer Nick Spencer's tenure on *All-New Captain America* tried to be political but was awash with both-sidesism and false equivalencies that ultimately cast Sam as a "failed replacement for Steve Rogers." Artistic depictions of Riri Williams were critiqued for their faulty understanding of Black hair and for hypersexualizing a fifteen-year-old girl, including another variant cover from J. Scott Campbell who called the critiques an "SJW [social justice warrior] whine-fest."

White creators crafting characters of color has been the norm at DC and Marvel for decades, but one of the few long-lasting success stories for increased representation on the page involved representation behind the scenes. The new *Ms. Marvel*, Kamala Khan, was a bevy of firsts for Marvel in 2014, not just in terms of gender and race but also religion. She was created by writer G. Willow Wilson, who is Muslim like Kamala, and editor Sana Amanat, who is Pakistani American and grew up in New Jersey like Kamala. These two women brought an authenticity to the character that, combined with great storytelling, has made her a staple of the Marvel universe. Ms. Marvel has headlined her own book since her debut, and appears in the teen team book *Champions* alongside Miles Morales, Riri Williams, and other young heroes. Kamala also starred in the *Marvel Rising* cartoons and comics aimed at young female fans, was the lead character in Square Enix's *Marvel's Avengers* video game, and launched her own live-action television show on Disney+ with Iman Vellani in the lead role.

The *Ms. Marvel* show marked a big step forward for live-action superhero adaptations, which have been starkly white for some time. While the *Blade* trilogy marked Marvel's first successful cinematic outing, Sony's *Spider-Man* films, 20th Century Fox's *X-Men* franchise, and Marvel's own film line have largely centered on white heroes, with people of color relegated to side characters. The first thirteen solo films in the Marvel Cinematic Universe were led by white, male heroes until *Black Panther* broke the trend, while early team-ups like the initial *Avengers* movie were exclusively Caucasian affairs. A second team franchise, *Guardians of the Galaxy*, starred actors of color like Dave Bautista, Vin Diesel, and Zoe Saldana, though they all played makeup-heavy or CGI aliens rather than characters who shared their own ethnic identities, a common trend across superhero films.

DC's focus for over forty years has been Batman and Superman, with multiple incarnations of each hero, though the current DC cinematic universe has been more inclusive. Jason Momoa's Aquaman and Ray Fisher's Cyborg starred in *Justice League*, and there were diverse casts in the *Suicide Squad* franchise and *Birds of Prey*. Still, the tentpoles of these blockbuster franchises remain unsurprisingly pale.

Because of the superhero industry's overwhelming volume of white characters, many live-action adaptations have enhanced diversity by casting actors of color in traditionally white roles. This racebending had been embraced by some fans and decried by others. Segments of fandom threw a fit when Michael B. Jordan was announced as Johnny Storm in *Fantastic Four*, with both Jordan and the film's director Josh Trank receiving online harassment and even death threats. It's not just movies either. Candice Patton, who plays Iris West-Allen on the CW's *The Flash* TV series, has faced daily harassment since the show began in 2014.

Support behind the scenes wavered as well. Jeph Loeb, the former head of Marvel television, has been accused of rejecting story lines for Asian characters on *Daredevil*, with actor Peter Shinkoda alleging that Loeb said, "Nobody cares about Chinese people and Asian people." DC has also faced backlash from actors, with Ray Fisher accusing *Justice League* director Joss Whedon, DC chief creative officer Geoff Johns, and producer Jon Berg of "gross, abusive, unprofessional, and completely unacceptable" racist behavior.

Champions #5, art by Toni Infante, Marvel Comics, 2021. A new generation of heroes of color, including Spider-Man, Ms. Marvel, Nova, and Ironheart.

When original *Justice League* director Zack Snyder left the project, Whedon, Johns, and Berg cut the bulk of Cyborg's story line, and Whedon refused to take notes from Fisher on how the character was being portrayed. Johns told him to smile more, while producers fretted about having "an angry Black man" at the center of the film. Johns had written Cyborg in comics before and was similarly unreceptive to notes from Fisher, and Fisher later said, "It was like he was assuming how Black people would respond rather than taking the advice from the only Black person—as far as I know—with any kind of creative impact on the project."

One major conflict involved Cyborg saying, "Booyah," the character's catchphrase from a *Teen Titans* cartoon for children. Fisher felt that it "played differently" in live action, especially since no one else in the movie had a catchphrase, and explained, "It seemed weird to have the only Black character say that." But Whedon and Johns insisted, and Fisher eventually conceded. David F. Walker, the writer of a recent *Cyborg* comic for DC, expressed solidarity with Fisher as a fellow Black man in a predominantly white creative environment and said, "the problem isn't so much with the term 'booyah,' the problem is when a white person tells a black person that they know more about what black people think, say, or do."

This, in a nutshell, has been the relationship between superhero media and people of color. The vast majority of nonwhite characters were written and drawn by white creators, shaped by this narrow lens for decades, and then reinforced by a predominantly white power structure when the creative ranks finally began to diversify. At the same time, segments of fandom entrenched in nostalgia and entitlement have vocally demanded that characters not change and that their old favorites remain in prominent positions, all while ignoring fans of color who have been clamoring for improved representation for ages. Male dominance and white dominance are baked into the fabric of the superhero genre, interwoven in ways the industry is only beginning to acknowledge, much less address.

CHAPTER 15

Assemble

Lynda Carter debuted as Wonder Woman in 1975, saving Steve Trevor and emerging as the champion of the Amazons in a TV movie that soon led to a full-time show. Her take on Wonder Woman highlighted the character in all her superhero might, and the program ran for three seasons as Carter and Wonder Woman became icons of the decade. In the years before Wonder Woman finally arrived on the small screen, Batman and Superman each had successful runs in film serials in the 1940s and on television in the 1950s and 1960s. After *Wonder Woman* ended in 1979, it took thirty-six years for another live-action Wonder Woman to debut, and over that span there were six new, different live-action versions of Batman and seven of Superman.

Such was the nature of superhero film and television. Male heroes took center stage repeatedly, regardless of previous success or failures, while female heroes were a rarity. It was true in the past and it remains true today, despite substantial strides in representation. Live-action superhero media replicated the sexist trends of its source material, resulting in limited roles for women. The most common of these roles was as the hero's girlfriend.

The first blockbuster superhero film was Richard Donner's *Superman* in 1978, with Christopher Reeve in the starring role. Margot Kidder played Lois Lane, depicting her as an absolute firecracker who fearlessly chased after big scoops, but despite Kidder's bold take on the character, her narrative purpose was clear. She was there to be rescued and fall for the hero, and Lois's death spurred the film's climactic solution in which Superman turned back time to save her. Lois also proved expendable, and she was largely left out of *Superman III* after Kidder publicly criticized Donner's firing from the sequel, replaced by Annette O'Toole as Lana Lang.

Batman followed suit, with Bruce Wayne dating a different woman in each installment of his four-film franchise starting in 1989. From Kim Basinger's

Vicki Vale to Michelle Pfeiffer's Selina Kyle to Nicole Kidman's Chase Meridian to Elle Macpherson's Julie Madison, there was always someone for the Dark Knight to romance. Pfeiffer broke the mold, at least, with Selina becoming the fiendish Catwoman in *Batman Returns*, but that film marked the end of Tim Burton's run as director. Joel Schumacher took over from there and his second film, *Batman & Robin*, expanded the female cast by introducing Alicia Silverstone as Batgirl and Uma Thurman as Poison Ivy, but also marked the end of the franchise.

The first superhero hit of the 2000s was *X-Men*, which initially appeared to buck the trend with four powerful women in the mix. Famke Janssen as Jean Grey, Anna Paquin as Rogue, and Halle Berry as Storm were some of the film's heroes, while Rebecca Romijn's Mystique worked with the villainous Magneto. But Hugh Jackman's Wolverine emerged as the film's breakout character, and he took center stage while the women moved into the background as the original trilogy continued, with Jean eventually killed in a half-hearted take on the Dark Phoenix story line. Wolverine received his own follow-up trilogy, snarling and slashing his way through scores of villains, while a revamped franchise focused largely on Professor X and Magneto. Jennifer Lawrence's Mystique played a sizable role, but her story revolved around the two men. Meanwhile, an adaptation of the *Uncanny X-Men* story line "Days of Future Past" removed Kitty Pryde from the lead role she had in the comics, replacing her with Wolverine, while *X-Men: Dark Phoenix* killed Jean again, this time with Sophie Turner in the role.

Christopher Nolan's *Dark Knight* trilogy also proved hazardous to female characters. Nolan adapted Batman's darkest, grittiest moments from the comics, with *Batman Begins* drawing from Frank Miller's *Batman: Year One*, *The Dark Knight* inspired by elements of *Batman: The Killing Joke*, and *The Dark Knight Rises* loosely adapting *Batman: Knightfall*. Rachel Dawes was the only major female character in the first two films, played by Katie Holmes then Maggie Gyllenhaal, and she served as Bruce's romantic interest in need of constant rescuing. She was his conscience in the first film, then was killed by the Joker in the sequel to further Bruce's angst. While the third film had two female characters, Anne Hathaway as Selina Kyle and Marion Cotillard as Talia al Ghul, Talia was killed and Selina became Bruce's prize for his happily ever after once he retired as Batman.

The glut of superhero films in the early 2000s offered few opportunities for female characters. Sam Raimi's blockbuster *Spider-Man* franchise had a male hero fighting male villains, while Kirsten Dunst's Mary Jane Watson watched worriedly from the sidelines or ended up captured. Heroes like Daredevil, Ghost Rider, Green Lantern, the Hulk, the Punisher, and more followed the same formula. Only two superhero movies had female leads, and they were both disasters before filming even started.

Catwoman starred Halle Berry, though the film had been in development for over a decade, originally with Michelle Pfeiffer reprising her role. Pitof, the film's director, had little experience, and he inherited a convoluted script that had gone through more than a dozen different drafts as the story morphed and changed following Pfeiffer's departure. The end result was a sloppy, corny mess that failed to earn back its production budget.

Elektra, a *Daredevil* spin-off with Jennifer Garner returning to the role, was fraught behind the scenes as well. Garner wasn't keen to do the project but she was contractually obligated, and production moved quickly, rushing ahead with a half-baked script so she could film between seasons of her TV series *Alias*. The end result was disjointed and fell flat with critics and audiences, earning back its budget but barely just.

Catwoman and *Elektra* weren't the only superhero flops in this era, but the pair had long-lasting ramifications. In leaked emails between Marvel CEO Ike Perlmutter and Sony CEO Michael Lynton, Perlmutter called *Elektra* "very, very bad" and *Catwoman* "a disaster," linking the two with the underwhelming 1984 *Supergirl* movie. In connecting these three films specifically, it was clear that Perlmutter believed they failed because they had female leads, not because of any other production issues, and his subsequent output reflected his distrust of female superheroes.

In 2005, Marvel formed Marvel Studios to independently produce their own films. Many of their characters were licensed to other studios, but Marvel still had the rights to the Avengers and planned to introduce them individually across a shared universe and then bring them together for team movies. *Iron Man* kicked things off in 2008, and was followed by *The Incredible Hulk*, *Thor*, and *Captain America: The First Avenger* before the heroes united in *Avengers* in 2012.

All the early solo films and their sequels had male leads, and followed the standard girlfriend formula. Well-known, critically acclaimed actresses were limited to romantic subplots, including Gwyneth Paltrow's Pepper Potts, Liv Tyler's Betty Ross, Natalie Portman's Jane Foster, and Hayley Atwell's Peggy Carter. Group films featured one female character on each team initially, with Scarlett Johansson's Natasha Romanoff a.k.a. Black Widow in *Avengers* and Zoe Saldana's Gamora in *Guardians of the Galaxy*, though their sequels added one additional woman each, Elizabeth Olsen's Wanda Maximoff and Pom Klementieff's Mantis, respectively.

Further solo films continued the girlfriend trend, adding Evangeline Lilly as Hope van Dyne in *Ant-Man* and Rachel McAdams as Christine Palmer in *Doctor Strange*. The Marvel Cinematic Universe's eighteenth film, *Black Panther* in 2018, was the first to feature a multitude of female characters in a variety of roles, with Lupita Nyong'o as the adventurous Nakia, Danai Gurira as the fierce

Avengers poster, Marvel Studios, 2012. Black Widow was the only female hero saving the world. *Walt Disney Studios Motion Pictures/Photofest © Walt Disney Studios Motion Pictures.*

Okoye, Letitia Wright as the inventive Shuri, and Angela Bassett as the regal Ramonda. Hope became the first female superhero to headline a film when she debuted as the Wasp, but she had to share the title in 2018's *Ant-Man and the Wasp*. Brie Larson's Carol Danvers was the first to have her own solo outing when *Captain Marvel* hit theaters in 2019 as the studio's twenty-first film.

Marvel tried to pay homage to their female heroes during the climactic battle in *Avengers: Endgame* when ten different women teamed up to ferry the Infinity Gauntlet through Thanos's forces. While some found the scene empowering, others found it forced. At *The AV Club*, Caroline Siede called the moment "glaringly patronizing," and wrote, "It misses the mark so badly it could only come from a studio that made 20 movies before it got to one with a female lead and then acted like we should all be grateful for its trailblazing feminism."

The studio's lack of women on-screen was paired with a stark absence of women behind the scenes. Men directed the first twenty Marvel films, and across the fifty writing credits in that span, only one belonged to a woman, Nicole Perlman, who penned an early draft of *Guardians of the Galaxy*. James Gunn received all the credit for the film's success after he rewrote her script and directed the film, and Perlman didn't return for the sequel. *Captain Marvel* marked the studio's first film with a female director, Anna Boden, though like the Wasp, she had to share the credit, with Ryan Fleck codirecting. Cate Shortland on *Black Widow* in 2021 was Marvel's first solo female director.

Marvel's treatment of Black Widow generally was emblematic of the studio's poor handling of its female characters. She debuted as a side character in *Iron Man 2*, and it took eleven years for her own movie to finally happen, despite Scarlett Johansson's high profile and many fans clamoring for more Black Widow. Natasha wasn't handled well in early outings either. She showed her superspy prowess in *Iron Man 2*, but also served as eye candy in a tight, conspicuously unzipped catsuit. Tony Stark's regular flirtation underscored her intended role, and Johansson later said of the film, "While it was really fun and had a lot of great moments in it, the character is so sexualized, you know? Really talked about like she's a piece of something, like a possession or a thing or whatever—like a piece of ass, really."

While Black Widow proved a fierce fighter in *Avengers*, writer/director Joss Whedon's handling of the character in the sequel was widely criticized. An out-of-the-blue romance with Bruce Banner left many fans scratching their heads, especially since she was the only woman on the core team. Saddling her with a romantic subplot seemed painfully clichéd. Whedon's treatment of her past didn't sit well with some fans either. Natasha described her training as an enemy spy, explaining to Bruce, "They sterilize you. It's efficient. One less thing to worry about. The one thing that might matter more than a mission. Makes everything easier. Even killing. You still think you're the only monster on the team?" Some were offended by the implication that infertility was in some way monstrous, while others were frustrated that the subject was brought up at all, with *Blastr*'s Tara Bennett wondering why "they chose to get the one damn developed female superhero we get in the MCU's ovaries involved."

Black Widow was ultimately killed off in *Avengers: Endgame*, sacrificing herself to spare her old friend Hawkeye. It was a poignant death, but one quickly forgotten in the chaos that followed as the remaining Avengers faced off against Thanos again. Natasha went largely unmourned, while Tony Stark's passing at the end of the final battle dominated the latter part of the film, from his dramatic death to a big funeral scene. The subsequent *Black Widow* was a prequel film, finally giving Natasha the spotlight only after her death in a movie many fans enjoyed but called too little, too late for a character they thought deserved much more.

While female characters were shuttled to the background, Marvel's male heroes reveled in snark and bravado, fighting with each other at every turn in an endless display of toxically masculine traits. Steve, Thor, and Tony all clashed in *Avengers* before ultimately coming together, while Steve and Tony's issues continued in *Captain America: Civil War* as a villain easily manipulated the duo into fighting each other like petulant children. This rift remained through *Avengers: Infinity War*, leaving the team ill prepared for Thanos's assault, and Tony continued to spar with his fellow heroes Doctor Strange and Star-Lord. When the story continued in *Avengers: Endgame*, Tony's fury at Steve lasted another five years before they reunited to defeat Thanos for good. Tony was the poster child for unaddressed anger and violent outbursts, but most of Marvel's male heroes were inclined to punch first and ask questions later. The macho posturing was constant, with few characters able to escape this aggressive, confrontational mindset.

Some of Marvel's fans exhibited similar traits. The audience for Marvel movies was broad and nearly evenly split along gender lines, but certain corners of the fandom grew angry when the studio moved away from male-led films. These predominantly male fans were incensed when *Captain Marvel* was announced, claiming that Marvel was caving to "PC culture" by having a female lead, and were particularly mad when early trailers showed a strong, determined Captain Marvel who they felt didn't smile enough. Many took issue with Brie Larson as well. She was a proud feminist, unafraid to speak up about inequality, especially in Hollywood. Larson had noted that the bulk of the journalists and critics she met were white men and "decided to make sure my press days were more inclusive." This simple statement about bringing "more seats up to the table" outraged many white, male Marvel fans, who made tanking *Captain Marvel* their life's mission.

Before the film was even released, these fans took to the site Rotten Tomatoes to leave bad reviews meant to lower its audience score in a practice known as "review bombing." They weren't subtle about their aims either. One reviewer complained that "Brie had to come out as a bore SJW," another explained, "Have no interest in watching a movie starring a man hating feminazi," and one unintentionally ironic review declared, "Once Brie went on an anti-White male tirade I lost interest in this movie. [. . .] She can wallow in her own hate filled life." The sheer volume of negative reviews tanked the film's score, prompting Rotten Tomatoes to change their policy on reviewing a movie before it was released and purge roughly fifty-eight thousand reviews of *Captain Marvel*. Ultimately, the plan proved ineffective. *Captain Marvel* made over $1.1 billion globally, Larson came back for *Avengers: Endgame*, and will return again in *The Marvels* with two new female superheroes, Ms. Marvel and Monica Rambeau, in 2023.

Ms. Marvel and Monica made their debut on Disney+, where Marvel's television series have spotlighted female characters like the Scarlet Witch, Kate Bishop's Hawkeye, She-Hulk, and more. The movie slate has grown as well, with a wealth of female characters in *The Eternals*, a female Thor in *Thor: Love and Thunder*, a return to Wakanda in *Black Panther: Wakanda Forever*, and the aforementioned *The Marvels*. Still, male characters are the leads in the majority of the Marvel Cinematic Universe's new projects. The studio has dug a deep hole in terms of female representation, one they are only now beginning to slowly address, fourteen years in.

After Marvel's blockbuster success, Warner Bros. and DC decided to develop their own shared cinematic universe, starting with Zack Snyder's *Man of Steel* in 2013. It took Marvel six films to get from *Iron Man* to *Avengers*, though, and Warner Bros. didn't want to wait that long. They brought their two biggest properties together right away in *Batman v Superman: Dawn of Justice*, aiming to wow fans with this historic meeting. Warner Bros. wanted to differentiate their films from Marvel as well, and eschewed bright colors and quips in favor of a muted palette and darker, more serious stories. The aim was to be the anti-Marvel, and yet Warner Bros. ended up replicating many of their competitor's less inclusive traits.

Warner Bros. avoided the girlfriend trope initially by emphasizing the reporting prowess of Amy Adams's Lois Lane. She discovered Superman's secret identity on her own halfway through *Man of Steel*, but after that the trope returned in full force. She trailed after Superman, breathlessly fearful, for the rest of *Man of Steel*, had to be saved multiple times in *Batman v Superman*, and was sidelined by her grief over Superman's death in *Justice League*, though Martha Kent inadvertently lightened the mood when she recounted Clark calling Lois "the thirstiest young woman he'd ever met."

Superman's death was indicative of the DC universe's darker, more violent nature. He'd killed General Zod in *Man of Steel*, despite the fact that killing was strictly against Superman's moral code in the comics, and *Batman v Superman* combined elements of Frank Miller's *The Dark Knight Returns* and the early 1990s "Death of Superman" arc to bring about Superman's demise. Both Batman and Superman were violent and angry, with Batman nursing a grudge that grew into hatred, and the climax of the film centered on the two heroes trying to beat each other to death. The aggressive posturing was toxic masculinity run amok, borrowing directly from some of comics' most macho-fueled moments, and Batman even taunted Superman, "It's time you learn what it means to be a man."

In the midst of all the male angst, *Batman v Superman* also introduced Gal Gadot as Wonder Woman, though the initial announcement of her casting hadn't gone over well with some fans. Those who were used to exaggerated comic book art found Gadot lacking. One commenter pointed out, "Wonder Woman is meant to be a voluptuous, full-figured Amazonian heroine," while another said of the model and former Miss Israel, "She's not drop dead gorgeous or full figured like Lynda Carter! Plain looking and no alluring qualities!" The core of these complaints was encapsulated by one commenter who plaintively asked, "Isn't Wonder Woman supposed to have bigger boobs??"

Despite these objections, Wonder Woman was the breakout character of *Batman v Superman* and starred in her own solo film the following year, directed by Patty Jenkins. The prequel took place a hundred years earlier, during World War I, and featured action set pieces that highlighted the martial prowess of the Amazons and Wonder Woman's bravery and power. Jenkins had to fight to ensure the film's empowering message shone through, nixing the studio's early plans for a traumatic mass rape backstory for the Amazons and arguing for the inclusion of what became the film's most memorable scene: Wonder Woman defiantly crossing No Man's Land. The end result was DC's first critical and commercial hit in this new era, and *Wonder Woman*'s domestic box office has yet to be topped by any of DC's other films.

After Jenkins and Gadot worked so hard to create compelling, respectful takes on Diana and the Amazons, *Justice League* promptly went in the other direction. Snyder returned to direct initially, then left the project due to perpetual disagreements with the studio and a family tragedy, with Joss Whedon taking over. The film recostumed the Amazons, swapping their original full-coverage armor for leather bikinis in a move that prompted noted cosplayer Kimi to lament "a really great design being thrown out in favor of something that would excite the cis male gaze." Whedon also rewrote the script to lighten the tone, adding slapstick jokes that objectified Wonder Woman, the team's only female character, like when the Flash fell and landed face first on her breasts. Gadot refused to film the scene and had issues with Whedon throughout production, so much so that she ultimately took her concerns to the head of the studio. Whedon shot the scene with a stunt double, and it made the theatrical cut.

Justice League **poster, Warner Bros., 2017. DC's premier superhero team was as unbalanced as the Avengers, with only Wonder Woman in the mix.** *Warner Bros./Photofest © Warner Bros.*

The hypersexualization of female characters was the norm in *Suicide Squad* as well, which literally depicted the male gaze when Margot Robbie's Harley Quinn had to change her clothes in front of a group of gawking male guards and teammates. She swapped her prison uniform for short shorts and a tight shirt with "Daddy's Lil Monster" written across the chest, and she wore the small, tight costume for the rest of the film along with a dog collar that read "Puddin'," her pet name for the Joker. Women were secondary characters in the next few DC films, with Amber Heard's Mera helping Jason Momoa's Arthur on his heroic journey in *Aquaman*, and *Shazam!* centered mainly on Billy and Freddy until the film's final fight. Meanwhile, *Joker* was a tedious look at the violent, lethal lengths an aggrieved white man will go to when he feels like society has wronged him.

In 2020, *Birds of Prey (and the Fantabulous Emancipation of One Harley Quinn)* brought back Robbie, with writer Christina Hodson and director Cathy Yan. Robbie produced the film, which focused on Harley assembling an all-female team that included Jurnee Smollett-Bell's Black Canary, Mary Beth Winstead's Huntress, Rosie Perez's Renee Montoya, and Ella Jay Basco's Cassandra Cain. Fans and critics noted how *Birds of Prey* deconstructed the male gaze, from costume choices to camera angles to the lack of gratuitous sexualization. Writing for *The Hollywood Reporter*, Ciara Wardlow pointed out that Harley swapped her possessive shirt and dog collar from *Suicide Squad* for a more independent "loose-fitting t-shirt patterned with her own name—all caps, bolded font."

Perhaps unsurprisingly, some male nerds weren't terribly pleased with the changes. In a widely shared tweet, novelist Matthew Kadish espoused the core of their complaints and predicted the film would bomb because "they've removed any sex appeal these characters had to appeal to a female 'girl power' audience instead of the core male comic book audience. [. . .] They even toned down Harley Quinn to make her less sexy." Another male fan agreed with his assessment and wrote, "These movies are appealing only to radical feminists and putting off everyone else." When *Birds of Prey* opened slightly lower than expected, these same nerds crowed that they were right and that catering to their prurient interests was the only way for female-led films to succeed. In reality, despite the film's R rating and the specter of a global pandemic limiting the film's audience, *Birds of Prey* ultimately earned more than twice its production budget, less than other DC properties but hardly a failure.

The entitlement these fans displayed in demanding sexy characters was echoed in a different, yearslong campaign to #ReleaseTheSnyderCut. After Snyder left *Justice League* and Whedon trimmed down his planned four-hour epic into a breezier two-hour feature, some disappointed fans became convinced that Snyder's original cut of the film was largely completed and hidden away by Warner Bros. executives. Wanting a return to the harsher, grittier feel of Snyder's earlier DC films, these fans started the hashtag #ReleaseTheSnyderCut on social media and agitated for the studio to let them see the original movie.

It was a fringe movement initially, but it grew over time, largely fueled by the targeted bullying of anyone who disagreed with them. Any criticism of the campaign or of Snyder's previous DC work was met with a barrage of insults and cruel trolling. This frequently devolved into full-on harassment, especially when female film writers drew their ire, escalating to rape threats, death threats, and encouraging critics to kill themselves. While some supporters were simply fans of Snyder's work, elements of the movement were so toxic that many pop culture writers stopped mentioning Snyder or the campaign at all lest the mob come after them.

Snyder himself eventually expressed his support for the hashtag, with some *Justice League* actors joining in as well. After the COVID-19 pandemic in 2020 led to a weaker than expected launch for Warner Bros.' streaming service, HBO Max, the studio tried to drum up interest when they announced that the Snyder cut would debut as an HBO Max exclusive in 2021. However, despite fans insisting for years that it was ready to go, the Snyder cut was nowhere near completed. Snyder only had a very rough cut put together, and it cost an additional $70 million to finish the film. This after Warner Bros. announced massive layoffs across their many subsidiaries, including the firing of nearly half of DC Comics' editorial staff.

While the four-hour *Zack Snyder's Justice League* premiered to better reviews than its predecessor, the praise was decidedly mixed. Fans behind the campaign rejoiced at their success, though if Warner Bros. executives thought they would be satisfied and move on from their toxic entitlement, they were sorely mistaken. Soon a new campaign emerged—#RestoreTheSnyderverse—demanding that Snyder be allowed to proceed with his original plans for a sequel. Other fans wanted Warner Bros. to #ReleaseTheAyerCut, director David Ayer's original cut of *Suicide Squad* free of the studio's changes to the theatrical release. Marvel fans even got in on the act, with Iron Man fans still upset over his death putting up a billboard that read #BringBackTonyStarkToLife.

That two studios with such different aesthetics hit the same pitfalls with gender representation and toxic fandom spoke to the degree to which these issues were ingrained in the superhero genre as a whole. Everything that had been building in and around the comics for decades continued into the movies, the tropes and trends seemingly unexamined by the predominantly male writers, directors, and studio heads. There were other sexist film franchises with aggressive, trolling fans, but none that managed the multimillion-dollar revision of a tentpole movie. That only happened with superheroes, the end result of decades spent catering to the whims of a select few.

CHAPTER 16

Power

The adage "With great power comes great responsibility" has been a pillar of superhero morality at both DC Comics and Marvel for decades. It's most commonly associated with Spider-Man, stated at the end of his 1962 debut appearance in *Amazing Fantasy* #15 as "With great power there must also come—great responsibility!" Later stories have attributed the line to Peter Parker's uncle Ben, who died in that issue because of Spider-Man's inaction. The phrase has a history with Superman as well, dating back to the first installment of the 1948 *Superman* film serial when Clark Kent's adopted father explained, "Because of these great powers—your speed and strength, your x-ray vision and super-sensitive hearing—you have a great responsibility."

Most superheroes hold to this advice, using their unique abilities not for their own gain but to help others. That's why the characters are cultural icons, revered by generations of fans. This reverence also extends to those who craft superhero stories. The writers and artists who create these narratives are admired by fans who support their work and look up to them as the architects of the genre they love. There is a power in this admiration, and thus a subsequent responsibility to treat others well, yet many creators have abused this power.

In recent years, several high-profile creators have been accused of misconduct with fans, aspiring creators, and colleagues. The allegations involve sexual harassment, sexual assault, sexual coercion, grooming minors, and more. Those named include *Red Wolf* writer Nathan Edmondson, *The Authority* writer Warren Ellis, *Superman: American Alien* writer Max Landis, *Spider-Gwen* writer Jason Latour, *Red Hood and the Outlaws* writer Scott Lobdell, *Batgirl* cowriter Cameron Stewart, *Ultimate X-Men* writer Brian Wood, and several others, as well as DC Comics editors Eddie Berganza and Mike Carlin and Dark Horse Comics editor in chief Scott Allie. This is not a new development in the superhero industry, however. Similar behavior goes back some time, and all the way to the top of DC Comics.

Julius Schwartz joined DC Comics as an editor in 1944, beginning a working relationship that lasted the rest of his life. He engineered the publisher's Silver Age renaissance, cocreated the Justice League of America, oversaw Batman's transition from camp figure to the Dark Knight, and modernized Superman over the course of the 1970s and 1980s before his retirement in 1986. Schwartz remained an editor emeritus at DC after his retirement, serving as the publisher's goodwill ambassador as he visited comic book conventions all around the world. Over the span of his career he won every major industry award and was inducted into multiple comic book Halls of Fame. He was also accused of being a serial sexual harasser.

The DC offices were a "testosterone pileup" in Schwartz's heyday, so much so that artist Ramona Fradon tried to get in and out as quickly as possible when dropping off her artwork in the 1960s, sneaking in the back and attempting to stay out of sight "for fear they'd all start teasing me or something. It was scary." A major reason she felt uncomfortable was "there was one jerk who used to come up behind me and kiss me on the neck." Such was the nature of the DC bullpen at the height of the Silver Age.

Reports show that Schwartz carried on the cavalierly sexist mindset of this era well into his elder years. Heidi MacDonald, a former editor at DC who started at the publisher in the mid-1990s, later recalled that Schwartz "regularly greeted me whenever I was near him with a big wet kiss on the mouth no matter how much I squirmed away." Artist Trina Robbins had similar experiences with Schwartz, so often that "I became an expert at turning my head so all he could get was my cheek. " Other female creators echoed their accounts, but to their male colleagues Schwartz was just "Uncle Julie," a shameless old flirt.

Writer Peter David said of Schwartz, "His talent for charming the most formidable of women is absolutely legendary. 'Tis a wonderment to behold." Another writer, Mark Evanier, agreed and said, "If you wanted to find the best-looking woman at any comic or science-fiction convention, just locate Schwartz and look who had his arm," while writer James Robinson called Schwartz "the biggest flirt you've ever met whenever there's a pretty woman around. And, an all-around good guy."

But many women claimed Schwartz was more than just a flirt, and that his casual disregard for women's bodily autonomy was part of a larger disrespect for female creators as a whole. Writer Poppy Z. Brite recalled meeting him at a convention where "he told me in a condescending tone, 'You don't look like a writer,' then attempted to cop a feel. I often glimpsed him treating other young women the same way at various cons." Artist Jill Thompson reported a comparable encounter with Schwartz at a convention when she was only seventeen years old, with Schwartz grabbing her breast immediately after a friend introduced her to him.

In 1985, Schwartz invited artist Colleen Doran out to dinner, and Doran later revealed that he had "offered to help her advance her career if she would be his companion to parties and other industry functions." Doran was twenty-one years old at the time, while Schwartz was seventy. Doran brought writer/editor Jo Duffy to the dinner, and both women recalled having to fight Schwartz to keep him off them throughout the evening. Doran said that his "hands [were] practically crawling up my dress under the table," and she even stabbed him with a fork at one point. When Duffy went to the washroom, Doran remembered, "He grabbed me and tried to shove his tongue down my mouth." The car ride to the train station was just as fraught, with Schwartz so aggressively handsy that Duffy "literally had to pull him off the top of [Doran]." Both women had bruises on their arms and legs by the end of the evening.

The incident left Doran shaken. She was talked out of any legal action by her editor at DC, but she recalled, "My career at that company came to a standstill. It was a nightmare." Doran and Duffy recounted the incident to the *Comics Journal* a decade later, but the publication decided not to print the story for yet another decade, waiting until after Schwartz had passed. Such was Schwartz's standing in the industry. Although his treatment of Doran and Duffy was known within DC Comics, he remained a key member of the team and editors underplayed his actions when they were mentioned, with some going so far as to dismiss Doran as "sexually confused." Schwartz was remembered far and wide as a legend of the superhero genre when he died in 2004, with DC printing a glowing eulogy and releasing several special comic issues as a tribute. None of the nearly seventy writers, artists, colorists, and letterers who worked on the eight tribute issues were women.

Schwartz was the editor of the Superman line when he retired in 1985, and two years later editor Mike Carlin took over the job. Carlin worked as an assistant editor at Marvel before joining DC, and his work on the Superman titles drew global attention when he oversaw the complicated "Death of Superman" crossover. He was promoted to executive editor in 1996, and dealt with special projects like 2004's *Identity Crisis*. At the same time that Carlin was working on *Identity Crisis*, he also allegedly sexually harassed his assistant editor Valerie D'Orazio to the point of emotional and physical breakdown.

Carlin was well respected within the industry, but there were reports that he was difficult to work with. He could be defensive and had a temper, particularly with female employees. Black assistant editors had trouble with Carlin as well, who felt he singled them out for unwarranted critiques and kept them from advancing within the company. Multiple reports were filed with human resources about Carlin's behavior over the years.

D'Orazio joined DC in 2000 after working at Acclaim Comics, and became an assistant editor two years later. In her memoir, she recalled that soon after she arrived at DC, Carlin began remarking on her figure and her appearance, and regularly asked her out. She tried to laugh off his comments and politely rebuff his advances, but he persisted, and only increased his harassment when D'Orazio was assigned to his department. Other editors who were aware of the situation tried to step in, joining D'Orazio and Carlin when they had meetings to ensure she wasn't alone with him and even calling Carlin out publicly when he made inappropriate remarks in group settings.

Meanwhile, D'Orazio was passed over for promotions while men with far less experience than her rose through the ranks. As she continued to refuse Carlin's invitations, she found that his attitude toward her shifted to "very loud, insulting, and emotionally violent" behavior. D'Orazio started having heart palpitations at work, then panic attacks and migraines, and these conditions worsened after she reported Carlin to human resources and his hostility escalated further. She took medical leave before ultimately exiting the publisher, and later learned she was one of several female employees at DC who had "been black-balled, fired or demoted for questionable & vague reasons, or forced to resign in order to not put up with harassment." Carlin remained a mainstay in DC editorial despite the various complaints filed against him, and was promoted to DC Entertainment's creative director of animation, where he continues to work today.

One of Carlin's colleagues, Eddie Berganza, carried on the trend of alleged harassment within the DC offices. Berganza was hired at the publisher in the early 1990s, and made a name for himself in the 2000s with high-profile books like *Green Lantern: Rebirth* and the event series *Infinite Crisis*, *Final Crisis*, and *Blackest Night*. He was promoted to executive editor in 2010 and helped oversee DC's line-wide New 52 relaunch the following year. Then in 2012, Berganza was abruptly demoted back down to group editor and put in charge of the Superman line.

The reason why was an open secret within the comics industry. There were rumors of internal human resources complaints against Berganza, as well as multiple, well-witnessed public incidents that included him grabbing a woman's breast at a corporate event and kissing a writer's girlfriend aggressively and without her consent in a hotel lobby during a major comic book convention. Along with his demotion, the DC brass barred him from conventions for a while, and instituted a policy that he couldn't work with female employees in the DC offices. Given that *Supergirl* and *Wonder Woman* were under the Superman editorial umbrella at the time, the lack of female staffers on his titles was rather glaring. Some writers and artists refused to work with Berganza because of his reputation, especially female creators, and when famed writer Greg Rucka was recruited to revamp the flagging *Wonder Woman* series, he insisted that the book move to a new editor.

Despite these issues, Berganza remained at DC through multiple corporate restructurings, and even began to rise in prominence again. In 2017, he edited the publisher's major summer event series *Dark Nights: Metal* from the superstar team of writer Scott Snyder and artist Greg Capullo. By this point, the open secret of Berganza's sexual harassment history was fully public knowledge. Multiple former employees and comic book journalists had called him out, and comic book news sites stopped dancing around the rumors and named him directly. Still, he continued to succeed within DC.

In November 2017, at the height of the #MeToo movement, Jessica Testa, Tyler Kingkade, and Jay Edidin published a lengthy article on *BuzzFeed* titled "The Comics Giant behind Wonder Woman Is Accused of Promoting an Editor after Women Accused Him of Sexual Harassment." The reporters spoke with several former DC staffers who detailed Berganza's misconduct in depth and shared similar stories of unwanted kissing, groping, and other sexual advances. All the women left DC, and none worked in the superhero industry at the time of the article's release. While Berganza's history had been reported on comic book news sites, *BuzzFeed* had a much broader reach and the story quickly gained traction. Three days after the article was published, *BuzzFeed* accomplished what a voluminous human resources file could not and DC fired Berganza.

DC wasn't the only publisher with editor problems. In 2015, former DC editor Janelle Asselin, one of many employees who had filed complaints against Berganza, published an article alleging years of abusive behavior by Dark Horse Comics editor in chief Scott Allie. Asselin spoke to several Dark Horse employees who described Allie's history of misbehavior, including drunken antics; groping, licking, and punching employees; and a penchant for biting. Multiple complaints had been filed, to no avail. Dark Horse demoted Allie to executive senior editor after another biting incident at San Diego Comic-Con that year, but new allegations surfaced five years later. Writer Shawna Gore accused Allie of sexually harassing and assaulting her, and she received public support from other Dark Horse employees and creators, including the publisher's most famous writer/artist, *Hellboy* creator Mike Mignola. Allie was fired soon after.

Another prominent institution, the Comic Book Legal Defense Fund, faced its own scandal that same year. The CBLDF is "a non-profit organization dedicated to the protection of the First Amendment rights of the comics art form," and it relies on the support of comic book creators and fans, with superhero icons like Jim Lee and Frank Miller on its Advisory Board. In 2002, Charles Brownstein became the CBLDF's executive director, and three years later he was accused of sexually assaulting cartoonist Taki Soma at a comic book trade association conference. The incident was yet another open secret within the industry, but Brownstein remained in his position. In 2020, during a new wave of sexual harassment allegations throughout the comics industry, Brownstein's past actions resurfaced and new accusations emerged, and he ultimately resigned.

Harassment wasn't limited to print media either. Live-action superhero adaptations have been littered with men who had a history of misconduct. Before taking on the *Avengers* franchise, Joss Whedon was a famed feminist with a sterling reputation for writing strong female characters on shows like *Buffy the Vampire Slayer* and *Firefly*. By the time he took over *Justice League*, his feminist brand was rapidly deteriorating. His ex-wife Kai Cole called him a "hypocrite preaching feminist ideals," alleging numerous infidelities, and many of Whedon's female stars have since accused him of creating a "hostile and toxic working environment" marked by explosive anger, threats, and body shaming. He was slated to write and direct a Batgirl film after *Justice League*, but he ultimately left the project.

Bryan Singer, the director of *X-Men*, *X2*, and *Superman Returns*, was a staple in superhero adaptations, despite a checkered history. In 1997, underage actors on his film *Apt Pupil* filed a lawsuit alleging that he had ordered them to appear naked in a shower scene. Troubling rumors followed the director for several years, and another lawsuit in 2014 accused him of sexual assault of a minor. More lawsuits and allegations continued over the next several years, but Singer stayed busy in the X-Men universe, directing *X-Men: Apocalypse* in 2016 and episodes of the Marvel TV series *The Gifted* in 2017. While eventually the allegations grew to such a degree that Singer has been largely benched from filmmaking, it took several years and numerous reports of him assaulting teenage boys for there to be any professional repercussions.

Another X-Men director, *X-Men: The Last Stand*'s Brett Ratner, also faced a bevy of accusations when multiple actors accused him of sexual harassment and assault in 2017, including *X-Men* franchise stars Olivia Munn and Elliot Page. Ratner was several years removed from his last superhero project at the time, and has largely faded from the Hollywood scene since. Meanwhile in television that same year, Andrew Kreisberg, a producer on the CW's *Arrow*, *Supergirl*, and *The Flash*, was accused of misconduct by nineteen employees, fifteen women and four men. The employees detailed a pattern of "sexual harassment and demeaning women" that was constant and pervasive, to such a degree that they no longer felt safe on set. Kreisberg, a cofounder of the CW's "Arrow-verse," was fired soon after.

That all of this was allowed to happen in so many high-level places at such frequency, with no consequences until recent years, explains in part why similar behavior has flourished among comic book writers and artists over the past two decades. With minimal accountability and accusers blackballed, few victims came forward, and it's only lately that they're being believed. It was an environment tailor made for abusers to thrive.

In 2013, cartoonist MariNaomi wrote an article about being sexually harassed by a writer during a convention panel, detailing the incident without naming the perpetrator. Scott Lobdell later outed himself as the writer and apologized, calling the situation a "failed attempt at humor," and DC took no action against him. He remained a fixture at the publisher for the next seven years, even as other allegations mounted and rumors swirled of him continuing to behave inappropriately in workplace settings. It was only in 2020, after yet another round of allegations, that he stopped working for DC, seemingly of his own volition. In a farewell post, he looked back on his time writing the violent, troubled Red Hood and remarked on the character, "I'm profoundly grateful for the last ten years on a book telling the story of a tragically flawed man in search of redemption."

Brian Wood was another writer who regularly avoided repercussions, despite repeat allegations. In 2013, artist Tess Fowler accused Wood of feigning interest in helping her career in order to proposition her, and noted that she'd been in contact with several other women who'd had similar demeaning experiences with Wood. He publicly apologized, and agreed that there was an "industry-wide discussion that needs to happen" about sexual harassment. Then, as this discussion unfolded over the next several years, Wood took a different tack. He wrote in a 2015 newsletter, "Public shaming can be treacherous," calling it "spectator sport style ugliness" and cautioning that "it's going to end with someone killing themselves," referring to those who were accused of sexual harassment, not the victims of the industry's pervasive abuse. His distaste for the discussion may well have been self-serving. Wood has been accused of the same sort of manipulative harassment repeatedly since, and after years of steady work seems to be fading out of the business as of late.

There was a tendency to dismiss, to downplay, and to undermine, both during and after public apologies, largely because it often worked. The accused were afforded the benefit of the doubt, and any graying of the subject served to their advantage. "I'm sorry, but it was a joke," or "I'm sorry, but this whole discussion is getting out of hand," obfuscated the issue.

Writer Warren Ellis took this to new heights in 2020. Ellis was an icon within the industry, with more than two decades of steady, highly praised work at DC and Marvel, along with many of his own successful creator-owned projects. He also hosted the Warren Ellis Forum, an online community in the early 2000s that was a who's who of future comic book stars like Kelly Sue DeConnick, Matt Fraction, and Kieron Gillen. By 2020 he was a showrunner, in charge of Netflix's popular *Castlevania* animated series. Ellis was enormously influential, a legendary hero to many and the godfather of an entire generation of superhero writers and artists.

Then a group of women and nonbinary individuals accused Ellis of "using his celebrity status and vast public platform as catalyst and shield to manipulate and groom targets under false pretenses, and to coerce private pornography and sexual exchanges." Over a twenty-year period, Ellis allegedly offered mentorship and support before taking the relationship into sexual territory and then abruptly cutting off contact once he got what he wanted. It was a manipulative pattern "refined and escalated" by Ellis, and almost one hundred people came forward to share their experiences in a private forum, with thirty-six of them posting public testimonials online.

Ellis issued an apology rife with excuses. He opened by saying, "I have never considered myself famous or powerful. [. . .] It had never really occurred to me that other people didn't see it the same way—that I was not engaging as an equal when gifted with attention, but acting from a position of power and privilege," before insisting, "Let me be clear, I have never consciously coerced, manipulated, or abused anyone." The denial of his obvious immense power and his refusal to take responsibility for his intentions fell flat with victims and fans, who called it "textbook gaslighting." While Ellis had a story removed from a DC anthology book after the allegations emerged, the publisher still released the last five issues of his series *The Batman's Grave* and he remained showrunner on the final season of *Castlevania*, which aired in 2021.

Accusations against Ellis emerged during a wave of allegations across the industry that included Charles Brownstein, Jason Latour, and Cameron Stewart. In response, a group of creators put together the #ComicsPledge and shared it across social media, promising to "never abuse, harass, groom, or manipulate" anyone, "to call out our friends and peers," and to "keep this conversation alive in the industry." The pledge was well intentioned, but more performative than actually constructive, and failed to address the structural issues that allowed predators to thrive within the community.

The superhero industry wasn't the only business with a sexual harassment problem, of course. It's rampant everywhere. But the enormous gap between the heroic ideals of its characters and the men who wrote, drew, edited, and directed their adventures was striking. All of these abusers were bad actors who used their positions to take advantage of those with less power than them, and while they didn't constitute the majority of male comic book editors and creators, they were certainly enabled by this majority. The industry is small and interconnected, and misbehavior was known and tolerated time and again, unpunished until very recently as prominent men chose to look the other way.

Meanwhile, female employees had to band together to protect themselves and guard new hires and interns as they entered the lions' den. Female freelancers had their own safety networks as well, warning each other about the known predators who stalked convention halls. So many female writers, artists, and editors left the industry, hurt and angry and traumatized by their treatment, while male abusers were allowed to thrive. There are also scores of men who remain protected by those at the top, their victims reticent to come forward on the record for fear of professional retribution and/or the stress of reliving their trauma. A full reckoning of this rampant abuse has yet to take place.

CHAPTER 17

Instigate

When a megalomaniac billionaire announced that he was running for president of the United States of America, nobody thought he had a chance. The businessman proved savvier than anyone expected, however, emphasizing his financial acumen and promising an era of prosperity for all Americans. Although he was from a big city and lived a life plagued with scandal, he connected with the heartland of the nation, even choosing a running mate from a midwestern state to emphasize this bond. He faced strong opposition from vocal, powerful critics who insisted he was too corrupt to lead, but the race proved tighter than expected. When all the votes were counted, the world was introduced to President Lex Luthor.

This eerily prescient story line spanned the Superman titles in late 2000, with the Man of Steel's archnemesis ascending to the highest office in the land sixteen years before another billionaire, Donald Trump, accomplished the same feat. The two tycoons have been closely tied for several decades now. Luthor was originally a mad scientist, but John Byrne's 1986 revamp of Superman turned him into a businessman, intentionally patterned on bloviating magnates like Donald Trump and Ted Turner. The 1989 comic *Lex Luthor: The Unauthorized Biography* further emphasized this connection, with a cover patterned on Trump's 1987 book *The Art of the Deal*.

President Luthor's tenure ended in disaster when his crimes were exposed, including colluding with evil intergalactic powers and his failure to act against the global threat posed by a Kryptonite asteroid hurtling toward the Earth. President Trump also faced charges of collusion and failure to act against a global threat, but he ultimately served his full term despite two impeachment trials. The superhero ties continued through Trump's presidency. Marvel president Ike Perlmutter was a mainstay at Trump's Mar-a-Lago resort, where he advised the president and helped make policy for the Department of Veterans Affairs.

The January 6, 2021, Capitol insurrection attempt to overturn Trump's election loss was also rife with Captain America imagery, from multiple rioters carrying Captain America shields to a flag with the president's head on Captain America's body to shirts that proclaimed "MAGA: Civil War, January 6, 2021" patterned on the logo for Marvel's *Captain America: Civil War* film.

The vitriol of the Capitol insurrection reflected the tone and tenor of President Trump, especially his social media presence. He frequently took to Twitter to insult and harass his critics, saving his harshest attacks for women and people of color. Mockery was a key component of his persona, prompting one publication to declare, "Donald Trump Is the World's Greatest Troll." His supporters followed suit, in lockstep with their leader as they flooded social media with discord and disinformation while openly bullying their political opponents and critics. This quasi-organized harassment campaign was mirrored in superhero fandom as well, as conservative fans banded together to take down the supposedly liberal superhero industry. Taking cues from their community leaders, they too employed hateful rhetoric and relentless trolling in their ongoing crusade to "Make Comics Great Again."

Early manifestations of this campaign predated Trump, and were much less organized. The discourse surrounding Milo Manara's hypersexualized *Spider-Woman* cover in 2014 and Rafael Albuquerque's traumatic *Batgirl* variant in 2015 revealed an aggrieved assortment of fans upset over censorship and publishers catering to "political correctness" and "social justice warriors." When former DC editor Janelle Asselin critiqued a *Teen Titans* cover for its exaggeratedly curvaceous take on Wonder Girl, a teenager, she was harassed on Twitter for days, including a barrage of rape threats. After Marvel released art for a *Mockingbird* cover with the hero wearing a T-shirt that said, "Ask Me about My Feminist Agenda," the book's writer Chelsea Cain faced so much abuse on Twitter that she quit the platform.

While there was a degree of coordination across these incidents, a rapid piling-on of like-minded fans, the movement didn't fully coalesce in the public eye until July 2017. After the passing of Flo Steinberg, a beloved fixture behind the scenes in the Marvel bullpen in the 1960s, Marvel editor Heather Antos posted a photo of her and several other female Marvel staffers getting milkshakes together as a joyful tribute to Flo's pioneering legacy. The responses quickly took a negative turn, with gatekeeping rhetoric calling them "Tumblr SJW fake geek girls" and "diversity window dressing." Other comments accused the women of being the reason for Marvel's momentarily slumping sales, with one asking, "Can we just get off of feminism and social justice and actually print stories?"

Mocking responses to Antos's post continued in this vein, along with a slew of cruel direct messages. In solidarity with Antos, many comic creators posted pictures of themselves enjoying milkshakes with the hashtag

#MakeMineMilkshake, a twist on Marvel's classic "Make Mine Marvel" slogan. Artists drew superheroes doing the same, and even DC tweeted out their support with all their female staffers banding together for a group photo. But something had changed. While male fans harassing female creators was nothing new, unfortunately, the volume and speed of this negative response was. These weren't disparate fans voicing their discontent. This was a unified crusade that soon became known as Comicsgate.

The name was a spin on Gamergate, a misogynistic harassment campaign that plagued the video game industry a few years before. Ostensibly about "ethics in games journalism," Gamergate began in 2014 when a jilted boyfriend posted a series of inflammatory and misleading posts about his game developer ex, Zoë Quinn, suggesting their game had gotten favorable press because they were dating reviewers. As the post made the rounds, Quinn was flooded with online harassment, including rape threats, death threats, and doxxing, the public release of one's address and other personal information. Soon the harassment spread to several notable women throughout the industry in organized, targeted attacks. The real issue wasn't ethics, but rather a long-simmering rage over "female encroachment on a traditionally male space," and male gamers lashed out in a coordinated attempt to keep women, feminism, and other progressive values out of their community.

Comicsgate had the same resentments, and the same objective. Its adherents claimed otherwise, arguing it was a positive movement that simply wanted to bring fun back to the superhero genre and keep politics and other weighty topics out of comics. Part of this involved working together to #MoveTheNeedle and support books that embraced the action and excitement they loved. In reality, Comicsgate was relentlessly negative, rooted in harshly criticizing comics they disliked and harassing anyone and everyone who disagreed with them. One supporter outlined their conspiracy-tinged conservative ideology, explaining that the movement was about standing up to the "left wing monopoly" in comics who wanted

> all books to force LGBTQWTF on children, none to have male or white lead characters (unless villains), and to push identity politics so that not only are the primary demographic of readers kicked out of comics, but so that they stir up anger to get white, Christian, Republican, men out of the country.

When Comicsgate targeted Antos, one account that got tagged repeatedly in the comments was the ironically named Diversity and Comics. The man behind the account was Richard C. Meyer, who began posting comic review videos on YouTube a few months earlier with titles like "SJW Marvel Comics is dying . . . and that's OK," "Captain Marvel is everything wrong with SJW Marvel," and

"AMERICA—SJW Marvel's Hip Hop Segregation Comic." His videos pined for the good old days when comics had "strict gender roles [and] the masculine hero saves the woman," and lamented that now "gender roles are blurred, masculinity is not prized."

Most of Meyer's ire was directed at Marvel initially, and his two most hated characters were Captain Marvel and America Chavez. He thought Carol Danvers was a "weirdly angry, super serious, hyper-masculine, humorless character" who was "haughty [and] proud" as well as a "pseudo lesbian." As artists put less emphasis on Carol's curves, Meyer took to calling her "Carl Manvers," suggesting she was turning into a man because, "we're watching her boobs disappear in every issue."

America Chavez was a superpowered, dimension-jumping, Latina lesbian, and Meyer absolutely despised her. He claimed her solo series was full of "racist, segregationist, woke minorities," and that her characterization made her "only brown and gay" and nothing else. Meyer criticized America's intelligence as well, calling her a "hostile, violent idiot" and "rude, condescending, and [. . .] just so dumb."

He was just as harsh toward *America* writer Gabby Rivera, labeling her a diversity hire who only got the job because she was, like America, "brown and gay." Rather than reading comics he enjoyed, he took the time to buy and review each issue of *America*, criticizing Rivera's writing ability and her supposed lack of comic book knowledge throughout before ripping the issue in half, literally, a treatment he tended to reserve for books with female and/ or POC leads. In one video, he asked, "Which SJW Marvel Writer Is Worse? Gabby Rivera (AMERICA) or Ta-Nehisi Coates?" and pit two of Marvel's few writers of color against each other despite the fact that Rivera was an award-winning YA novelist and Coates was a recipient of a MacArthur Genius Grant for his writing.

Another of Meyer's favorite targets was Magdalene Visaggio, an indie comics writer who was starting to get work at DC and Marvel in 2017. Visaggio was transgender and Meyer not only dismissed her as another diversity hire, he also misgendered her constantly and referred to her as a "man in a wig." He later called her a "fucking crazy person," "a criminal," and "a full-time pervert" who "came along just at the right time that there were all the trans issues and [the publishers were] like, 'Oh, we can weaponize this.'"

The theme was clear. Meyer didn't care for women, real or fictional, and was especially angry about queer women and people of color. He spread his views in videos and across social media, and soon had thousands of followers. His first Captain Marvel video was so popular that (at the time of this writing) it's been watched more than 670,000 times since it was posted. Before long, Meyer was the de facto leader of the Comicsgate campaign. Anyone he criticized became a target for the larger group, and an army of trolls immediately blasted them with hate-fueled posts and comments.

As Comicsgate grew, some disaffected creators joined its ranks. After receiving criticism when they revealed they'd voted for Donald Trump, colorist Elizabeth Breitweiser and her artist husband Mitch allied themselves with the movement. So did artist Jon Malin after he equated progressive leftists to Hitler and decried "the vipers nest that is the growing SJW infestation of this industry that is killing creative voices that politically differ." Mike S. Miller, an artist and a conservative Christian whose public comments got him uninvited to a convention for "very disparaging remarks [he] made in regards to minorities and women," also found a home there. So too did inker Art Thibert, who had a falling-out with Marvel and later accused the company of having an "SJW agenda."

The most prominent creator to board the movement was Ethan Van Sciver, an artist best known for *Green Lantern: Rebirth* and *The Flash: Rebirth*. He flirted with fascism before joining Comicsgate, including titling one of his sketchbooks *My Struggle*, the English translation of *Mein Kampf*, Adolf Hitler's manifesto. Van Sciver frequently posted alt-right memes, aligning himself with far right nationalism, and asserted that Donald Trump was "cleaning up [the] queer globalist mess." Before pivoting to Comicsgate, he developed a following by criticizing the diversity of the latest *Star Wars* trilogy on YouTube, most famously purchasing several toys of Rose Tico, a woman of color, and cutting off their heads.

When Van Sciver joined Comicsgate, he jumped in wholeheartedly and explained, "The comic book industry has been taken over by far left wing weirdos, and by the way the most vile, hateful people." He claimed that these social justice warriors were "ruining comics. They ruin everything that they touch," and cast himself as a moderate voice of reason. Meanwhile, he continued on with his sexism and bigotry, interviewing white nationalist Vox Day on his YouTube channel, mocking a female Comicsgate critic who got cancer, and "joking" about killing Chinese people at the height of anti-Asian sentiment during the coronavirus epidemic.

A staple of far right movements is the grift, in which those at the top profit financially from the support of their followers. Donald Trump was famous for it, so much so that *GQ* declared, "The Trump Presidency Is One Long Grift." Comicsgate swiftly shifted into moneymaking mode as well, launching crowdfunding campaigns for comic books from their top luminaries. Richard C. Meyer introduced *Jawbreakers: Lost Souls* with Jon Malin on art, Ethan Van Sciver debuted *Cyberfrog*, Vox Day teamed up with writer Chuck Dixon for *Alt-Hero*, and Mike S. Miller launched *The MAGAnificent 7*, alongside scores of other titles. The campaigns were promoted heavily within the Comicsgate community and many proved extremely lucrative, including nearly $200,000 for *Jawbreakers* and over half a million dollars for *Cyberfrog*. Several of the books shipped late and were of dubious quality, but the fervor of Comicsgate's supporters didn't let up.

Meanwhile, the movement continued its constant torment of female creators on social media as it moved into publishing, and soon expanded its target list. Some comic book retailers chose not to sell Comicsgate books in their shops because of the campaign's unsavory history of harassment. In response, Meyer posted a list of these shops along with employee information for his followers, who then flooded the retailers and employees with online abuse. One store was even vandalized and robbed. *Jawbreakers* was due to be published by Antarctic Press, but when fans and industry professionals, including writer Mark Waid, explained the nature of the movement to the publisher they quickly canceled their plans, incensing Meyer further. He sued Waid for defamation, launching a barrage of harassment against Waid as he proceeded to raise nearly $170,000 for his suit from Comicsgate supporters over the next two years before abruptly dropping the case.

Despite Comicsgate's constant complaints about "SJW cancel culture," trying to cancel others was a key component of the movement. Beyond going after women, Waid, and comic book shops, they also targeted creators with political differences. When *GI Joe* writer Aubrey Sitterson tweeted about the performative grief that often accompanied the anniversary of the September 11 attacks each year, he drew the ire of Meyer, a former Marine. He rallied his followers to complain to Sitterson's employer, IDW Publishing, and got him fired. Comicsgate supporters also took aim at writer Chuck Wendig after he was vocal about his disgust with the Trump administration and he was then fired by Marvel, where he was working on multiple *Star Wars* titles. These were bad-faith complaints, faux outrage meant to take down prominent liberals who valued inclusivity. Both Sitterson and Wendig introduced female and queer characters into what had been largely straight, male-dominated franchises, which was the true reason for Comicsgate's anger. Eventually publishers caught on, and these attempts to cancel liberal creators became less effective.

Rifts within the movement also limited effectiveness. By 2020, infighting among top Comicsgate personalities had caused divisions as insufficiently militant members lost followers, others were accused of co-opting the movement for financial gain, and prominent voices butted heads to control the larger narrative. Meyer and Van Sciver distanced themselves from the term "Comicsgate" at different times, though Van Sciver quickly returned to the fold and both have kept up their crusades against social justice warriors in the comic industry. Online harassment remains a constant, however, slightly less than at the movement's peak but still a persistent component of superhero fandom.

An early Comicsgate figure, Edwin Boyette, quit the campaign after the infighting began, deleting his YouTube and Twitter accounts to focus on his work as vice chair of communications for the Republican Party in Hawaii. He had to leave that job in 2021 after posting his support for QAnon, a conspiracy theory that alleges, among other things, that a Satanic pedophile cult conspired against President Trump. The leap from Comicsgate to QAnon was a logical one. Both were far right movements against imaginary leftist media cabals, with virulent harassment at the core of their tactics.

Much like Comicsgate supporters comprised a small but vocal segment of superhero fandom, QAnon supporters comprised a small but vocal segment of Republican voters. They backed President Trump wholeheartedly, but weren't the majority of his base. Trump's best demographic was white men, who voted for him at proportions far higher than any other group. Most of these men didn't harass people online, or openly mock anyone who disagreed with them. They were simply men who, when faced with the prospect of a woman in the White House, saw in Trump the best opportunity to maintain a system that explicitly benefited them. The blatant sexism and racism of Trump's campaign didn't deter them because their primary goal was self-preservation, to keep the power structure of society the same as it had been their entire lives. These voters had a lot in common with the superhero industry.

For all of Comicsgate's talk of liberals running DC and Marvel, we've seen repeatedly how publishers did not care about women, people of color, or the queer community, be they characters, creators, or fans. Investments in stories about these marginalized groups were rare and fleeting, frequently undone to return to the white, straight, male status quo. Editors were openly contemptuous of critics and fans who wanted better representation, employing a slew of male writers and artists and then insisting that they were simply "hiring the best creators." It's only very recently that we've seen actual commitment to inclusive storytelling from DC and Marvel.

As more diverse voices entered fandom in the early 2000s, many creators handled the new perspectives poorly. The superhero community was relatively small, and most writers and artists interacted with fans regularly on social media and online forums. They developed loyal followings, little fiefdoms that became echo chambers of enthusiastic support. When new fans began to point out the sexism and racism inherent in the superhero genre, some of these creators took the criticisms personally, reacting defensively with outraged indignation. "Quote tweeting" was a common response, wherein the creator shared a critic's comment with his own aggrieved reaction, posting it for all his followers who then inevitably began sending angry responses to the critic. Daring to criticize a prominent male creator, however thoughtful or well intentioned the remarks, could blow up your social media for days.

Marginalized fans, especially people of color and queer readers, were bullied and harassed within the superhero community for years, long before Comicsgate. Publishers ignored them, some male creators were actively hostile to them deigning to have opinions, and segments of fandom followed their lead. Marginalized creators were in a similar boat, subject to sexist, racist, and homophobic fan backlash and often not supported by their publishers when the onslaught came.

It spoke volumes that the first major public response to Comicsgate came when Heather Antos, a cisgender white woman, was targeted. Creators like Gabby Rivera and Mags Visaggio had been subjected to online abuse from the same sources for months before that, with nary a peep from the rest of the superhero world. Then after a flurry of #MakeMineMilkshake posts, the conversation quickly faded while the harassment continued unabated. The Antos incident sparked a reaction, but nothing sustained.

The industry stood up against Comicsgate again a year later when yet another cisgender white woman was in the crosshairs. In August 2018, a Comicsgate supporter posted a video of acclaimed writer/artist Darwyn Cooke, who had passed away two years earlier, and declared that "he would have been #ComicsGate." Cooke's widow Marsha quickly replied, "I can guarantee he thought you comics gate idiots were a bunch of crybaby losers ruining comics. Because you are," calling the movement a "racist homophobic woman hating club" and insisting that Cooke saw them as "a bunch of angry losers with no lives, harassing women because they were too angry to meet any IRL." In response, Comicsgate members attacked her with such vitriol that she disabled her Twitter account.

Some creators took a strong stance against this latest round of harassment, with writer Jeff Lemire declaring that "Comicsgate is based on fear, intolerance, bigotry and anger" and artist Bill Sienkiewicz calling the movement "hateful, misogynistic and plain-old-ugly dogma." Both writer Aleš Kot and artist Ramon Villalobos labeled Comicsgate a "white supremacist hate group," but the most common response was more generic. Writer Tom Taylor posted, "There is no place for homophobia, transphobia, racism or misogyny in comics criticism," and many of his fellow creators did the same, borrowing the phrase in a well-meaning albeit tepid stand against the movement. Much like the industry's pledge against sexual harassment, the intentions were good but the statement did little to actually solve the larger problem.

Some didn't even go that far. DC and Marvel remained quiet about Comicsgate, saying nothing about the far right hate group while simultaneously imploring their creators to write comics that would "appeal more to Trump voters." Both publishers had a long history of ignoring the far right appropriation of their heroes, like when the Punisher logo became a Blue Lives Matter symbol or the white nationalist Proud Boys used DC's logo for a pro-Trump march in the nation's capital. Smaller publishers like Dynamite Comics even worked directly with Comicsgate until public outcry made them reconsider, while others like Alterna Comics continued supporting the campaign despite the backlash.

Several creators also refused to speak out against Comicsgate, either due to a degree of support for the movement's aims or a mercenary approach to business whereby they didn't want to lose any potential readers, no matter how vile their behavior. Some walked a fine line, using dog whistles to appeal to Comicsgate supporters like decrying politics in comics, disparaging social justice warriors, or sharing #MoveTheNeedle. Others worked with well-known pro-Comicsgate creators, saying nothing about the movement themselves but hoping that supporters would interpret this association as a tacit endorsement and go buy their work. Some stayed out of things entirely, perhaps encouraging a general civility in fandom but otherwise refusing to take a specific stance. Sitting on the fence while staying neutral about hate speech to protect your own profits is the very definition of privilege, yet many took that path.

The Trump presidency and the subsequent rise of hate-fueled alt-right movements didn't come out of nowhere. They were the result of decades of catering to the self-serving interests of a narrow base and valuing performative masculinity and limited gender roles above inclusivity. So too was Comicsgate the result of similar trends within the superhero industry, taken to extremes. It wasn't an outlier or an aberration, but rather the heinous culmination of the genre's worst impulses. While Comicsgate is beginning to fade now, it's inevitable that similar campaigns will arise unless fans and publishers address the history of toxic masculinity at the root of the superhero genre and build a new way forward together.

Conclusion

Superheroes are everywhere right now. They lead multiple film franchises that are shattering box office records, star in television shows across most major networks and streaming services, and have headlined some of the most popular video games of the past few years. And that's all on top of their home base in publishing, where hundreds of new comic books and graphic novels are released each month. Superheroes are at the forefront of multibillion-dollar empires, ubiquitous in modern popular culture as they take down villains and save the world time and again. They have arguably never been more popular, across all age groups and demographics.

But as much as these superhero narratives can be inspirational and empowering, the genre is built on a shaky foundation. Many of its core tenets are antiquated at best, and actively harmful at worst. We've seen the deep-rooted sexism that runs through the history of the superhero industry, along with the continued presence of racism and homophobia. The genre has constantly idealized one group above all else, elevating straight white men who are good at punching things as the ultimate paragons of heroism. It is a narrow paradigm that becomes more outdated with each passing day.

Writing for *Vulture* in October 2020, Abraham Riesman reflected on the genre as a whole in a piece about the second season of *The Boys*, Amazon's darkly satirical deconstruction of superheroes based on the comic book series by Garth Ennis and Darick Robertson. Superheroes are the villains in *The Boys*, adored public figures who present a friendly exterior to society that belies their true selfish, sinister motivations. Riesman argued that these villainous superheroes revealed a fatal flaw in the genre because "superhero fiction has perpetually been about characters who believe that the laws don't apply to them and that violence is justified when your opponent is scary enough." Digging into the supposed values behind this vigilantism, he wrote:

The core pantheon of superheroes have always, always ended up upholding the status quo, and we are finally waking up to the fact that that status quo is morally indefensible. Of what use is Superman when it's been revealed that truth and justice were always the opposite of the American way?

Riesman suggested that we might be at "the end of the superhero as we know it," and that this could be a good thing. Finding the lofty ideals of the genre unattainable, he concluded, "In our world, superheroes can never be what we've dreamed them to be. Maybe we never should have had those dreams in the first place. No one is flying to the rescue." It was a bold argument that led to much discussion and debate across superhero fandom, and it bears further consideration.

To judge the genre's viability as a relevant, worthwhile force in modern popular culture, we must face the reality of the superhero industry and its legacy. From its very inception, women have been treated as objects who existed for male pleasure. Every woman, real or fictional, was seen through this lens, whether they were characters who manifested their creators' desires, hyperexaggerated figures in minuscule and/or impossibly tight outfits, cosplayers who built impressively detailed costumes, or employees at major publishers. Objectification and harassment were commonplace, and went hand in hand, all of it rooted in a lack of respect for women. Throughout time, this evolved into hostility for anything outside of a restrictive masculine norm, be it feminine, queer, or otherwise different from the standard fare.

Meanwhile, male heroes became increasingly violent power fantasies, embodiments of toxic masculinity run amok as they abandoned empathy and justice for vengeance and death. Their opponents were often people of color, like gang members or ninja hordes, there only to be brutally dispatched. Heroes of color rarely took center stage and were quickly discarded when they did, benched to allow classic characters to return and thus reinforce the white, male power structure.

Fans have internalized these messages for decades. Some take it to extremes, lashing out with hate speech and harassment. Others passively absorb it, not doing active, intentional harm but nonetheless ignoring the genre's faults because they are so wrapped up in nostalgia. They defend the long-established status quo of superhero narratives while failing to recognize that this status quo excludes and dehumanizes so many.

All these issues are baked into the superhero genre, so much so that it's not unreasonable to wonder if they can ever be extricated. Beyond the historical baggage, both DC and Marvel are owned by corporations known for their reticence to change. Their business model relies on appealing to as much of the population as possible, and so they place their content firmly in the middle of societal and cultural issues, adapting only when it is financially advantageous to do so. This is not an environment conducive to reckoning with complicated matters surrounding gender.

But the fandom crises of the past decade have left the superhero genre on a precipice. Some fans want the industry to move forward with better representation and inclusivity, while others want the genre to return to the tone and tenor of their youth. In this moment, the question of whether superheroes can ever move beyond simply reinforcing the status quo has never been more relevant, and fandom could provide the answer.

If the recent past is any indication, little is likely to change if the industry is left to its own devices, abandoned by the fans who want it to evolve. Piecemeal representation will continue, with occasional breakthrough characters and moments that hint at a more relevant future, but the inherent conservatism of corporate America, bolstered by a vocal corner of fandom who wholly embrace the antiquated values built into the genre, will keep the industry in stasis. Nostalgic limitations will further calcify and everything will remain the same, the inspirational and empowering elements of the genre tempered by its exclusionary limitations.

Or fans can keep pushing for superheroes to embrace their full potential. At their best, superheroes represent our highest ideals, in their own fantastical ways. They use their abilities for the good of others, stand up for the downtrodden and the forgotten, and choose hope over fear, all while inspiring generations of readers to do the same. If fans embrace the core of what makes the genre exciting, uplifting, and relevant and push publishers to do so as well, change is a possibility. By tackling sexism and toxic masculinity head-on, elevating new voices and perspectives, and being proactive instead of reactive to social and societal growth, the superhero industry could make a new way forward. The future of superheroes remains undecided, and will hinge on whether the genre clings to its past or learns from it.

Acknowledgments

This was a big book. A normal length, yeah, but expansive for someone used to deep dives on particular characters. As such, I drew from a lot of different places.

All the charts and data came from information gathered on a variety of fan-run websites. The Grand Comics Database (comics.org) is unparalleled for comic book credits, Mike's Amazing World of Comics (mikesamazingworld .com) was instrumental for understanding what came out when, and the DC (dc.fandom.com) and Marvel (marvel.fandom.com) Database Wikis proved a great resource for credits, first appearances, and similarly finicky and obscure details. Without all of this excellent data, I'd still be thumbing through back issues trying to figure out when Terra first appeared or when *Ms. Marvel*'s lost issues were finally printed.

Given that this was an overview of the superhero genre as a whole, I'm indebted to scholars and historians who have studied its past and made it all easily understandable. In particular, I'd like to thank Bart Beaty, Les Daniels, Sean Howe, Amy Kiste Nyberg, Trina Robbins, Carol Tilley, Larry Tye, Glen Weldon, and Bradford Wright for their work, though many others have been instrumental as well.

The book transitions from the past to the present, and the comic book news websites that monitor this bizarre industry were pivotal as well. From regular news coverage on sites like *Comic Book Resources* and *Newsarama* to in-depth pieces on *Comics Alliance* (RIP) and *The Beat*, this record of the genre's recent past was extremely helpful. I'd also like to single out *The Mary Sue*, *Polygon*, and *Women Write about Comics* for years of thoughtful pieces from unique perspectives.

Big thanks as always to Strange Adventures, the best comic shop in the world, where I get all of my many, many comic books. Everyone at Photofest has been great as well, always keen to track down my weirdly specific requests for images.

I'm so glad to be back with the excellent team at Rowman & Littlefield for our second book together. Christen Karniski and Deni Remsberg have been fantastic to work with on the editorial front, and this book has benefitted massively from their involvement. Much appreciation as well for the stellar contributions of Veronica Dove in marketing, Nicole Carty in production, and cover designer Kathi Ha.

My best friend Nicole has to hear about whatever minutia of comic book history I'm currently lost in when thinking about it no longer works and I have to talk it out. She always asks smart questions and offers good advice. Plus she tells me what words to use to accurately describe the weird mishmash of outfits male artists tend to put their female characters in.

Thanks to you as well, readers, for going on this weird trip through comic book history with me. We've only just scratched the surface of sexism and toxic masculinity in superhero media here, honestly. This book could be ten times longer and still not address it all, it's so central to the genre as a whole. So many fascinating characters and stories didn't make the cut! But I hope this gave you a taste of the issues at play, and that what you learned will illuminate your future superhero reading and watching.

Finally, all the thanks in the world to my family, who are endlessly supportive of me and my work. My parents are the best, my sister and brother-in-law are also great, and my nieces Lennie and Josie are my favorite people in the whole world, even though they are too adorable and thus extremely detrimental to my writing process. Playing Barbies, building towers, and reading stories are much more important than whatever old comic I'm blathering on about, though.

Notes

Superhero comic books are collected in various editions, from larger Archive, Essentials, Masterworks, Omnibus, and Showcase volumes for older material to paperback and hardcover collections of more recent story lines. The bulk of DC's and Marvel's comics from the past eight decades are also available in digital form via Comixology. Comic books will be cited here based on the original issue, with the issue number and cover date.

Chapter 1: Origins

1   "champion of the oppressed" . . . *Action Comics* #1 (June 1938).

1   **they were bullied often** . . . Brad Ricca, *Super Boys: The Amazing Adventures of Jerry Siegel and Joe Shuster—the Creators of Superman* (New York: Macmillan, 2013), 198.

1   **Ohio was also a hotbed** . . . Michael Cikraji, *The Cleveland Nazis: 1933–1945* (Cleveland, OH: MSL Academic Endeavors, 2014).

3   **groups like America First** . . . Sarah Churchwell, *Behold, America: The Entangled History of "America First" and "the American Dream"* (New York: Basic Books, 2018).

3   **stood up for workers'** . . . *Action Comics* #3 (August 1938).

3   **evacuated and then demolished** . . . *Action Comics* #8 (January 1939).

3   **Superman stopped swindlers** . . . *Action Comics* #11 (April 1939).

3   **corrupt politicians** . . . *Action Comics* #1 (June 1938), *Action Comics* #12 (May 1939).

3   **cruel judges** . . . *Action Comics* #1 (June 1938).

3   **didn't care for Superman** . . . Larry Tye, *Superman: The High-Flying History of America's Most Enduring Hero* (New York: Random House, 2012), 35.

3   **"friend of the helpless"** . . . *Action Comics* #7 (December 1938).

3   **Superman became the permanent** . . . *Action Comics* #19 (December 1939).

3   **The Man of Steel smashed** . . . Jerry Siegel and Joe Shuster, "How Superman Would End the War," *Look*, February 27, 1940.

3   **The publishing business was a tough** . . . Nirit Anderman, "Supermensches: Comic Books' Secret Jewish History," *Haaretz*, January 24, 2016.

4   **the Shield, a star-spangled** . . . *Pep Comics* #1 (January 1940).

4   **Uncle Sam** . . . *National Comics* #1 (July 1940).

4   **Steve Rogers** . . . *Captain America Comics* #1 (March 1941).

4   **raided a German concentration** . . . *Captain America Comics* #2 (April 1941).

4   **One of the threats** . . . Mark Evanier, *Kirby: King of Comics* (New York: Abrams, 2008), 56.

4   **millionaire Bruce Wayne** . . . *Detective Comics* #27 (May 1939).

6   **the Scarlet Horde** . . . *Detective Comics* #33 (November 1939).

6   **leveraged his superior power** . . . *Action Comics* #2 (July 1938).

6   **expressing no remorse** . . . *Detective Comics* #28 (June 1939).

7   **"a fate [they] well"** . . . *Captain America Comics* #1 (March 1941).

7   **"yellow rats"** . . . *Detective Comics* #1 (March 1937).

7   **"[He] can make a harmonica"** . . . *Young Allies* #1 (Summer 1941).

7   **Japanese characters were dehumanized** . . . Mark Fertig, *Take That, Adolf! The Fighting Comic Books of the Second World War* (Seattle, WA: Fantagraphics, 2017), 25–27.

8   **captured by villains** . . . See *Action Comics* #2 (July 1938), *Action Comics* #3 (October 1938).

8   **stumble into peril** . . . See *Captain America Comics* #5 (August 1941) for one example.

8   **then quickly phased out** . . . *Detective Comics* #49 (March 1941).

8   **"I'd advise you not"** . . . *Action Comics* #1 (June 1938).

8   **he regularly stole scoops** . . . *Superman* #3 (Winter 1940), *Action Comics* #47 (April 1942).

8   **gaslit her time and again** . . . See *Superman* #17 (July 1942) for a classic example.

8   **"Quiet or papa spank"** . . . *Batman* #1 (Spring 1940).

8   **didn't trust her in a fight** . . . *Captain America Comics* #2 (April 1941).

8   **Fiction House had a handful** . . . Including Fran Hopper, Lily Renee, Ruth Roche, and more.

8   **Hall worked on *Black Cat*** . . . Starting with *Speed Comics* #17 (April 1942).

8   **June Tarpé Mills wrote** . . . Starting with *Miss Fury* #1 (Winter 1943).

8   **Black Widow** . . . *Mystic Comics* #4 (August 1940).

8   **Mary Marvel** . . . *Captain Marvel Adventures* #18 (December 1942).

8   **Phantom Lady** . . . *Police Comics* #1 (August 1941).

9   **wisely suggested a heroine** . . . "Elizabeth H. Marston, Inspiration for Wonder Woman, 100" (obituary), *New York Times*, April 3, 1993.

9   **"America, the last citadel"** . . . *All Star Comics* #8 (December 1941).

9   **"blood-curdling masculinity"** . . . William Moulton Marston, "Why 100,000,000 Americans Read Comics," *American Scholar* 13 (January 1944): 42.

9   **one of DC's bestselling** . . . Les Daniels, *Wonder Woman: The Complete History* (San Francisco: Chronicle Books, 2000), 61.

9   **"women, as a sex"** . . . William Moulton Marston, *Emotions of Normal People* (New York: Harcourt, Brace, 1928), 258–59.

9   **"psychological propaganda for"** . . . Daniels, *Wonder Woman*, 22.

11   **bondage imagery in over** . . . Tim Hanley, *Wonder Woman Unbound: The Curious History of the World's Most Famous Heroine* (Chicago: Chicago Review Press, 2014), 46.

11   **Marston dismissed their qualms** . . . Daniels, *Wonder Woman*, 68–72.

12   **Joe Shuster was immediately** . . . Ricca, *Super Boys*, 141–44.

12   **Bob Kane based Catwoman** . . . Eric Obenzinger, "Ruth Steel Interview (Age 96)—May 22, 2011," YouTube, May 27, 2011.

Chapter 2: Codification

13   **By the early 1950s, crime** . . . Bradford W. Wright, *Comic Book Nation: The Transformation of Youth Culture in America* (Baltimore: Johns Hopkins University Press, 2001), 156.

13   **Delinquency levels were no** . . . James Gilbert, *A Cycle of Outrage: America's Reaction to the Juvenile Delinquent in the 1950s* (Oxford: Oxford University Press, 1986), 71.

13   **"Slowly, and at first"** . . . Fredric Wertham, *Seduction of the Innocent* (New York: Rinehart, 1954), 10.

13   **excerpted in *Ladies' Home Journal*** . . . Fredric Wertham, "What Parents Don't Know about Comic Books," *Ladies' Home Journal*, November 1953, 50–53.

13   ***Reader's Digest*** . . . Fredric Wertham, "Comic Books—Blueprints for Delinquency!" *Reader's Digest*, May 1954.

14   **"self-righteous shrink"** . . . Max Allan Collins, "Lady, Go Die! A Behind the Scenes Look at Completing Mickey Spillane's Lost 'Mike Hammer' Novels," *Lit Reactor*, May 7, 2012.

14   **"Josef Mengele of funnybooks"** . . . Mark Evanier, *Wertham Was Right!* (Raleigh, NC: TwoMorrows, 2003), 189.

14   **"publicity-seeking German quack"** . . . Charles Brownstein, "1954: The Year Comics Almost Died," *Comic Book Legal Defense Fund Defender* no. 1 (Spring 2015): 8.

14   **remarkably progressive** . . . Bart Beaty, *Fredric Wertham and the Critique of Mass Culture* (Jackson: University Press of Mississippi, 2005), 82–90.

14   **the books served as how-to** . . . Wertham, *Seduction*, 118.

14   **should be reading "real"** . . . Ibid., 65.

14   **Wertham conflated and** . . . Carol L. Tilley, "Seducing the Innocent: Fredric Wertham and the Falsifications That Helped Condemn Comics," *Information & Culture* 47, no. 4 (2012): 394.

14   **"If I were asked to express"** . . . Wertham, *Seduction*, 265.

15   **"At home they lead"** . . . Ibid., 190.

15   **"only someone ignorant"** . . . Ibid., 189–90.

15   **"homosexual and anti-feminine"** . . . Ibid., 191.

15   **cited a teen who was** . . . Tilley, "Seducing," 394.

15   **"a horror type"** . . . Wertham, *Seduction*, 34.

15   "the Lesbian counterpart" . . . Ibid., 192.
15   "While she is a frightening" . . . Ibid., 34.
15   "extremely sadistic hatred" . . . Ibid., 193.
16   "They do not work" . . . Ibid., 234.
16   "A homoerotic attitude" . . . Ibid., 188.
16   "smut and trash" . . . "Testimony of Dr. Fredric Wertham, Psychiatrist, Director, Lafargue Clinic, New York, N.Y.," April 21, 1954.
16   "within the bounds of good" . . . "Testimony of William S. Gaines, Publisher, Entertaining Comics Group, New York, N.Y.," April 21, 1954.
16   the *New York Times* . . . Peter Khiss, "No Harm in Horror, Comics Issuer Says; Comics Publisher Sees No Harm in Horror, Discounts 'Good Taste,'" *New York Times*, April 22, 1954.
16   consortium of publishers . . . Wright, *Comic Book Nation*, 172.
17   "violations of standards" . . . 1954 Comics Code, in Amy Kiste Nyberg, *Seal of Approval: The History of the Comics Code* (Jackson: University Press of Mississippi, 1998), 166–68.
17   "if crime is depicted" . . . Ibid.
17   "illicit sex relations" . . . Ibid.
17   Many publishers went out . . . Nyberg, *Seal of Approval*, 124–25.
17   homosexuality was essentially illegal . . . Fred Fejes, *Gay Rights and Moral Panic: The Origins of America's Debate on Homosexuality* (New York: Palgrave Macmillan, 2008), 16–17.
18   She was Kathy Kane . . . *Detective Comics* #233 (July 1956).
18   their union had improved . . . Dave Truesdale, "Review: The Collected Edmond Hamilton, Volume One: The Metal Giants and Others," *SF Gate*, 2010.
18   "This is no place for" . . . *Detective Comics* #233 (July 1956).
18   Bat-Woman became the butt . . . *Batman* #105 (February 1957).
20   a series of "imaginary stories" . . . See *Batman* #131 (April 1960), *Batman* #163 (May 1964).
20   Kathy Kane's niece Bette . . . *Batman* #139 (April 1961).
20   "I can't marry you" . . . *Wonder Woman* #99 (July 1958).
20   "How can I become" . . . *Wonder Woman* #137 (April 1963).
20   "It would be unfair" . . . *Wonder Woman* #133 (October 1962).
21   introduced a Wonder Girl feature . . . *Wonder Woman* #105 (April 1959).
22   convince Green Lantern to marry . . . *Green Lantern* #26 (January 1964).
22   her outings ended in tears . . . Tim Hanley, *Investigating Lois Lane: The Turbulent History of the Daily Planet's Ace Reporter* (Chicago: Chicago Review Press, 2016), 87–92.
22   Supergirl debuted in 1959 . . . *Action Comics* #252 (May 1959).
22   Man of Steel kept her . . . *Action Comics* #258 (November 1959).

Chapter 3: Marvelous

23   **one all-star series** . . . *Justice League of America* #1 (October/November 1960).
23   **chased trends** . . . Sean Howe, *Marvel Comics: The Untold Story* (New York: Harper, 2012), 28.
23   **He wanted a superteam** . . . Ibid., 1.
23   **Lee was burnt out** . . . Ronin Ro, *Tales to Astonish: Jack Kirby, Stan Lee, and the American Comic Book Revolution* (New York: Bloomsbury, 2004), 71–72.
24   **Lee claimed it was all** . . . Howe, *Marvel Comics*, 2.
24   **which had strong similarities** . . . Chris Tolworthy, "Challengers of the Unknown = Fantastic Four," *The Fantastic Four 1961–1989 was the Great American Novel*, n.d.
24   **Their new team premiered** . . . *Fantastic Four* #1 (November 1961).
24   **functional blue uniforms** . . . *Fantastic Four* #3 (March 1962).
25   **"Hmmm, I think I'd"** . . . *Fantastic Four* #14 (May 1963).
25   **"Bah! How can you"** . . . *Fantastic Four* #1 (November 1961).
25   **"Well! Here is a prize"** . . . *Fantastic Four* #4 (May 1962).
25   **they did in 1965** . . . *Fantastic Four Annual* #3 (October 1965).
25   **"Wives should be kissed"** . . . *Fantastic Four* #65 (August 1967).
27   **"the sight of that monster"** . . . *Fantastic Four* #12 (March 1963).
27   **"Reed . . . dearest! I've been"** . . . *Fantastic Four Annual* #2 (November 1964).
27   **"I think Susan Storm"** . . . *Fantastic Four* #6 (September 1962).
27   **"If you ever throw"** . . . *Fantastic Four* #8 (November 1962).
27   **"the most important person"** . . . *Fantastic Four* #11 (February 1963).
27   **"A pretty young lady"** . . . *Fantastic Four* #12 (March 1963).
27   **"Some artists, such as Jack"** . . . Ted White, "A Conversation with the Man behind Marvel Comics, Stan Lee," *Castle of Frankenstein* no. 12 (1968): 60.
28   **Kirby showed Sue pointing** . . . Kate Willaert, "Fantastic Four #8 (Page 15)," *Kirby without Words*, July 11, 2015.
28   **With dialogue, Sue simply** . . . *Fantastic Four* #8 (November 1962).
28   **Kirby had Sue sneak** . . . Kate Willaert, "Fantastic Four #29 (Page 21)," *Kirby without Words*, November 17, 2015.
28   **"Sue, honey . . . you didn't"** . . . *Fantastic Four* #29 (August 1964).
28   **Kirby's margin notes** . . . Kate Willaert, "Fantastic Four #43 (Page 14)," *Kirby without Words*, December 28, 2016.
28   **"Stop him, Reed!"** . . . *Fantastic Four* #43 (October 1965).
29   **"So much like Maria!"** . . . *Tales to Astonish* #44 (June 1963).
29   **"If he thinks I became"** . . . *Tales to Astonish* #50 (December 1963).
29   **"I can't see why you"** . . . *Avengers* #1 (September 1963).
31   **she tried to help** . . . *Avengers* #2 (November 1963).
31   **"We are writing to ask"** . . . *Avengers* #13 (February 1965).
31   **The entire configuration** . . . *Avengers* #16 (May 1965).
31   **feature in *Tales to Astonish* ended** . . . *Tales to Astonish* #69 (July 1965).
31   **"homo sapiens bow to"** . . . *X-Men* #1 (September 1963).
32   **"a most attractive young lady"** . . . Ibid.

32   **"I can never tell her!"** . . . *X-Men* #3 (January 1964).

32   **caused her to faint** . . . *X-Men* #7 (September 1964).

32   **"almost numb with fear!"** . . . *X-Men* #10 (March 1965).

32   **Kirby's art showed Jean** . . . Kate Willaert, "X-Men #3 (Pages 21 & 22)," *Kirby without Words*, August 5, 2015.

32   **"Marvel Girl! How did you"** . . . *X-Men* #3 (January 1964).

Chapter 4: Mania

35   **Superman quickly emerged** . . . Joel Eisner, *The Official Batman Batbook* (Bloomington, IN: AuthorHouse, 2008), 10.

35   **on the verge of cancellation** . . . Julius Schwartz, *Man of Tomorrow: My Life in Science Fiction and Comics* (New York: Harper, 2000), 114.

35   **"New Look" era for Batman** . . . Began with *Detective Comics* #327 (May 1964).

36   **Dozier envisioned the show** . . . Eisner, *Official Batman Batbook*, 11.

36   **executives were not impressed** . . . Ibid., 12.

36   **"Tomorrow night! Same time"** . . . "Hi Diddle Diddle," *Batman*, season 1, episode 1, directed by Robert Butler (Warner Bros., 1966).

36   **"KRUNCH! ZLONK! BAM!"** . . . "Smack in the Middle," *Batman*, season 1, episode 2, directed by Robert Butler (Warner Bros., 1966).

36   **"very square, hard-nosed"** . . . Eisner, *Official Batman Batbook*, 15.

37   **"Odd, the new discotheque"** . . . "Hi Diddle Diddle," *Batman*.

37   **"You've done it again"** . . . Ibid.

37   **"I have only one regret"** . . . "Smack in the Middle," *Batman*.

37   **ploy to garner more screen time** . . . Burt Ward, *Boy Wonder: My Life in Tights* (Los Angeles: Logical Figments, 1995), 69.

37   **A Batman craze ensued** . . . Glen Weldon, *The Caped Crusade: Batman and the Rise of Nerd Culture* (New York: Simon & Schuster, 2016), 89.

37   **West appeared on the cover** . . . *Life*, March 11, 1966.

38   **Batusi, his awkward dance** . . . Weldon, *The Caped Crusade*, 91.

38   **"Meet the *new* Batgirl!"** . . . *Detective Comics* #359 (January 1967).

39   **"Holy interference! She's ruining"** . . . Ibid.

39   **"feminine weakness betrayed me"** . . . *Detective Comics* #371 (January 1968).

39   **Catwoman fought her to prove** . . . *Batman* #197 (December 1967).

39   **Wonder Woman then faced** . . . *The Brave and the Bold* #78 (July 1968).

39   **Penguin kidnapping Barbara** . . . "Enter Batgirl, Exit Penguin," *Batman*, season 3, episode 1, directed by Oscar Rudolph (Warner Bros., 1967).

39   **"How could a woman"** . . . "Zelda the Great," *Batman*, season 1, episode 9, directed by Norman Foster (Warner Bros., 1966).

40   **"I don't know who"** . . . "Enter Batgirl," *Batman*.

40   **"Well, that winds that up"** . . . "Ring around the Riddler," *Batman*, season 3, episode 2, directed by Sam Strangis (Warner Bros., 1967).

40   **"Batman and Robin took care"** . . . "The Wail of the Siren," *Batman*, season 3, episode 3, directed by George Waggner (Warner Bros., 1967).

40   **"Perhaps crimefighting is better"** . . . "The Ogg Couple," *Batman*, season 3, episode 15, directed by Oscar Rudolph (Warner Bros., 1967).

40   **"Where did you come from?"** . . . Debuted in "The Wail of the Siren," *Batman*.

41   *Batman* **almost found new life** . . . Eisner, *Official Batman Batbook*, 445.

41   **Schwartz returned to the grittier** . . . Began with *Batman* #204 (August 1968).

42   **"The Secret of the Waiting Graves"** . . . *Detective Comics* #395 (January 1970).

42   **"What a perfect story!"** . . . Letters from *Detective Comics* #399 (May 1970).

44   **dating different women** . . . Superman dated Lois while Clark dated Lana beginning in *Superman* #321 (March 1978).

Chapter 5: Divergence

45   **Books like** *Captain Marvel* . . . Ben Morse, "Thunderstruck," *Wizard* 179 (September 2006): 38.

45   *Superman* . . . Larry Tye, *Superman: The High-Flying History of America's Most Enduring Hero* (New York: Random House, 2012), 38.

45   *Wonder Woman* . . . Olive Richard, "Our Women Are Our Future," *Family Circle*, August 14, 1942.

45   **each issue was read** . . . Adrian Hill, "Superman Then and Now: The Story of Comics," *Graphically Inclined*, March 25, 2010.

45   **Readership was evenly split** . . . Shirley Biagi and Marilyn Kern-Foxworth, *Facing Difference: Race, Gender, and Mass Media* (Thousand Oaks, CA: Pine Forge, 1997), 249.

45   **Advertisements bore this out** . . . Tim Hanley, *Wonder Woman Unbound: The Curious History of the World's Most Famous Heroine* (Chicago: Chicago Review Press, 2014), 154–57.

46   **Some editors were even** . . . Sean Howe, *Marvel Comics: The Untold Story* (New York: Harper, 2012), 144.

46   **The chart below shows** . . . Data for DC and Marvel originally published in Tim Hanley, "The Evolution of Female Readership: Letter Columns in Superhero Comics," *Gender and the Superhero Narrative*, ed. Michael Goodrum, Tara Prescott, and Philip Smith (Jackson: University Press of Mississippi, 2018), 221–50. Series were chosen based on popularity and longevity. Every letter column was tabulated, using the traditionally associated gender of each name unless the text suggested otherwise. Gender-neutral names, pseudonyms, or initials weren't counted unless the letter made the gender clear.

48   **"I have yet to see any representation"** . . . *Fantastic Four* #57 (December 1966).

48   **1966 poll in** *Esquire* . . . Bradford W. Wright, *Comic Book Nation: The Transformation of Youth Culture in America* (Baltimore: Johns Hopkins University Press, 2001), 223.

48   **Marvel's sales had eclipsed** . . . Howe, *Marvel Comics*, 16.

48   **Black Panther, the leader** . . . *Fantastic Four* #52 (July 1966).

48   **Sam Wilson was introduced** . . . *Captain America* #117 (September 1969).

49   **"Bigotry and racism are"** . . . From Marvel comic books cover dated December 1968.

49   **"Only there's skins you"** . . . *Green Lantern/Green Arrow* #76 (April 1970).

49   **John Stewart was given** . . . *Green Lantern* #87 (December 1971/January 1972).

49   **Harry Osborn took stimulant** . . . *Amazing Spider-Man* #96 (May 1971).

49   **CCA to revamp its** . . . Reed Tucker, *Slugfest: Inside the Epic 50-Year Battle between Marvel and DC* (New York: Da Capo, 2017), 77.

49   **Speedy was addicted** . . . *Green Lantern/Green Arrow* #85 (August/September 1971).

49   **Diana gave up her** . . . The mod era began with *Wonder Woman* #178 (September/October 1968).

50   **she lobbied the editors** . . . Yohana Desta, "How Gloria Steinem Saved Wonder Woman," *Vanity Fair*, October 10, 2017.

50   **"Wonder Woman for President"** . . . *Ms.* 1, no. 1 (1972).

50   **"the feminism and strength"** . . . Gloria Steinem, introduction, *Wonder Woman* (New York: Holt, Rinehart and Winston, 1972), 5.

50   **"I'm no longer the girl"** . . . *Superman's Girl Friend Lois Lane* #121 (April 1972).

50   **"Will they clean up the slums?"** . . . *Detective Comics* #423 (May 1972).

50   **"a militant Women's Lib"** . . . *Superman's Girl Friend Lois Lane* #126 (August 1972).

50   **"Why must every ish"** . . . *Superman's Girl Friend Lois Lane* #128 (December 1972).

50   **"obnoxious dame"** . . . *Superman's Girl Friend Lois Lane* #124 (July 1972).

50   **"Women should know their"** . . . Ibid.

51   **"Who knows what evil"** . . . *Superman's Girl Friend Lois Lane* #126 (August 1972).

51   **"Dottie Cottonman"** . . . *Wonder Woman* #204 (January/February 1973).

51   **"Diana Prince's liberated"** . . . *Wonder Woman* #209 (December 1973/January 1974).

51   **"Don't let her get bogged"** . . . *Wonder Woman* #208 (October/November 1973).

51   **"All right, girls—that finishes"** . . . *Avengers* #83 (December 1970).

52   **the Cat was Greer Nelson** . . . *The Cat* #1 (November 1972).

52   **"At last! A bold new"** . . . *Ms. Marvel* #1 (January 1977).

52   **"the modern woman's quest"** . . . Ibid.

52   **"new diets, and fashions"** . . . Ibid.

52   **"should be action-oriented"** . . . *Ms. Marvel* #3 (March 1977).

52   **"are so indoctrinated"** . . . *Ms. Marvel* #4 (April 1977).

52   **"We've been trying to eliminate"** . . . *Ms. Marvel* #8 (August 1977).

54   **black bathing suit** . . . *Ms. Marvel* #20 (October 1978).

54   **weren't published for another** . . . Beginning in *Marvel Super-Heroes* #10 (July 1992).

54   **"Do less females read"** . . . Stan Lee, introduction, *The Superhero Women* (New York: Simon & Schuster, 1977), 7.

Chapter 6: Overpowered

57   **"Fourth World"** . . . Began with *Superman's Pal Jimmy Olsen* #133 (October 1970) and soon expanded to several other series.

57   **yearlong "Korvac Saga"** . . . Began with *Avengers* #167 (January 1978).

57   **Captain America hung up** . . . *Captain America* #180 (December 1974).

57   **Tony Stark addressed his alcoholism** . . . Began with *Invincible Iron Man* #120 (March 1979).

57   **Newsstands were unreliable** . . . Bradford W. Wright, *Comic Book Nation: The Transformation of Youth Culture in America* (Baltimore: Johns Hopkins University Press, 2001), 258–59.

58   **Direct market comic book shops** . . . Ibid., 259–62.

58   **Professor X recruited a new** . . . *Giant Size X-Men* #1 (May 1975).

58   **Jean Grey sacrificed herself** . . . *X-Men* #100 (August 1976).

58   **"I am fire!"** . . . *X-Men* #101 (October 1976).

58   **"My . . . god. Jean used to be"** . . . *X-Men* #105 (June 1977).

58   **"nexus of realities"** . . . *X-Men* #108 (December 1977).

59   **letters in *Uncanny X-Men*** . . . My own count, based on the same criteria as in chapter 5. The letters span *X-Men* #97 (February 1976) to *Uncanny X-Men* #140 (December 1980).

59   **"no more than a second-rate"** . . . *X-Men* #110 (April 1978).

59   **sparing only herself and Beast** . . . *X-Men* #113 (September 1978).

59   **"I want a superheroine of limitless"** . . . *Uncanny X-Men* #117 (January 1979).

59   **"Phoenix's power was reduced"** . . . *Uncanny X-Men* #123 (July 1979).

59   **"she wasn't the girl I'd"** . . . *X-Men* #114 (October 1978).

59   **began dating Colleen Wing** . . . *Uncanny X-Men* #120 (April 1979).

59   **Jean met a mysterious man** . . . *Uncanny X-Men* #122 (June 1979).

59   **began having visions** . . . *Uncanny X-Men* #125 (September 1979).

60   **became the Black Queen** . . . *Uncanny X-Men* #132 (April 1980).

60   **"No longer am I the woman"** . . . *Uncanny X-Men* #134 (June 1980).

60   **reminiscent of romance novels** . . . Kelly Williams, "Female Readership and Corruption in the Dark Phoenix Saga (1980) and Dark Phoenix (2019)," *The Vault of Culture*, May 23, 2019.

60   **"The emotions he stirs"** . . . *Uncanny X-Men* #129 (January 1980).

60   **"Every facet of her being"** . . . *Uncanny X-Men* #130 (February 1980).

60   **"psychic seduction"** . . . *Uncanny X-Men* #132 (April 1980).

60   **"tailor[ing] your illusions"** . . . *Uncanny X-Men* #134 (June 1980).

60   **"There is no joy"** . . . *Uncanny X-Men* #135 (July 1980).

62   **agree to his implied proposal . . .** *Uncanny X-Men* #136 (August 1980).

62   **trope as old as time . . .** Williams, "Female Readership," and Joshua Wilson, "Elana Levin on Jean Grey, the X-Men's Feminist Icon," *The Fabulist,* June 21, 2019.

62   **Claremont's original plan . . .** *Phoenix: The Untold Story* #1 (April 1984).

62   **"didn't like Phoenix" . . .** Ibid.

62   **"It's better this way" . . .** *Uncanny X-Men* #137 (September 1980).

62   **"How could you do" . . .** *Uncanny X-Men* #139 (November 1980).

63   **Robin, Kid Flash, and Wonder Girl . . .** *New Teen Titans* #1 (November 1980).

63   **letter columns in the early . . .** My own count, based on the same criteria as above. Letters span *New Teen Titans* #15 (January 1982) to *Tales of the Teen Titans* #49 (December 1984).

63   **trapped in a hellish vision . . .** *New Teen Titans* #31 (May 1983).

63   **debuted as a villain . . .** *New Teen Titans* #26 (December 1982).

64   **"We went out of" . . .** Dan Greenfield, "Crafting the Judas Contract—and the Irredeemable Terra," *13th Dimension,* September 5, 2018.

64   **"I wanted her to be cute" . . .** Eric Nolen-Weathington, *Modern Masters Volume Two: George Perez* (Raleigh, NC: TwoMorrows, 2007), 128.

64   **"we could always head up" . . .** *New Teen Titans* #30 (April 1983).

64   **earned their approval . . .** *New Teen Titans* #34 (August 1983).

64   **Terra in a low-cut robe . . .** Ibid.

64   **"I wanted her to look" . . .** Nolen-Weathington, *Modern Masters,* 128.

64   **capture all of the Teen Titans . . .** *Tales of the Teen Titans* #43 (June 1984).

64   **"Your pwetty widdle girlfriend" . . .** *Tales of the Teen Titans Annual* #3 (July 1984).

65   **"But I—I thought he cared" . . .** Ibid.

65   **"That girl was loony" . . .** Ibid.

65   **"It was difficult to see" . . .** *Tales of the Teen Titans* #47 (October 1984).

66   **"make certain that we" . . .** Ibid.

66   **"the first girl to break" . . .** Brad Meltzer, "How I Spent My Summer Vacation with the Judas Contract," *Give Our Regards to the Atomsmashers* (New York: Pantheon, 2004), 97.

Chapter 7: Despair

67   **on a Spider-Man book . . .** *Peter Parker: The Spectacular Spider-Man* #27 (February 1979).

67   **Miller took over drawing . . .** *Daredevil* #158 (May 1979).

68   **let Miller write it . . .** *Daredevil* #168 (January 1981).

68   **"the external reality represents" . . .** Peter Sanderson, "The Frank Miller/Klaus Janson Interview," *Daredevil by Frank Miller & Klaus Janson, Vol. 2* (New York: Marvel, 2019).

68   **"action where people don't" . . .** Ibid.

68   **"I enjoy the fact" . . .** Ibid.

68   the futuristic samurai tale . . . Began with *Ronin* #1 (July 1983).

68   DC decided not to even . . . Peter Sanderson, "The Ronin Forum," *Amazing Heroes* 25 (June 15, 1983): 53.

68   new "Born Again" arc . . . Began with *Daredevil* #227 (February 1986),

69   victim of a violent sexual . . . *Daredevil* #173 (August 1981).

69   and also introduced . . . *Daredevil* #168 (January 1981).

69   then killed off Elektra . . . *Daredevil* #181 (April 1982).

69   "I have never read" . . . Susana Polo, "The Writer Who Made Me Love Comics Taught Me to Hate Them," *Polygon*, March 1, 2016.

69   Miller wanted to return . . . *Comic Book Confidential*, directed by Ron Mann (Cinecom, 1988).

69   "good soldier" . . . *Batman: The Dark Knight* #2 (July 1986), *Batman: The Dark Knight* #4 (December 1986).

70   severely beaten by the Joker . . . *Batman: The Dark Knight* #3 (August 1986).

70   "makes me sick" . . . *Batman: The Dark Knight* #1 (June 1986).

70   "darling" and "my sweet" . . . *Batman: The Dark Knight* #3 (August 1986).

70   "The homophobic nightmare" . . . Will Brooker, Roberta Pearson, and William Uricchio, *Many More Lives of the Batman* (London: Palgrave Macmillan, 2015), 36.

72   the character's definitive origin . . . Began with *Batman* #404 (February 1987).

72   that Moore come up with . . . Frank Plowright, "Watchmen," *Amazing Heroes* 97 (June 15, 1986): 44.

73   Nite Owl and Doctor Manhattan decided . . . *Watchmen* #12 (October 1987).

73   Randian views of Steve Ditko . . . Susana Polo, "Alan Moore Created Rorschach to Dunk on Randian Superheroes," *Polygon*, October 24, 2019.

73   "The entire world is just" . . . Plowright, "Watchmen," 47.

73   "morally blank world" . . . *Watchmen* #6 (February 1987).

74   "accumulated filth" . . . *Watchmen* #1 (September 1986).

74   "felt cleansed" . . . *Watchmen* #6 (February 1987).

74   Moore predicted that fans . . . Plowright, "Watchmen," 48.

74   unwell murderer was cheered . . . Steven Surman, "Alan Moore's Watchmen and Rorschach: Does the Character Set a Bad Example?" *Steven Surman Writes*, January 20, 2015.

74   "The Silk Spectre was just" . . . Jon B. Cooke, "Toasting Absent Heroes: Alan Moore Discusses the Charlton-Watchmen Connection," *Comic Book Artist*, August 2000.

74   grew dissatisfied with the . . . *Watchmen* #3 (November 1986).

74   connected with Nite Owl . . . *Watchmen* #5 (January 1987).

74   curing of his impotence . . . *Watchmen* #7 (March 1987).

74   Her role within *Watchmen* . . . Anna C. Marshall, "Not So Revisionary: The Regressive Treatment of Gender in Alan Moore's Watchmen," *Downtown Review* 3 no. 2 (December 2016).

74   "She thinks she's a coffee table" . . . *Batman: The Killing Joke* (July 1988).

75   in his original artwork . . . Paul Jaissle, "Original, More Explicit Artwork for *The Killing Joke* Surfaces," *Sequart Organization*, December 3, 2013.

75   "Yeah, okay, cripple the bitch" . . . Mike Cotton, "Last Call," *Wizard* 147 (January 2004): 62–64.

75   retired the character . . . *Batgirl Special* #1 (July 1988).
75   "clumsy [and] misjudged" . . . George Khoury, *The Extraordinary Works of Alan Moore* (Raleigh, NC: TwoMorrows, 2003), 123.
75   "should've reined me in" . . . Cotton, "Last Call," 64.
75   "I must admit I had to" . . . Brian Bolland, afterword, *Batman: The Killing Joke—The Deluxe Edition* (New York: DC Comics, 2008).
75   brought her back a few . . . *Suicide Squad* #23 (January 1989).
75   a fixed point that . . . *Booster Gold* #5 (February 2008), *The Brave and the Bold* #33 (June 2010).
76   the lifeless body . . . *Batman* #428 (Holiday 1988).

Chapter 8: Caliber

77   "by the book" . . . *Batman: The Killing Joke* (July 1988).
77   "He's different! He's deadly!" . . . *Amazing Spider-Man* #129 (February 1974).
78   slept with the only . . . *The Punisher* #2 (February 1986).
78   shot her Jeep . . . *The Punisher* #5 (May 1986).
78   "left one breathing" . . . *The Punisher* #1 (July 1987).
78   infiltrated a drug operation . . . *The Punisher* #2 (August 1987).
78   exposed white supremacists . . . *The Punisher* #3 (October 1987).
78   gunned down Middle Eastern . . . *The Punisher* #7 (March 1988).
78   reverend based on Jim Jones . . . *The Punisher* #4 (November 1987).
78   "I hate to cause animals" . . . *The Punisher* #6 (February 1988).
80   action movie of his . . . *The Punisher*, directed by Mark Goldblatt (New World Pictures, 1989).
80   grief-stricken husband . . . *The Punisher* #4 (November 1987).
80   first he had sex . . . *The Punisher* #5 (January 1988).
80   only to have her die . . . *The Punisher* #7 (March 1988).
80   whopping 99 percent male . . . My own count, based on the same criteria as in chapter 5. The letters span *The Punisher* #1 (July 1987) through *The Punisher* #36 (August 1990).
80   "Few comics today offer" . . . *The Punisher* #11 (September 1988).
80   "an American comic where" . . . *The Punisher* #10 (August 1988).
80   "refreshing jolt" . . . *The Punisher* #12 (October 1988).
80   "If there had been" . . . *The Punisher* #9 (June 1988).
81   "some might say it's" . . . *The Punisher Magazine* #1 (September 1989).
81   "The Punisher seems to have" . . . Ibid.
81   The Punisher's skull logo . . . Benjamin Linzy, "The Badge and the Skull: Cops, Militants, and a Punisher Fetish," *Activist History Review*, June 22, 2000.
82   "I'm the best there is" . . . *Wolverine* #1 (September 1982).
82   "the part I can't control" . . . *Kitty Pryde and Wolverine* #6 (April 1985).
82   "good people. Idealists." . . . *Wolverine* #1 (November 1988).
84   Giffen reintroduced his character . . . *Lobo* #1 (November 1990).

84   the artists only received . . . George Khoury, *Image Comics: The Road to Independence* (Raleigh, NC: TwoMorrows, 2007), 11.

85   "Have to make 'em" . . . *WildC.A.T.s* #1 (August 1992).

85   rollout of the new publisher . . . Patrick A. Reed, "On This Day in 1992: The Start of the Image Comics Revolution," *Comics Alliance*, February 1, 2016.

85   the publisher accounted . . . John Jackson Miller, "January 1995 Comic Book Sales to Comics Shops," *Comichron*, n.d.

86   sales for the Superman line . . . Jermaine Mclaughlin, "An Oral History of the Death and Return of Superman, 25 Years Later," *SYFY Wire*, August 10, 2018.

86   a massive brawl . . . Began with *Superman: The Man of Steel* #18 (December 1992).

86   inspired by Image Comics' . . . Michael Bailey, "Doomsday: Ten Years Later," *Superman Homepage*, December 2002.

86   died in Lois's arms . . . *Superman* #75 (January 1993).

86   original Superman inevitably returned . . . *Superman* #81 (September 1993).

86   began in 1993 . . . Began with *Batman* #492 (May 1993).

86   snapping his spine . . . *Batman* #497 (July 1993).

87   the latter ultimately conceding . . . *Batman: Legends of the Dark Knight* #63 (August 1994).

87   Green Lantern went mad . . . *Green Lantern* #48 (January 1994).

87   Wonder Woman had to relinquish . . . *Wonder Woman* #93 (January 1995).

87   Aquaman lost his hand . . . *Aquaman* #2 (September 1994).

87   Green Arrow died . . . *Green Arrow* #101 (October 1995).

Chapter 9: Exaggeration

90   Black Canary with her . . . Debuted in *Flash Comics* #86 (August 1947).

90   midriff-baring Namora . . . The look debuted in *Sub-Mariner Comics* #23 (Summer 1947).

90   Wertham to decry . . . The cover of *Phantom Lady* #17 (April 1948) was reprinted in the photo insert of Fredric Wertham, *Seduction of the Innocent* (New York: Rinehart, 1954).

90   Supergirl donned a low-cut . . . Debuted in *Adventure Comics* #410 (September 1971).

90   special pinup pages . . . *Savage She-Hulk* #24 (January 1982).

90   "The Naked Truth" . . . *Fantastic Four* #275 (February 1985).

91   Kevin Nowlan pinup . . . *Marvel Fanfare* #18 (January 1985).

91   barrage of alien weapon . . . *Sensational She-Hulk* #2 (June 1989).

91   "I have had the biggest" . . . *Sensational She-Hulk* #1 (May 1989).

91   "I know it's insane" . . . *Sensational She-Hulk* #7 (November 1989).

91   "beautiful" . . . *Sensational She-Hulk* #12 (February 1990).

91   "gorgeous" . . . *Sensational She-Hulk* #13 (March 1990).

91   "sexy" . . . *Sensational She-Hulk* #24 (February 1991).

91   **"I'm proud to say I'm addicted"** . . . *Sensational She-Hulk* #7 (November 1989).

91   **male fans comprised over 90 percent** . . . My own count, based on the same criteria as in chapter 5. The letters span *Sensational She-Hulk* #1 (May 1989) to *Sensation She-Hulk* #60 (February 1994).

91   **Moore's famous *Vanity Fair*** . . . *Vanity Fair*, August 1991.

91   **She-Hulk in a tiny bikini** . . . *Sensational She-Hulk* #34 (December 1991).

91   **"This is it! Because you"** . . . *Sensational She-Hulk* #40 (June 1992).

91   **"a giant green porn star"** . . . Sean O'Connell, "David S. Goyer Dismisses She-Hulk as 'A Giant Green Porn Star,'" *Cinema Blend*, May 22, 2014.

93   **"an avenging angel"** . . . *WildC.A.T.s* #1 (August 1992).

93   **similar look to the Amazons** . . . *Wonder Woman* #90 (September 1994).

93   **Diana shifted to a new outfit** . . . *Wonder Woman* #93 (January 1995).

93   **The editor had to regularly** . . . Joseph P. Illidge (@JosephPIllidge), "Do not even get me started . . . ," Twitter, October 18, 2015.

93   **a take on *Sports Illustrated*'s** . . . *Marvel Illustrated: Swimsuit Issue* #1 (January 1991).

93   **In the same month** . . . Among all books cover dated January 1991.

93   **women accounted for 60 percent** . . . My own count.

94   **"Why is Catwoman so busty?"** . . . *Catwoman* #8 (March 1994).

94   **"Catwoman's chest looks"** . . . *Catwoman* #6 (January 1994).

94   **"Please reconsider your stand"** . . . *Catwoman* #12 (July 1994).

94   **"Shirtless men with abnormal"** . . . *Catwoman* #8 (March 1994).

94   **"Well said"** . . . Ibid.

95   **sales dropped immediately** . . . Tim Hanley, *The Many Lives of Catwoman: The Felonious History of a Feline Fatale* (Chicago: Chicago Review Press, 2017), 141.

95   **a useful distraction** . . . *Superman/Batman* #4 (January 2004).

95   **an identity crisis** . . . *JSA: Classified* #2 (October 2005).

95   **Sue Storm uncharacteristically** . . . Look debuted in *Fantastic Four* #384 (January 1994).

95   **Emma Frost took the idea** . . . Look debuted in *New X-Men* #114 (July 2001).

95   **The Star Sapphires extended** . . . Look debuted in *Green Lantern* #18 (May 2007).

95   **Male Star Sapphires were fully** . . . *Green Lantern Corps* #36 (January 2015).

97   **"Human prudishness still baffles"** . . . *Titans* #1 (June 2008).

97   **Scott Lobdell tied it to** . . . *Red Hood and the Outlaws* #1 (November 2011).

97   **Selina Kyle undressed** . . . *Catwoman* #1 (November 2011).

97   **lead character stripping** . . . *Voodoo* #1 (November 2011).

97   **swapping out Harley Quinn's** . . . *Suicide Squad* #1 (November 2011).

97   **for negligees** . . . See *Superman* #219 (September 2005), *Superman* #654 (September 2006), *Action Comics* #848 (May 2007).

97   **Lois's thong was clearly** . . . *Adventures of Superman* #644 (November 2005).

97   **the return of Supergirl** . . . *Superman/Batman* #8 (May 2004).

98   **Black Widow and Hawkeye** . . . *Marvel Adventures Super Heroes* #17 (October 2011).

98   **"for real though look"** . . . HoursAgo, "for real though look me . . . ," *needless procedures* (Tumblr blog), December 1, 2012.

98   **"how to fix every Strong"** . . . ND Stevenson (@gingerhaze), "how to fix every Strong . . . ," *How Are You I'm Fine Thanks* (Tumblr blog), December 2, 2012.

98   **contorted artwork of Ms. Marvel** . . . ND Stevenson (@gingerhaze), "weirdly enough, upon drawing this . . . ," *How Are You I'm Fine Thanks* (Tumblr blog), December 2, 2012.

98   **and Psylocke** . . . ND Stevenson (@gingerhaze), "I tested my hypothesis . . . ," *How Are You I'm Fine Thanks* (Tumblr blog), December 2, 2012.

98   **"range from comics where"** . . . Ben Quinn, "Ker-pow! Women Kick Back against Comic-Book Sexism," *Guardian*, December 28, 2011.

99   **Ms. Marvel became Captain** . . . *Captain Marvel* #1 (September 2012).

99   **Batgirl swapped her tight** . . . *Batgirl* #35 (December 2014).

99   **Spider-Woman hung up** . . . *Spider-Woman* #5 (May 2015).

99   **Squirrel Girl embraced her** . . . *Unbeatable Squirrel Girl* #1 (March 2015).

99   **plus-size female lead** . . . *Faith* #1 (January 2016).

99   **Batgirl is in tight spandex** . . . As of *Batgirl* #27 (November 2018), though *Nightwing* #84 (November 2021) introduced a new costume for Batgirl that combines her two recent styles.

99   **So is Spider-Woman** . . . Beginning with *Strikeforce* #1 (November 2019).

Chapter 10: Breakdown

101   **young women were the fastest** . . . Shannon O'Leary, "Despite Early Sales Slump, Comics Retailers Remain Upbeat," *Publishers Weekly*, March 21, 2014.

101   **"[Based on] analysis that Disney"** . . . Milton Griepp, "ICv2 Interview: Marvel's David Gabriel—Part 2: Mass Test, Digital, Changing the Characters, and Kids," *ICv2*, August 16, 2016.

102   **This data was assembled** . . . The charts cover all DC and Marvel single issues released in January and August from 1960 to 2020, using dates from *Mike's Amazing World of Comics*. Data for each issue was garnered from the Grand Comics Database or the DC and Marvel Fandom wiki pages. "Writers" included anyone with a writing credit, while "artists" included pencilers and inkers. To be counted, a story had to be at least three pages in length or a creator's credits had to amount to at least three pages cumulatively across multiple features in the same issue. Creators were tabulated based on the gender they identified as at time of publication.

102   **worked on romance comics** . . . Unlike superhero comics, credits for romance comics are quite spotty on online databases. It's likely there were many more female writers and artists working on these romance titles, but they remain unknown and uncredited.

103   **"Although the company"** . . . Trina Robbins and Catherine Yronwode, *Women and the Comics* (n.p.: Eclipse Books, 1985), 106–8.

103   A handful of other . . . Including Jo Duffy, Tamsyn Flynn, Barbara Kesel, and Mindy Newell.

103   artists Colleen Doran . . . *Sandman* #20 (October 1990), *Sandman* #34 (January 1992).

103   and Jill Thompson . . . *Sandman* #40 (August 1992) to *Sandman* #49 (May 1993).

103   Nancy Collins . . . Began with *Swamp Thing* #110 (August 1991).

103   Rachel Pollack . . . Began with *Doom Patrol* #64 (March 1993).

103   Mindy Newell cowrote . . . Began with *Wonder Woman* #36 (November 1989).

103   including Jo Duffy . . . Began with *Catwoman* #1 (August 1993).

103   and Devin Grayson . . . Began with *Catwoman* #56 (April 1998).

103   and added *Nightwing* . . . Began with *Nightwing* #71 (September 2002).

103   Gail Simone took over . . . Began with *Birds of Prey* #56 (August 2003).

104   "We're just trying to hire" . . . Heidi MacDonald, "SCOOP: What Really Happened at the Infamous Dan DiDio/Hire More Women Incident," *The Beat*, July 29, 2011.

104   The predominantly male panel . . . "An Interview with the Batgirl of the SDCC Panels," *DC Women Kicking Ass*, July 27, 2011.

104   of their many weekly . . . Began with *Earth 2: World's End* #1 (December 2014).

104   Babs Tarr drew . . . Began with *Batgirl* #35 (December 2014).

104   Hope Larson, Mairghread Scott . . . Began with *Batgirl* #1 (September 2016).

104   *Wonder Woman* featured writers . . . Including Meredith Finch, Shea Fontana, G. Willow Wilson, Mariko Tamaki, and Becky Cloonan from 2015 onward.

104   written by Marguerite Bennett . . . Two volumes, beginning with *DC Comics Bombshells* #1 (October 2015) and *Bombshells United* #1 (November 2017).

106   She was a veteran of the industry . . . David Sims, "Remembering the Woman Who Changed Marvel Comics," *The Atlantic*, August 31, 2018.

106   Severin got the gig . . . Work appeared in *Esquire* (September 1966).

106   Lee assigned her to . . . Began with *Strange Tales* #153 (February 1967).

106   Linda Fite wrote . . . Began with *The Cat* #1 (November 1972).

106   written by Jean Thomas . . . Began with *Night Nurse* #1 (November 1972).

106   penned by Carole Seuling . . . Began with *Shanna the She-Devil* #1 (December 1972).

106   "Why is a man writing" . . . *Ms. Marvel* #1 (January 1977).

107   lengthy runs on *Power Man* . . . Began with *Power Man* #56 (April 1979).

107   and *Star Wars* . . . Began with *Star Wars* #70 (April 1983).

107   books like *Power Pack* . . . Began with *Power Pack* #1 (August 1984).

107   and *X-Factor* . . . Began with *X-Factor* #6 (July 1986).

107   run on *Daredevil* . . . Began with *Daredevil* #236 (November 1986).

107   not a single issue . . . Based on my own count, using the same criteria as the chapter's larger count but with every issue in Marvel's entire Ultimate line tabulated.

108   female creators in occasional . . . Began with *Girl Comics* #1 (May 2010).

108   DeConnick writing Carol Danvers . . . Began with *Captain Marvel* #1 (September 2012).

108   **written by G. Willow Wilson** . . . Began with *Ms. Marvel* #1 (April 2014).

108   **Reeder and Natacha Bustos** . . . Began with *Moon Girl and Devil Dinosaur* #1 (January 2016).

108   **Leth and Brittany L. Williams** . . . Began with *Patsy Walker a.k.a. Hellcat* #1 (February 2016).

108   **Stacey Lee and Tana Ford** . . . Began with *Silk* #1 (April 2015).

108   **Erica Henderson** . . . Began with *Unbeatable Squirrel Girl* #1 (March 2015).

108   **Thompson is a constant presence** . . . Thompson is so prolific that she was writing or cowriting eight different issues at Marvel in December 2018.

108   **"Sure—some women get"** . . . Robbins and Yronwode, *Women and the Comics,* 106.

108   **"an economic ghetto"** . . . Ibid., 108.

109   **women accounted for 15 percent** . . . From 2017 to 2019, based on statistics tabulated for my website.

109   **Most editors at DC** . . . From 2017 to 2019, again based on my own statistics.

109   **"Barcon"** . . . Heidi MacDonald, "Barcon, That Starts with 'B' and That Rhymes with 'T' and That Stands for Trouble," *The Beat,* June 19, 2014.

109   **Men account for at least 97 percent** . . . My own count, based on credits listed in each creator's detailed Wikipedia bibliography.

110   **Becky Cloonan wrote** . . . Began with *The Punisher* #1 (July 2016).

110   **Kelly Thompson wrote** . . . Began with *Deadpool* #1 (January 2020).

110   **Mariko Tamaki recently became** . . . Began with *Detective Comics* #1034 (May 2021).

Chapter 11: Frozen

111   **"It occurred to me that"** . . . Gail Simone, "Front Page," *Women in Refrigerators,* March 1999.

111   **murdered and stuffed into** . . . *Green Lantern* #54 (August 1994).

112   **vivacious redhead Mary Jane** . . . Debuted in *Amazing Spider-Man* #42 (January 1967).

112   **Green Goblin threw Gwen** . . . *Amazing Spider-Man* #121 (June 1973).

112   **and then wed** . . . *Amazing Spider-Man Annual* #21 (September 1987).

112   **Ms. Marvel was mind-controlled** . . . *Avengers* #200 (October 1980).

112   **Spider-Woman perished** . . . *Spider-Woman* #50 (June 1983).

112   **Supergirl died to inspire** . . . *Crisis on Infinite Earths* #7 (October 1985).

113   **Black Canary, was captured** . . . *Green Arrow: The Longbow Hunters* #2 (September 1987).

113   **no longer able to bear** . . . Revealed in *Green Arrow* #34 (July 1990).

113   **Mike Grell disagrees** . . . Brian Cronin, "Comic Book Urban Legends Revealed #54," *Comic Book Resources,* June 8, 2006.

113   **He attacked her captors** . . . *Green Arrow: The Longbow Hunters* #2 (September 1987).

113   **Her powers eventually returned** . . . *Birds of Prey* #35 (November 2001).

113   **Raven went mad** . . . *New Titans* #100 (August 1993).

113   **Patsy Walker, a.k.a. Hellcat** . . . *Hellstorm: Prince of Lies* #14 (May 1994).

113   **Mockingbird was killed** . . . *Avengers West Coast* #100 (November 1993).

113   **Illyana Rasputin, died** . . . *Uncanny X-Men* #303 (August 1993).

113   **replaced by Stephanie Brown** . . . *Robin* #126 (July 2004).

114   **set out to implement** . . . *Batman: The 12 Cent Adventure* #1 (October 2004).

114   **"You're pretty as a peach"** . . . *Batman: Legends of the Dark Knight* #183 (November 2004).

114   **"I treated you to a few"** . . . *Robin* #131 (December 2004).

114   **Black Mask shot Stephanie** . . . Ibid.

114   **Stephanie had been promoted** . . . Rich Johnston, "'Spoiler Was Gonna Die'—Inside the DC Writer Meeting That Killed Stephanie Brown," *Bleeding Cool*, July 15, 2011.

114   **Dr. Thompkins had killed** . . . *Batman* #644 (October 2005).

114   **"she was never really"** . . . Julia Savoca Gibson, "80 Years of Robin: The Forgotten History of the Most Iconic Sidekick," *Guardian*, March 18, 2020.

117   **The first issue started cheerily** . . . *Identity Crisis* #1 (August 2004).

117   **Dr. Light hacked the transport** . . . *Identity Crisis* #2 (September 2004).

117   **"The rape pages are in!"** . . . Valerie D'Orazio, *Memoirs of an Occasional Superheroine* (self-pub., 2009), 81.

118   **"I've brought us together"** . . . *Identity Crisis* #7 (February 2005).

118   **Jean was later possessed** . . . *Day of Vengeance* #1 (June 2005).

118   **lost her marriage to Vision** . . . *Avengers West Coast* #63 (October 1990).

118   **as well as their two children** . . . *Avengers West Coast* #52 (December 1989).

118   **"Avengers Disassembled"** . . . Began with *Avengers* #500 (September 2004).

118   **the only safe response** . . . *House of M* #1 (August 2015).

118   **"No more mutants"** . . . *House of M* #7 (November 2005).

118   **teaching at Avengers Academy** . . . *Avengers Academy* #1 (August 2010).

118   **part of the ruling council** . . . *Power of X* #6 (December 2019).

119   **A solo series in 2016** . . . Began with *Scarlet Witch* #1 (February 2016).

119   **killed by Carnage** . . . *Ultimate Spider-Man* #62 (September 2004).

119   **killed off at the beginning** . . . *Ultimates 3* #1 (February 2008).

119   **victim of domestic assault** . . . *Avengers* #213 (November 1981).

119   **Hank assaulting Janet** . . . *Ultimates* #6 (August 2002).

119   **Janet was then killed** . . . *Ultimatum* #2 (January 2009).

119   **"We'll all miss him"** . . . *Final Crisis* #2 (August 2008).

120   **a new Supergirl debuted** . . . *Superman* #16 (April 1988).

120   **Kara later returned** . . . *Superman/Batman* #8 (May 2004).

120   **Gwen Stacy returned** . . . *Edge of Spider-Verse* #2 (September 2014).

120   **Stephanie Brown came back** . . . *Gotham Underground* #3 (February 2008).

120   **top creators weren't allowed** . . . Andy Hunsaker, "Scott Snyder on the Return of the Joker," *Crave Online*, July 9, 2012.

120   **appearance in an alternate** . . . Corinna Lawson, "Dead Again! Smallville Season 11 Revamped to Exclude Stephanie Brown," *Wired*, July 17, 2012.

120   returned as Spoiler . . . *Batman* #28 (April 2014).

121   "It didn't really even" . . . Abraham Riesman, "Deadpool 2 Writers Defend Treatment of Female Characters," *Vulture*, May 18, 2018.

121   Copycat, who was fridged . . . *Deadpool* #59 (December 2001).

Chapter 12: Barriers

123   "This is what we" . . . Noelle Stevenson(@gingerhaze), "Oh, I know I have it . . . ," *How Are You I'm Fine Thanks* (Tumblr blog), February 10, 2014. Stevenson identified as a woman at this time, but has since transitioned.

124   "geek" and "fan" . . . Jay Edidin, "Geek Masculinity and the Myth of the Fake Geek Girl," *Comics Alliance*, November 15, 2012.

125   "the false notion of limited" . . . Drea Letamendi, "The Psychology of the Fake Geek Girl: Why We're Threatened by Falsified Fandom," *The Mary Sue*, December 21, 2012.

126   "pretentious females who have" . . . Tara Tiger Brown, "Dear Fake Geek Girls: Please Go Away," *Forbes*, March 26, 2012.

126   "a growing chorus" . . . Joe Peacock, "Booth Babes Need Not Apply," *CNN Geek Out*, July 24, 2012.

126   "so sick and tired" . . . Archived in Donna Dickens, "Comic Book Illustrator Tony Harris Hates Women (Cosplayers)," *BuzzFeed*, November 13, 2012.

126   sexually harassed by aggressive . . . Andrea Romano, "Cosplay Is Not Consent: The People Fighting Sexual Harassment at Comic Con," *Mashable*, October 15, 2014.

126   "6 of 9" . . . Peacock, "Booth Babes."

127   "Some of us are aware" . . . Dickens, "Comic Book Illustrator."

127   "Cosplay is not consent" . . . Romano, "Cosplay Is Not Consent."

128   "If you have, like me" . . . Albert Ching, "EXCLUSIVE: Geoff Johns Details 'Rebirth' Plan, Seeks to Restore Legacy to DC Universe," *Comic Book Resources*, February 18, 2016.

128   The cover showed Jessica . . . *Spider-Woman* #1 (January 2015).

128   an homage to one of . . . *Penthouse Comix* #17 (November 1996).

128   "I honestly don't know" . . . Jill Pantozzi, "Marvel, This Is When You Send an Artist Back to the Drawing Board," *The Mary Sue*, August 19, 2014.

128   "You have my word" . . . Dennis Hopeless (@HopelessDent), "@PositivelyB I don't have any input . . . ," Twitter, August 20, 2014.

128   "his body of work" . . . Tom Brevoort, "Well, I think a couple . . . ," *New Brevoort Formspring*, August 21, 2014.

128   "a false controversy" . . . Dan Slott (@DanSlott), "Shame on certain gossip sites . . . ," Twitter, August 20, 2014.

128   "for the mixed messaging" . . . Axel Alonso, "The Mixed Message of Manara's 'Spider-Woman' Variant, Reason for No 'Big Hero 6' Plans," *Comic Book Resources*, August 29, 2014.

129   **Manara's original artwork** . . . Samuel Gelman, "Milo Manara's Controversial Spider-Woman Cover Just Sold for over $37K," *Comic Book Resources*, October 15, 2020.

129   **"The cover was not seen"** . . . Albert Ching, "DC Comics Cancels 'Batgirl' Joker Variant Cover at Artist's Request," *Comic Book Resources*, March 16, 2015.

129   **false memory implanted** . . . *Batgirl* #49 (May 2016).

129   **pull up her skintight** . . . *Heroes in Crisis* #4 (March 2019).

129   **the "Joker War" event** . . . Began with *Batgirl* #47 (September 2020).

129   **Barbara flashing back** . . . *Batman: Three Jokers* #1 (October 2020).

130   **"ALL ages, gender identities"** . . . "About Us," Geek Girl Con.

130   **Jamie McKelvie's flight suit** . . . Patrick A. Reed, "This Woman, This Warrior: Celebrating Carol Danvers, Captain Marvel," *Comics Alliance*, December 12, 2016.

130   **"Carol falls down all the"** . . . Susana Polo, "Captain Marvel, Explained by the People Who Reimagined Her," *Polygon*, December 4, 2018.

130   **DeConnick provided merchandise** . . . Melissa Leon, "How Kelly Sue DeConnick Made 'C-List' Captain Marvel the Most Powerful Superhero in Hollywood," *The Daily Beast*, December 20, 2018.

130   **"No one gets to"** . . . Alex Abad-Santos, "Meet the Woman Who's Taking On the Sexism of the Comic Book Industry and Winning," *Vox*, October 13, 2014.

130   **hit the top of the list** . . . Heidi MacDonald, "Ms. Marvel Is Marvel's '#1 Digital Seller,'" *The Beat*, November 4, 2014.

132   **sales of over half a million** . . . Rich Johnston, "Ms. Marvel Has Sold Half a Million Trade Paperbacks," *Bleeding Cool*, August 31, 2018.

Chapter 13: Pride

133   **"disruptive behaviors such as"** . . . American Psychological Association, *APA Guidelines for Psychological Practice with Boys and Men*, August 2018.

134   **"A Very Personal Hell"** . . . *Hulk* #23 (October 1980).

134   **allegedly instituted a policy** . . . Andy Mangels, "Out of the Closet and into the Comics—Part 1," *Amazing Heroes* 143 (June 15, 1988): 39–54.

134   **John Byrne intended** . . . Mike Avila, "How Northstar Helped Make Comics History as Marvel's First Gay Character," *SYFY Wire*, June 4, 2021.

134   **Arnie Roth was very fond** . . . *Captain America* #268 (April 1982).

134   **Storm and Yukio** . . . Met in *Uncanny X-Men* #172 (August 1983).

134   **Mystique and Destiny's** . . . First appeared together in *Uncanny X-Men* #141 (January 1981).

134   **Extraño** . . . Debuted in *Millennium* #2 (January 1988).

134   **"I am gay!"** . . . *Alpha Flight* #106 (March 1992).

134   **Terry Berg was gay** . . . Came out in *Green Lantern* #137 (June 2001).

134   **Lee and Li** . . . Debuted in *Green Lantern* #69 (December 1995).

134   **Supergirl's friend Andy Jones** . . . Came out in *Supergirl* #26 (October 1998).

134   **Holly Robinson** . . . Came out in *Catwoman* #6 (June 2002).

134   **Maggie Sawyer** . . . Came out in *Superman* #15 (March 1988).

134   **Renee Montoya . . .** Outed in *Gotham Central* #6 (June 2003).

134   **Terry nearly beaten . . .** *Green Lantern* #154 (November 2002).

134   **"roommate" Michael died . . .** *Captain America* #279 (March 1983).

134   **Destiny was killed off . . .** *Uncanny X-Men* #255 (December 1989).

134   **Extraño contracted AIDS . . .** *New Guardians* #1 (September 1988).

134   **Northstar was stabbed . . .** *Wolverine* #25 (April 2005).

135   **"we've had more gay" . . .** Brian Cronin, "Comic Book Legends Revealed #213," *Comic Book Resources*, June 25, 2009.

135   **Freedom Ring was killed . . .** *Marvel Team-Up* #24 (November 2006).

135   **revealed their romance . . .** *The Authority* #8 (December 1999).

135   **proper kiss was . . .** *Jenny Sparks: The Secret History of the Authority* #2 (September 2000).

135   **Levitz vetoed the artwork . . .** Rich Johnston, "When DC Comics Censored a Kiss between Apollo and Midnighter," *Bleeding Cool*, April 6, 2017.

135   **when they got married . . .** *The Authority* #29 (July 2002).

135   **"a sharp dresser" . . .** *Rawhide Kid* #1 (April 2003).

135   **"Ugh, niiiiightmare" . . .** *Rawhide Kid* #2 (May 2003).

135   **Quesada faced questions . . .** "Joe Fridays: Week 37," *Newsarama*, February 10, 2006.

135   **"More on that" . . .** *Young Avengers* #2 (May 2005).

135   **"tired of seeing heterosexual" . . .** Ibid.

135   **"For once, I'd like" . . .** Ibid.

135   **"If something like that" . . .** *Young Avengers* #3 (June 2005).

136   **"couldn't agree with" . . .** *Young Avengers* #2 (May 2005).

136   **"Now, I'm not some" . . .** *Young Avengers* #3 (June 2005).

136   **fan did later reply . . .** *Young Avengers* #5 (August 2005).

136   **"Due to the very" . . .** *Young Avengers* #6 (September 2005).

136   **"We are constantly" . . .** Ibid.

136   **"I am anti-homosexuality" . . .** *Young Avengers* #7 (October 2005).

136   **ordered an art gallery . . .** Lester Haines, "DC Comics Takes Big Stick to Gay Batman," *The Register*, August 23, 2005.

137   **"buxom lipstick lesbian" . . .** George Gene Gustines, "Straight (and Not) out of the Comics," *New York Times*, May 28, 2006.

137   ***Batwoman* series was abandoned . . .** D. M. Grant, "TBU Exclusive: Devin Grayson on Her Batman Universe Work," *The Batman Universe*, May 20, 2014.

137   **debuted in the pages . . .** *52* #7 (August 2006).

137   **she finally took over . . .** *Detective Comics* #854 (August 2009).

137   **quitting the book . . .** Steve Morris, "JH Williams III and W. Haden Blackman Quit Batwoman over Editorial Interference," *The Beat*, September 5, 2013.

137   **Catwoman was bisexual . . .** *Catwoman* #39 (April 2015).

139   **confirming a past relationship . . .** *Wonder Woman* #12 (February 2017).

139   **two women eventually became . . .** While writers confirmed they were in a relationship in 2015, Harley and Ivy kissed for the first time in canon in *Harley Quinn* #25 (October 2017).

139   **duo's miniseries ended . . .** *Harley Quinn & Poison Ivy* #6 (April 2020).

139   **"first official statue"** . . . Kelly Knox, "Harley and Ivy Make a Lovely Pair in New DC Collectible Statue," *Nerdist*, February 7, 2020.

139   **"the epitome of what"** . . . Amanda Levine, "A Leafy Kind of Love: DC Collectibles Celebrates Harley and Ivy," *DC Comics*, February 14, 2020.

139   **married his boyfriend** . . . *Astonishing X-Men* #51 (August 2012).

139   **Hercules was shown** . . . *X-Treme X-Men* #9 (March 2013).

139   **"took place in a unique"** . . . Axel Alonso, "Course-Correcting Diversity Problems, Bendis' Iron Man Expansion," *Comic Book Resources*, July 31, 2015.

139   **teen Bobby was gay** . . . *All-New X-Men* #40 (June 2015).

139   **his adult counterpart** . . . *Uncanny X-Men* #600 (January 2016).

139   **took issue with Bobby's** . . . Alenka Figa, "In Plain Sight: On the Authenticity of Queer Characters," *Women Write about Comics*, June 8, 2015.

140   **subsequent *Iceman* miniseries** . . . Began with *Iceman* #1 (August 2017).

140   **"too gay"** . . . Sina Grace, "As Pride Month Comes to a . . . ," *Sina Grace* (Tumblr blog), June 28, 2019.

140   **Shvaughn Erin** . . . *Legion of Super-Heroes* #31 (July 1992).

140   **Jessie Drake** . . . *Marvel Comics Presents* #150 (March 1994).

140   ***Doom Patrol*** . . . Kate Godwin/Coagula debuted in *Doom Patrol* #70 (September 1993).

140   ***Invisibles*** . . . Lord Fanny debuted in *The Invisibles* #2 (October 1994).

140   ***Sandman*** . . . Wanda in *Sandman* #32 (November 1991).

140   **introduced Alysia Yeoh** . . . *Batgirl* #1 (November 2011).

140   **"the first non-fantasy-based"** . . . Gail Simone, "Erasing other characters like this . . . ," *Ape in a Cape* (Tumblr blog), April 10, 2013.

140   **consulted with trans** . . . Chris Spargo, "'Batgirl' Exclusive: Writer Gail Simone Talks New Transgender Character," *NewNowNext*, April 10, 2013.

140   **Her coming-out scene** . . . *Batgirl* #19 (June 2013).

140   **She planned for Alysia** . . . Gail Simone, "About That Alysia News Thingie," *Ape in a Cape* (Tumblr blog), April 15, 2015.

140   **"soundly rejected"** . . . Gail Simone, "I did pitch Alysia . . . ," *Ape in a Cape* (Tumblr blog), April 14, 2015.

140   **"the idea was turned"** . . . Simone, "About That Alysia News."

141   **Commissioner Gordon took over** . . . *Batman* #41 (August 2015).

141   **pre–New 52 Superman** . . . *Action Comics* #976 (May 2017).

141   **Alysia got to be a Batgirl** . . . *DC Comics Bombshells* #7 (February 2016).

141   **Koi Boi** . . . Debuted in *Unbeatable Squirrel Girl* #2 (February 2015).

141   **Sera** . . . Debuted in *Angela: Asgard's Assassin* #1 (December 2014).

141   **Tong** . . . Debuted in *Fantastic Four* #575 (January 2010), came out in *FF* #6 (June 2013).

141   **Porcelain** . . . Debuted in *Secret Six* #1 (February 2015).

141   **Lee Serano** . . . Debuted in *Supergirl* #19 (May 2018).

141   **Nia Nal, a.k.a. Dreamer** . . . Debuted in "American Alien," *Supergirl*, season 4, episode 1, directed by Jesse Warn (Warner Bros., 2018).

141   **cowrote a story** . . . "Date Night," *DC Pride* #1 (August 2021).

141 *Black Panther* **filmed a scene** . . . Joanna Robinson, "Black Panther Footage Reveals the Ferocious Female Warriors of Wakanda," *Vanity Fair*, April 18, 2017.

141 **"shipping" of Steve Rogers** . . . Kaila Hale-Stern, "Steve Rogers/Bucky Barnes Is the Most Popular MCU Ship Ever," *The Mary Sue*, April 22, 2019.

141 **"She's a woman who loves"** . . . Brent Land, "Gal Gadot Dishes on the New 'Wonder Woman' Film," *Variety*, October 11, 2016.

142 **supposed fans were outraged** . . . Clyde Hughes, "Batwoman's a Lesbian Now, Played by Ruby Rose," *Newsmax*, August 8, 2018.

142 **it was review bombed** . . . Paul Tassi, "'Batwoman' Is Getting IMDB and Rotten Tomato Review Bombed for Its Lesbian Lead," *Forbes*, October 9, 2019.

Chapter 14: Supremacy

143 **killed off in 1996** . . . *The Final Night* #4 (November 1996).

143 **became the new Green Lantern** . . . Debuted in *Green Lantern* #48 (January 1994).

143 **Hal was resurrected** . . . *Green Lantern: Rebirth* #1 (December 2004).

143 **Barry Allen a.k.a. the Flash** . . . *The Flash: Rebirth* #1 (June 2009).

143 **Barry had died** . . . *Crisis on Infinite Earths* #8 (November 1985).

143 **Wally West, took over** . . . *Crisis on Infinite Earths* #12 (March 1986).

143 **Wally was reinvented** . . . *The Flash Annual* #3 (June 2014).

144 **brought back the classic Wally** . . . *DC Universe: Rebirth* #1 (June 2016).

145 **first comic with a Black female lead** . . . Would have debuted in *The Vixen* #1 (November 1978) but the book was canceled. Later debuted in *Action Comics* #521 (July 1981).

145 **"Worlds Collide" event** . . . Began in *Superman: The Man of Steel* #35 (July 1994).

145 **Milestone's Shadow Cabinet** . . . *Justice League of America* #27 (January 2009).

145 **more aliens than people of color** . . . Based on my own count, tabulated from a handful of issues from the start of 1965, 1975, 1985, 1995, 2005, and 2015.

145 **Vibe and Vixen** . . . *Justice League of America Annual* #2 (October 1984).

145 **Mantis did join the team** . . . *Avengers* #112 (June 1973).

145 **Baz became a Green Lantern** . . . Debuted in *The New 52 Free Comic Book Day Special Edition* #1 (May 2012).

145 **Khalid Nassour** . . . Debuted in *Doctor Fate* #1 (June 2015).

145 **technopathic mutant Trinary** . . . Debuted in *X-Men: Red* #2 (May 2018).

145 **proper, non-superheroic name** . . . Ritesh Babu, "Trinary & the Aesthetics of Representation," *ComicsXF*, May 17, 2021.

146 **X-Men's Dani Moonstar** . . . Debuted in *The New Mutants* (September 1982).

146 **Apache Chief** . . . Debuted in "The Antidote," *The All-New Super Friends Hour*, season 2, episode 2, directed by Charles A. Nichols (Warner Bros., 1977).

146 **Cree hero Equinox** . . . Debuted in *Justice League United* #9 (June 2014).

146 **Red Wolf** . . . Series began with *Red Wolf* #1 (February 2016).

146   I Ching taught martial . . . Debuted in *Wonder Woman* #179 (December 1968).

146   O-Sensei . . . Debuted in *Richard Dragon, Kung-Fu Fighter* #1 (May 1975).

146   the Ancient One . . . Debuted in *Strange Tales* #110 (April 1963).

146   placed in the body of Kwannon . . . Debuted in *Uncanny X-Men* #256 (December 1989), though the full story wasn't revealed until *X-Men* #32 (May 1994).

147   two were finally separated . . . *Hunt for Wolverine: Mystery in Madripoor* #4 (October 2008).

147   "sexy-ninja" costume . . . Wendy Browne, "The Re-re-invention of Psylocke," *Women Write about Comics*, August 27, 2018.

147   a variant cover for a new *Joker* . . . *Joker* #1 (May 2021).

147   the fictional Sian Cong War . . . Rosie Knight, "Mark Waid Crafted the Fake Siancong War to Keep Marvel Characters Young . . . and It's Even Worse Than It Sounds," *Women Write about Comics*, September 17, 2019.

147   "Akira Yoshida" . . . Asher Elbein, "The Secret Identity of Marvel Comics' Editor," *The Atlantic*, December 17, 2017.

147   Robbie Reyes . . . Debuted in *All-New Ghost Rider* #1 (March 2014).

147   Sam Alexander . . . Debuted in *Marvel Point One* #1 (November 2011).

147   Jaime Reyes . . . Debuted in *Infinite Crisis* #3 (February 2006).

147   Jessica Cruz . . . Debuted in *Justice League* #30 (July 2014).

148   Catwoman . . . Revealed as Latina in *Catwoman* #81 (June 2000).

148   Lois Lane . . . *Superman: Lois Lane* #1 (April 2014) strongly implied her mother was Latina, and Lois is Cuban American in the "Bombshells" universe, *DC Comics Bombshells* #13 (July 2016).

148   Brazilian Yara Flor . . . Debuted in *Dark Knights: Death Metal* #7 (March 2021).

148   Miles Morales . . . Debuted in *Ultimate Fallout* #4 (August 2011).

148   his own solo title . . . Began with *Spider-Man* #1 (April 2016).

148   "disgraceful" . . . Comment on Germaine Lussier, "Marvel Introduces Half-Black, Half-Hispanic Spider-Man: Miles Morales," *SlashFilm*, August 2, 2011.

148   "straight white male bashing" . . . Ibid.

148   "This is a brilliant" . . . Comment on Rob Richards, "The New Ultimate Spider-Man Identity Revealed," *iFanboy*, August 2, 2011.

148   "It really seems as if" . . . Comment on Daniel Bates, "Marvel Comics Reveals the New Spider Man Is Black—and He Could Be Gay in the Future," *Daily Mail*, August 3, 2011.

148   "These guys believe something" . . . Dave Gibson, "You Can't Understand White Supremacists without Looking at Masculinity," *Mother Jones*, July 2018.

148   Sam Wilson took over the role . . . *Captain America* #25 (December 2014).

148   "disgustingly cynical" . . . Comments on Kwame Opam, "Marvel Is Replacing Steve Rogers with the New, Black Captain America," *The Verge*, July 16, 2014.

149   teen genius Riri Williams . . . Took over for Stark in *Invincible Iron Man* #1 (January 2017).

149   **"feels like racism"** . . . Comments on Abraham Riesman, "Geeks Are Angry about Iron Man Becoming a Black Girl—but Not for the Reason You'd Think," *Vulture*, July 7, 2016.

149   **"Any character that was diverse"** . . . Milton Griepp, "Marvel's David Gabriel on the 2016 Market Shift," *ICv2*, March 31, 2017.

149   **criticized by fans of color** . . . Alex Abad-Santos, "The Biggest Drama in Comic Books Right Now Is over Spider-Man and Race," *Vox*, March 7, 2016.

149   **"failed replacement for Steve"** . . . Vishal Gullapalli, "My Secret History with Secret Empire: Looking Back at Nick Spencer's Captain America," *ComicsXF*, March 11, 2021.

149   **Artistic depictions of Riri Williams** . . . Olivia Stephens, "Mantles, Crowns, and Knowledge: What RiRi Williams Needs," *Women Write about Comics*, August 22, 2016.

149   **"SJW [social justice warrior] whine-fest"** . . . J. Scott Campbell (@JScott Campbell), "Ha! Nope, Nope. Sitting this . . . ," Twitter, October 19, 2016.

150   **Michael B. Jordan was announced** . . . Mannie Holmes, "Michael B. Jordan on 'Fantastic Four' Casting Backlash: I'll 'Shoulder All This Hate,'" *Variety*, May 22, 2015.

150   **Candice Patton, who plays** . . . Jahkotta Lewis, "Candice Patton Ignores the Trolls and Focuses on the Importance of Representation," *Black Girl Nerds*, April 6, 2018.

150   **"Nobody cares about Chinese"** . . . Akhil Arora, "Marvel Television Head Didn't Care about Asian Characters, Daredevil Actor Says," *Gadgets 360*, July 27, 2020.

150   **"gross, abusive, unprofessional"** . . . Ray Fisher (@ray8fisher), "Joss Wheadon's on-set treatment . . . ," Twitter, July 1, 2020.

152   **"It was like he was"** . . . Kim Masters, "Ray Fisher Opens Up about 'Justice League,' Joss Whedon and Warners: 'I Don't Believe Some of These People Are Fit for Leadership,'" *The Hollywood Reporter*, April 6, 2021.

152   **"played differently"** . . . Ibid.

152   **"the problem isn't so much"** . . . David F. Walker (@DavidWalker1201), "I'll say this one more . . . ," Twitter, April 9, 2021.

Chapter 15: Assemble

153   **Lynda Carter debuted** . . . *The New Original Wonder Woman*, directed by Leonard Horn (Warner Bros., 1975).

153   **live-action versions of Batman** . . . Michael Keaton in *Batman*, Val Kilmer in *Batman Forever*, George Clooney in *Batman & Robin*, Christian Bale in *Batman Begins*, David Mazouz in *Gotham*, and Ben Affleck in *Batman v Superman: Dawn of Justice*.

153   **seven of Superman** . . . Christopher Reeve in *Superman*, John Haymes Newton and Gerard Christopher in *Superboy*, Dean Cain in *Lois & Clark: The New Adventures of Superman*, Tom Welling in *Smallville*, Brandon Routh in *Superman Returns*, and Henry Cavill in *Man of Steel*.

153   **first blockbuster superhero** . . . *Superman*, directed by Richard Donner (Warner Bros., 1978).

153   largely left out of *Superman III* . . . Nathan Rabin, "Random Roles: Margot Kidder," *AV Club*, March 3, 2009.

154   Vicki Vale . . . *Batman*, directed by Tim Burton (Warner Bros., 1989).

154   Selina Kyle . . . *Batman Returns*, directed by Tim Burton (Warner Bros., 1992).

154   Chase Meridian . . . *Batman Forever*, directed by Joel Schumacher (Warner Bros., 1995).

154   Julie Madison . . . *Batman & Robin*, directed by Joel Schumacher (Warner Bros., 1997).

154   first superhero hit of the 2000s . . . *X-Men*, directed by Bryan Singer (20th Century Fox, 2000).

154   Jean eventually killed in a half-hearted . . . *X-Men: The Last Stand*, directed by Brett Ratner (20th Century Fox, 2006).

154   a revamped franchise . . . Began with *X-Men: First Class*, directed by Matthew Vaughn (20th Century Fox, 2011).

154   removed Kitty Pryde . . . *X-Men: Days of Future Past*, directed by Bryan Singer (20th Century Fox, 2014).

154   killed Jean again . . . *Dark Phoenix*, directed by Simon Kinberg (20th Century Fox, 2019).

154   Katie Holmes . . . *Batman Begins*, directed by Christopher Nolan (Warner Bros., 2005).

154   Maggie Gyllenhaal . . . *The Dark Knight*, directed by Christopher Nolan (Warner Bros., 2008).

154   While the third . . . *The Dark Knight Rises*, directed by Christopher Nolan (Warner Bros., 2012).

155   *Catwoman* starred Halle Berry . . . *Catwoman*, directed by Pitof (Warner Bros., 2004).

155   inherited a convoluted script . . . Tim Hanley, *Many Lives of Catwoman: The Felonious History of a Feline Fatale* (Chicago: Chicago Review Press, 2017), 169.

155   *Elektra*, a *Daredevil* spin-off . . . *Elektra*, directed by Rob Bowman (Marvel, 2005).

155   Garner wasn't keen . . . Bernardo Sim, "15 Things You Never Knew about the Disastrous Elektra Movie," *ScreenRant*, August 18, 2017.

155   "very, very bad" . . . Jason Bailey, "Leaked Sony Email Confirms Marvel's Just as Clueless about 'Female Movies' as You Thought," *Flavor Wire*, May 5, 2015.

155   Pepper Potts . . . Debuted in *Iron Man*, directed by Jon Favreau (Marvel, 2008).

155   Betty Ross . . . Debuted in *The Incredible Hulk*, directed by Louis Leterrier (Marvel, 2008).

155   Jane Foster . . . Debuted in *Thor*, directed by Kenneth Branagh (Marvel, 2011).

155   Peggy Carter . . . Debuted in *Captain America: The First Avenger*, directed by Joe Johnston (Marvel, 2011).

155   Natasha Romanoff . . . *Avengers*, directed by Joss Whedon (Marvel, 2012).

155   Gamora . . . *Guardians of the Galaxy*, directed by James Gunn (Marvel, 2014).

155   Wanda Maximoff . . . *Avengers: Age of Ultron*, directed by Joss Whedon (Marvel, 2015).

155   **Mantis . . .** *Guardians of the Galaxy Vol. 2*, directed by James Gunn (Marvel, 2017).

155   **Hope van Dyne . . .** Debuted in *Ant-Man*, directed by Peyton Reed (Marvel, 2015).

155   **Christine Palmer . . .** Debuted in *Doctor Strange*, directed by Scott Derrickson (Marvel, 2016).

155   ***Black Panther* in 2018 . . .** *Black Panther*, directed by Ryan Coogler (Marvel, 2018).

157   **Hope became the first . . .** *Ant-Man and the Wasp*, directed by Peyton Reed (Marvel, 2018).

157   **Brie Larson's Carol Danvers . . .** *Captain Marvel*, directed by Anna Boden and Ryan Fleck (Marvel, 2019).

157   **Marvel tried to play homage . . .** *Avengers: Endgame*, directed by Anthony and Joe Russo (Marvel, 2019).

157   **some found the scene empowering . . .** Vivian Kane, "Let's Talk about *Avengers: Endgame*'s Big Moment of Pandering/Female Empowerment," *The Mary Sue*, May 2, 2019.

157   **"glaringly patronizing" . . .** Caroline Siede, "*Avengers: Endgame* Doesn't Earn Its Big 'Girl Power' Moment," *AV Club*, April 29, 2019.

157   **Marvel's first solo female director . . .** *Black Widow*, directed by Cate Shortland (Marvel, 2021).

157   **debuted as a side character . . .** *Iron Man 2*, directed by Jon Favreau (Marvel, 2010).

157   **"While it was really" . . .** Ashley Robinson, "Scarlett Johansson on the Sexualization of Natasha Romanoff and Why It Took 10 Years to Make 'Black Widow,'" *Collider*, June 15, 2021.

157   **"They sterilize you" . . .** *Avengers: Age of Ultron* (2015).

158   **infertility was in some . . .** Emily VanDerWerff, "A guide to the Growing Controversy over Joss Whedon's Avengers and Marvel's Gender Problem," *Vox*, May 11, 2015.

158   **"they chose to get" . . .** Krystal Clark and Tara Bennett, "How Avengers: Age of Ultron Dropped the Ball with Black Widow," *Blastr*, June 25, 2015.

158   **Black Widow was ultimately killed . . .** *Avengers: Endgame* (2019).

158   **Steve, Thor, and Tony all clashed . . .** *Avengers* (2012).

158   **Steve and Tony's issues continued . . .** *Captain America: Civil War*, directed by Anthony and Joe Russo (Marvel, 2016).

158   **This rift remained . . .** *Avengers: Infinity War*, directed by Joe and Anthony Russo (Marvel, 2018).

158   **Tony's fury at Steve . . .** *Avengers: Endgame* (2019).

158   **audience for Marvel . . .** Joe Comicbook, "Guardians of the Galaxy Had Highest Percentage of Female Viewers of Any Marvel Studios Movie," *Comic Book*, September 1, 2016.

158   **male fans were incensed . . .** Melissa Leon, "How Brie Larson's 'Captain Marvel' Made Angry White Men Lose Their Damn Minds," *The Daily Beast*, March 6, 2019.

158   **didn't smile enough . . .** Sarah El-Mahmoud, "Captain Marvel's Brie Larson Clapped Back at Haters Telling Her to Smile," *Cinema Blend*, September 22, 2018.

158   **"decided to make sure"** . . . Keah Brown, "Brie Larson on Superheroes, Success and Her Hollywood Sisterhood," *Marie Claire*, February 7, 2019.

158   **"more seats up to"** . . . Kate Gardner, "Brie Larson Shouldn't Have to Clarify Her Comments about the *Captain Marvel* Press Tour," *The Mary Sue*, February 22, 2019.

159   **"Brie had to come out"** . . . Comments saved in David Pountain, "Internet Trolls Trying to Sabotage Captain Marvel's Rotten Tomatoes Score," *We Got This Covered*, January 8, 2019.

159   **Rotten Tomatoes to change their policy** . . . David Sims, "A Change for Rotten Tomatoes ahead of *Captain Marvel*," *The Atlantic*, March 4, 2019.

159   **Monica made their debut** . . . *WandaVision*, created by Jac Schaeffer (Marvel, 2021).

159   **a wealth of female characters** . . . *Eternals*, directed by Chloé Zhao (Marvel, 2021).

159   **starting with Zack Snyder's** . . . *Man of Steel*, directed by Zack Snyder (Warner Bros., 2013).

159   **brought their two biggest** . . . *Batman v Superman: Dawn of Justice*, directed by Zack Snyder (Warner Bros., 2016).

159   **"the thirstiest young woman"** . . . *Justice League*, directed by Zack Snyder (Warner Bros, 2017).

160   **"It's time you learn"** . . . Warner Bros. Pictures, "Batman v Superman: Dawn of Justice—Official Trailer 2 [HD]," YouTube, December 3, 2015.

160   **"Wonder Woman is meant"** . . . Corrye Van Caeseele-Cook, "WTF Hollywood??? Why Casting Gal Gadot as Wonder Woman Is a Horrible Idea," *Funk's House of Geekery*, December 7, 2013.

160   **"She's not drop dead gorgeous"** . . . Ibid.

160   **"Isn't Wonder Woman supposed"** . . . Comment on Bryan Bishop, "Gal Gadot Cast as Wonder Woman in 'Batman vs. Superman,'" *The Verge*, December 4, 2013.

160   **starred in her own solo** . . . *Wonder Woman*, directed by Patty Jenkins (Warner Bros., 2017).

160   **traumatic mass rape backstory** . . . Perri Nemiroff, "'Wonder Woman': Connie Nielsen Explains How Patty Jenkins Stopped the Amazons' Original, Traumatic Origin Story," *Collider*, March 12, 2021.

160   **arguing for the inclusion** . . . Erik Davis, "'Wonder Woman' Director Patty Jenkins on How the Film's Most Memorable Scene Almost Didn't Happen," *Fandango*, May 31, 2017.

160   **"a really great"** . . . Kimi, "The Amazons' New Clothes," *Golden Lasso*, November 11, 2017.

160   **Gadot refused to film** . . . Grace Randolph (@GraceRandolph), "I doubt we'll ever get . . . ," Twitter, July 1, 2020.

161   **Margot Robbie's Harley** . . . *Suicide Squad*, directed by David Ayer (Warner Bros., 2016).

161   **Amber Heard's Mera** . . . *Aquaman*, directed by James Wan (Warner Bros., 2018).

161   **mainly on Billy and Freddy** . . . *Shazam!*, directed by David F. Sandberg (Warner Bros., 2019).

161   *Joker* was a tedious . . . *Joker*, directed by Todd Phillips (Warner Bros., 2019).

161   **Robbie produced the film** . . . *Birds of Prey*, directed by Cathy Yan (Warner Bros., 2020).

162   **"loose-fitting t-shirt"** . . . Ciara Wardlow, "How 'Birds of Prey' Deconstructs the Male Gaze," *The Hollywood Reporter*, February 8, 2020.

162   **"They've removed any sex appeal"** . . . Matthew Kadish (@MatthewKadish), "You know why #BirdsOfPrey is going . . . ," Twitter, January 25, 2020.

162   **"These movies are appealing"** . . . Jar Jar Abrams (@JarJarAbramss), "Hollywood is hiring feminist writers . . . ," Twitter, January 26, 2020.

162   **targeted bullying** . . . Alex Abad-Santos, "The Fight to #ReleaseTheSnyderCut of Justice League (Which May Not Even Exist), Explained," *Vox*, December 4, 2019.

162   **an additional $70 million** . . . Graeme Guttman, "Justice League Snyder Cut's Budget Is Reportedly $70 Million," *ScreenRant*, September 23, 2020.

163   **firing of nearly half** . . . Graeme McMillan and Borys Kit, "DC Comics, DC Universe Hit by Major Layoffs," *The Hollywood Reporter*, August 10, 2020.

163   **#RestoreTheSnyderverse** . . . Brad Curran, "#RestoreTheSnyderVerse Campaign Reaches over 1 Million Tweets," *ScreenRant*, March 25, 2021.

Chapter 16: Power

165   **"With great power there must"** . . . *Amazing Fantasy* #15 (September 1962).

165   **"Because of these great powers"** . . . "Superman Comes to Earth," *Superman*, part 1, directed by Spencer Gordon Bennet and Thomas Carr (Columbia, 1948).

165   **Nathan Edmondson** . . . Brett Schenker, "On Nathan Edmondson, Marvel, and the Cycle of Harassment," *Graphic Policy*, September 10, 2015.

165   **Warren Ellis** . . . Adi Robertson, "Warren Ellis Abused Star Power in Fan Relationships, Say Dozens of Women," *The Verge*, July 13, 2020.

165   **Max Landis** . . . Gene Maddaus, "Max Landis Accused of Rape, Assault and Psychological Abuse," *Variety*, June 18, 2019.

165   **Jason Latour** . . . Joe Grunenwald, "Multiple Women Accuse SPIDER-GWEN Co-creator Jason Latour of Misconduct," *The Beat*, June 23, 2020.

165   **Scott Lobdell** . . . Joe Grunenwald, "New Allegations against Scott Lobdell Surface after RED HOOD Departure Announcement," *The Beat*, June 30, 2020.

165   **Cameron Stewart** . . . Joe Grunenwald, "Multiple Women Accuse Cameron Stewart of Sexual Misconduct," *The Beat*, June 16, 2020.

165   **Brian Wood** . . . Kayleigh Hearn, "Tess Fowler, Brian Wood, and Harassment in the Comic Industry," *Women Write about Comics*, November 15, 2013.

165   **Eddie Berganza** . . . Jay Edidin, Tyler Kingkade, and Jessica Testa, "The Comics Giant behind Wonder Woman Is Accused of Promoting an Editor after Women Accused Him of Sexual Harassment," *BuzzFeed*, November 10, 2017.

165   **Mike Carlin** . . . Duna Haller and Travis Hedge Coke, "The Sounds of Silence: CBLDF and Systemic Toxicity in Comics," *Comicwatch*, June 25, 2020.

165   **Scott Allie** . . . Janelle Asselin, "Enough Is Enough: Dark Horse's Scott Allie's Assaulting Behavior," *Graphic Policy*, October 1, 2015.

166   **"testosterone pileup"** . . . Gwynne Watkins, "The Woman Who Made Aquaman a Star," *Vulture*, September 24, 2018.

166   **"for fear they'd all start"** . . . Jim Amash, "'It Was a Daily Identity Crisis,'" *Alter Ego* 69 (June 2007): 38.

166   **"there was one jerk"** . . . Watkins, "The Woman Who Made Aquaman."

166   **"regularly greeted me"** . . . Heidi MacDonald, "How a Toxic History of Harassment Has Damaged the Comics Industry," *The Beat*, October 1, 2015.

166   **"I became an expert"** . . . Comment on Aria Baci, "A Brief Timeline of Harassment and Sexual Assault in the Comics Industry," *The Mary Sue*, November 29, 2017.

166   **"His talent for charming"** . . . Michael Dean, "Two Sides of Julie the Ladies' Man," *Comics Journal* 259 (April 2004): 22.

166   **"If you wanted to find"** . . . Mark Evanier, "More Schwartz," *News from Me*, February 8, 2004.

166   **"the biggest flirt"** . . . Doug Zawisza, "James Robinson Interview," *Hawkman Companion* (Raleigh, NC: TwoMorrows, 2008), 157.

166   **"he told me in"** . . . Dean, "Two Sides of Julie."

166   **Thompson reported a comparable** . . . Ibid.

167   **"offered to help her"** . . . Ibid.

167   **"hands [were] practically"** . . . Ibid.

167   **"He grabbed me"** . . . Ibid.

167   **"literally had to pull him"** . . . Ronee Garcia Bourgeois, "What a Girl Wants #14—The Tit Grab Heard 'round the World (Part 1)," *Pop Culture Shock*, January 1, 2008.

167   **"My career at the"** . . . Ibid.

167   **"sexually confused"** . . . Valerie D'Orazio, *Memoirs of an Occasional Superheroine* (self-pub., 2009), 82.

167   **None of the nearly** . . . Numbers based on my own count of the credits for all of the issues.

167   **Black assistant editors** . . . See Rich Johnston, "Talking with Joe Illidge about DC Comics," *Comics Bulletin*, and Travis Clark, "Two Black Former DC Comics Editors Describe the Career Obstacles They Faced," *Business Insider*, October 28, 2020.

168   **D'Orazio joined DC** . . . This account comes from D'Orazio, *Memoirs*, and Valerie D'Orazio, *Valerie D'Orazio's Chronology for Working at DC Comics/Time Warner*, https://www.dropbox.com/s/5x6ba4gx5rdbpa0/Chronology.pdf?dl=0.

168   **"very loud, insulting"** . . . D'Orazio, *Memoirs*, 89.

168   **"been blackballed, fired"** . . . D'Orazio, *Chronology*, 13.

168   **rumors of internal human** . . . All incidents in this paragraph are cited in Edidin, Kingkade, and Testa, "The Comics Giant Behind."

168   **writer Greg Rucka** . . . Caitlin Rosberg, "DC Has Finally Fired Eddie Berganza—but Abuse and Harassment Go Much Deeper in the Tight-Knit Comics Industry," *AV Club*, November 14, 2017.

169   **a lengthy article on *BuzzFeed*** . . . Edidin, Kingkade, and Testa, "The Comics Giant Behind."

169   **Asselin spoke to several . . .** Asselin, "Enough Is Enough."

169   **Writer Shawna Gore . . .** Meagan Damore, "Dark Horse Editor Scott Allie Accused of Prolonged Sexual Abuse," *Comic Book Resources*, June 24, 2020.

169   **"a non-profit organization" . . .** "About," Comic Book Legal Defense Fund, 2021.

169   **sexually assaulted cartoonist . . .** Michael Dean, "No Oversight Leads to a History of Sexual Misconduct and Bullying at the CBLDF," *Comics Journal*, July 6, 2020.

170   **Brownstein's past actions resurfaced . . .** Ibid.

170   **"hypocrite preaching feminist ideals" . . .** Kai Cole, "Joss Whedon Is a 'Hypocrite Preaching Feminist Ideals,' Ex-wife Kai Cole Says," *The Wrap*, August 20, 2017.

170   **"hostile and toxic working" . . .** Sandy Schaefer, "All the Joss Whedon Abuse & Misconduct Allegations Explained," *ScreenRant*, February 20, 2021.

170   **underage actors on his film . . .** Rebecca Ascher-Walsh, "Was an Indecent Proposal Made on Bryan Singer's *Apt Pupil* Set?" *Entertainment Weekly*, May 2, 1997.

170   **another lawsuit in 2014 . . .** Alex French and Maximillian Potter, "Nobody Is Going to Believe You," *The Atlantic*, March 2019.

170   **multiple actors accused him . . .** Brent Lang and Cynthia Littleton, "Brett Ratner Accused of Sexual Harassment or Misconduct by Six Women," *Variety*, November 1, 2017.

170   **"sexual harassment and" . . .** Maureen Ryan, "'Supergirl,' 'Arrow' Producer Suspended amid Sexual Harassment Allegations by Warner Bros.," *Variety*, November 10, 2017.

171   **"failed attempt at humor" . . .** Heidi MacDonald, "Scott Lobdell: I Apologize to MariNaomi," *The Beat*, December 19, 2013.

171   **"I'm profoundly grateful" . . .** Grunenwald, "New Allegations."

171   **artist Tess Fowler accused . . .** Hearn, "Tess Fowler, Brian Wood."

171   **"industry-wide discussion" . . .** Albert Ching, "Brian Wood Responds to Misconduct Allegations," *Comic Book Resources*, November 15, 2013.

171   **"Public shaming can be" . . .** Rich Johnston, "So, Brian Wood Put Out a Newsletter . . . ," *Bleeding Cool*, September 17, 2015.

171   **Wood has been accused . . .** Samantha Puc, "Brian Wood Accused of Sexual Misconduct (Again)," *The Beat*, August 30, 2019.

172   **"using his celebrity status" . . .** "Our Statement," *So Many of Us*, December 2020.

172   **"I have never considered" . . .** Robertson, "Warren Ellis Abused Star Power."

172   **"textbook gaslighting" . . .** Christopher Chiu-Tabet, "Warren Ellis Responds to Sexual Allegations," *Multiversity Comics*, June 19, 2020.

172   **"never abuse, harass, groom" . . .** Gavia Baker-Whitelaw, "The Comic Book Industry Is Facing Another Wave of Sexual Abuse Allegations," *Daily Dot*, June 26, 2020.

172   **female employees had to . . .** Edidin, Kingkade, and Testa, "The Comics Giant Behind."

173   **their victims reticent . . .** Nick Hanover, "A Chorus of Silence: On the Impossibility of Reporting on Chronic Abusers in Comics," *Loser City*, September 8, 2015.

Chapter 17: Instigate

175   **ascending to the highest office . . .** *Superman: Lex 2000* #1 (January 2001).

175   **intentionally patterned on bloviating . . .** Melissa Leon, "The Many Ways Donald Trump Is a Real-Life Lex Luthor," *The Daily Beast*, August 14, 2016.

175   **a cover patterned . . .** *Lex Luthor: The Unauthorized Biography* (July 1989).

175   **ended in disaster . . .** *Superman/Batman* #6 (March 2004).

175   **advised the president . . .** Michael Cavna, "Before He Was a Trump Veterans Affairs 'Shadow Ruler,' Ike Perlmutter Transformed Marvel," *Washington Post*, August 8, 2018.

176   **Captain America shields . . .** Sian Cain, "Captain America Creator's Son Hits Out at Capitol Mob's Use of Superhero Imagery," *Guardian*, January 14, 2021.

176   **flag with the president's head . . .** Tobias Hoonhout, "Woman Shot in Capitol Riot Dies," *National Review*, January 6, 2021.

176   **"MAGA: Civil War" . . .** Mallory Simon and Sara Sidner, "Decoding the Extremist Symbols and Groups at the Capitol Hill Insurrection," CNN, January 11, 2021.

176   **"Donald Trump Is the" . . .** Nate Silver, "Donald Trump Is the World's Greatest Troll," *FiveThirtyEight*, July 20, 2015.

176   **Asselin critiqued a *Teen Titans* . . .** Janelle Asselin, "Let's Talk about How Some Men Talk to Women in Comics," *Janelle Rambles*, April 14, 2014.

176   **Cain faced so much abuse . . .** Noelene Clark, "Chelsea Cain: Mockingbird Writer Receives Support after Cover Backlash," *Entertainment Weekly*, October 26, 2016.

176   **Antos posted a photo . . .** Heather Antos (@HeatherAntos), "It's the Marvel milkshake crew . . . ," Twitter, July 28, 2017.

176   **"Tumblr SJW fake geek" . . .** Parker Molloy, "Marvel Writer Harassed for Having a Milkshake with Coworkers? It's as Silly as It Sounds," *Upworthy*, July 31, 2017.

176   **"Can we just get" . . .** Tori Preston, "#MakeMineMilkshake: When Marvel & DC Both Agree You're Being an A**hole, You're Probably Being an A**hole," *Pajiba*, August 2, 2017.

177   **even DC tweeted . . .** DC (@DCComics), "Cheers @Marvel ladies . . . ," Twitter, August 1, 2017.

177   **Gamergate began in 2014 . . .** Emily VanDerWerff, "#Gamergate: Here's Why Everybody in the Video Game World Is Fighting," *Vox*, October 13, 2014.

177   **"female encroachment on a" . . .** Jessica Valenti, "Anita Sarkeesian Interview: 'The Word "Troll" Feels Too Childish. This Is Abuse,'" *Guardian*, August 29, 2015.

177   **#MoveTheNeedle . . .** Rachael Krishna, "There's an Online Harassment Campaign Underway against People Advocating for Diversity in Comics," *BuzzFeed*, March 22, 2018.

177   **"left wing monopoly" . . .** Jon Del Arroz, "The ComicsGate Grifters," *Jon Del Arroz*, June 24, 2019.

177   **"SJW Marvel Comics" . . .** Comics MATTER w/Ya Boi Zack, "SJW Marvel Comics is dying . . . and that's OK," YouTube, April 15, 2017. Channel previously known as "Diversity and Comics."

177   "Captain Marvel is everything" . . . Comics MATTER w/Ya Boi Zack, "Captain Marvel is everything wrong with SJW Marvel," YouTube, May 11, 2017.

178   "AMERICA—SJW Marvel's Hip Hop" . . . Comics MATTER w/Ya Boi Zack, "AMERICA—SJW Marvel's Hip Hop Segregation Comic," YouTube, May 15, 2017.

178   "strict gender roles" . . . Comics MATTER, "SJW Marvel Comics."

178   "weirdly angry, super serious" . . . Comics MATTER, "Captain Marvel."

178   "we're watching her" . . . Megan Fox, "Secret Facebook Page Reveals Marvel, DC Comics Writers Conspiring to Harass Comic-Con Conservatives," *PJ Media*, September 21, 2017.

178   "racist, segregationist, woke" . . . Comics MATTER, "AMERICA—SJW Marvel's."

178   before ripping the issue . . . See Comics MATTER w/Ya Boi Zack, "SJW Marvel's Hot Trash 'Heroes' like AMERICA Are Now Teaming Up With Themselves," YouTube, June 22, 2017.

178   "Which SJW Marvel Writer" . . . Comics MATTER w/Ya Boi Zack, "Which SJW Marvel Writer Is Worse? Gabby Rivera (AMERICA) or Ta-Nehisi Coates?" YouTube, July 10, 2017.

178   "man in a wig" . . . Asher Elbein, "#Comicsgate: How an Anti-diversity Harassment Campaign in Comics Got Ugly—and Profitable," *The Daily Beast*, April 2, 2018.

178   "fucking crazy person" . . . This and subsequent quotes from Rich Johnston, "No Enemy but Peace—Richard Meyer, Antarctic Press, and Jawbreakers," *Bleeding Cool*, May 13, 2018.

178   colorist Elizabeth Breitweiser . . . ComicArtistPro Secrets, "COMICSGATE LIVE," YouTube, June 16, 2018.

179   "the vipers nest that is" . . . Susana Polo, "Marvel Comics Artist Draws Ire with 'SJW Hitler' Tweet about the X-Men," *Polygon*, January 25, 2018.

179   "very disparaging remarks" . . . Blacklist Universe, "GRAND RAPIDS COMIC-CON bans ME??? ALOHA!" YouTube, September 19, 2018.

179   "SJW agenda" . . . Art Thibert, "Marvel; they tried to destroy me!" YouTube, December 11, 2019.

179   He flirted with fascism . . . Krishna, "There's an Online Harassment Campaign."

179   "cleaning up the queer" . . . Ibid.

179   purchasing several toys . . . ComicArtistPro Secrets, "1 Hour of NonStop ROSE TICO Unboxings," April 27, 2018.

179   "The comic book industry has" . . . ComicArtistPro Secrets, "COMICSGATE LIVE."

179   Vox Day . . . ComicArtistPro Secrets, "EVS vs VOX DAY," YouTube, January 15, 2018.

179   mocking a female . . . ComicArtistPro Secrets, "KICKSTARTER FIRES SJW GATEKEEPER CAMILLA ZHANG! Ultimate Victory! LIVE!" YouTube, May 11, 2020.

179   "joking" about killing . . . YouTube removed the video for hate speech. Clip available at the Playlist (@YrOnlyHope), "Holy fucking shit. ComicsGate guys . . . ," Twitter, March 18, 2021.

180   Meyer posted a list . . . Corissa Haury, "Previously on Comics: Comicsgate Gets Aggressive (and Other News)," *Women Write about Comics*, May 14, 2018.
180   sued Waid for defamation . . . Brian Cronin, "Jawbreakers' Richard Meyer Drops Lawsuit against Mark Waid," *Comic Book Resources*, December 22, 2020.
180   Sitterson tweeted about . . . Teresa Jusino, "IDW Actually Considering Taking Action against Writer . . . Based on the Whims of Right-Wing Harassers," *The Mary Sue*, September 14, 2017.
180   He rallied his followers . . . Krishna, "There's an Online Harassment Campaign."
180   writer Chuck Wendig . . . Marcus Jones, "'Star Wars' Comics Writer Says He Was Fired by Marvel for His Vulgar Tweets," *BuzzFeed*, October 12, 2018.
181   An early Comicsgate figure . . . Rich Johnston, "Comicsgate Figure Quits Republican Vice Chair after QAnon Gaffe," *Bleeding Cool*, January 26, 2021.
181   conspiracy theory that alleges . . . Julia Carrie Wong, "QAnon Explained: The Antisemitic Conspiracy Theory Gaining Traction around the World," *Guardian*, August 25, 2020.
181   Trump's best demographic . . . Saadia McConville, "Call Out Karen, but Don't Forget about Kevin. They Chose Trump Twice," *Time*, November 16, 2020.
181   Daring to criticize a prominent . . . See J. A. Micheline, "Comicsgate Is the Latest Front in the Ongoing Culture Wars," *Guardian*, September 11, 2018.
182   "he would have been #ComicsGate" . . . Post since deleted, archived at Tim Midura, "Marsha Cooke Guarantees Darwyn Thought 'Comics Gate Idiots Were a Bunch of Crybaby Losers Ruining Comics,'" *The Outhousers*, August 23, 2018.
182   "I can guarantee" . . . Marsha Cooke (@Nicest_Girl_Evr), "Hi guys, this is Darwyn's wife . . . ," Twitter, August 21, 2018.
182   "racist homophobic woman hating" . . . Marsha Cooke (@Nicest_Girl_Evr), "Hi, definitely me on my actual . . . ," Twitter, August 21, 2018.
182   "a bunch of angry losers" . . . Screengrabbed in Midura, "Marsha Cooke Guarantees."
182   "Comicsgate is based on fear" . . . Jeff Lemire (@JeffLemire), "Comicsgate is based on fear . . . ," Twitter, August 23, 2018.
182   "hateful, misogynistic, and plain-old-ugly" . . . Bill Sienkiewicz, "To Comicsgaters—but also: to general . . . ," Facebook, August 23, 2018.
182   Aleš Kot and artist Ramon . . . Kieran Shiach, "Top Comics Creators Denounce 'Comicsgate' for the First Time," *Polygon*, August 28, 2018.
182   "There is no place for" . . . Tom Taylor (@tomtaylormade), "I believe comics are for . . . ," Twitter, August 26, 2018.
182   "appeal more to Trump voters" . . . Phil Jimenez (@philjimeneznyc), "Ah, #Superwoman. What a strange . . . ," Instagram, February 22, 2021.
182   Proud Boys used DC's logo . . . Rich Johnston, "The Proud Boys Use DC Comics Logo for Washington Protests This Weekend," *Bleeding Cool*, November 11, 2020.
182   Dynamite Comics even worked . . . Liam McGuire, "Dynamite Comics CEO Allegedly Worked with Comicsgate in Secret," *ScreenRant*, July 20, 2020.

183   Alterna Comics continued supporting . . . Corissa Haury, "Previously, on Comics: Controversy and Comicsgate," *Women Write about Comics*, September 17, 2018.

Conclusion

185   "superhero fiction has perpetually" . . . Abraham Riesman, "*The Boys* Is the End of the Superhero as We Know It," *Vulture*, October 9, 2020.

Bibliography

This is a select bibliography of the most important and relevant sources that informed substantial portions of the book. A full, detailed bibliography is available on the author's website, thanley.wordpress.com.

Abad-Santos, Alex. "Meet the Woman Who's Taking On the Sexism of the Comic Book Industry and Winning." *Vox*, October 13, 2014. https://www.vox.com/2014/10/13/6961965/marvel-kelly-sue-deconnick-writer-carol-corps.

Baci, Aria. "A Brief Timeline of Harassment and Sexual Assault in the Comics Industry." *The Mary Sue*, November 29, 2017. https://www.themarysue.com/comics-assault-timeline/.

Beaty, Bart. *Fredric Wertham and the Critique of Mass Culture*. Jackson: University Press of Mississippi, 2005.

Dean, Michael. "Two Sides of Julie the Ladies' Man." *Comics Journal* 259 (April 2004): 22.

Edidin, Jay. "Geek Masculinity and the Myth of the Fake Geek Girl." *Comics Alliance*, November 15, 2012. https://comicsalliance.com/geek-masculinity-and-the-myth-of-the-fake-geek-girl/.

Edidin, Jay, Tyler Kingkade, and Jessica Testa. "The Comics Giant behind Wonder Woman Is Accused of Promoting an Editor after Women Accused Him of Sexual Harassment." *BuzzFeed*, November 10, 2017. https://www.buzzfeednews.com/article/jtes/dc-comics-editor-eddie-berganza-sexual-harassment.

Eisner, Joel. *The Official Batman Batbook*. Bloomington, IN: AuthorHouse, 2008.

Evanier, Mark. *Kirby: King of Comics*. New York: Abrams, 2008.

Haller, Duna, and Travis Hedge Coke. "The Sounds of Silence: CBLDF and Systemic Toxicity in Comics." *Comicwatch*, June 25, 2020. https://comic-watch.com/news/the-sounds-of-silence-cbldf-and-systemic-toxicity-in-comics.

Hanley, Tim. "The Evolution of Female Readership: Letter Columns in Superhero Comics." In *Gender and the Superhero Narrative*, edited by Michael Goodrum, Tara Prescott, and Philip Smith, 221–50. Jackson: University Press of Mississippi, 2018.

Howe, Sean. *Marvel Comics: The Untold Story*. New York: Harper, 2012.

Krishna, Rachael. "There's an Online Harassment Campaign Underway against People Advocating for Diversity in Comics." *BuzzFeed*, March 22, 2018. https://www.buzzfeednews.com/article/krishrach/comicsgate#.ldWr3aDgV6.

Letamendi, Drea. "The Psychology of the Fake Geek Girl: Why We're Threatened by Falsified Fandom." *The Mary Sue*, December 21, 2012. https://www.themarysue.com/psychology-of-the-fake-geek-girl/.

MacDonald, Heidi. "How a Toxic History of Harassment Has Damaged the Comics Industry." *The Beat*, October 1, 2015. https://www.comicsbeat.com/how-a-toxic-history-of-harassment-has-damaged-the-comics-industry/.

Micheline, J. A. "Comicsgate Is the Latest Front in the Ongoing Culture Wars." *Guardian*, September 11, 2018. https://www.theguardian.com/commentisfree/2018/sep/11/poison-comicsgate-racism-misogyny-take-a-stand.

Nyberg, Amy Kiste. *Seal of Approval: The History of the Comics Code*. Jackson: University Press of Mississippi, 1998.

Ricca, Brad. *Super Boys: The Amazing Adventures of Jerry Siegel and Joe Shuster—the Creators of Superman*. New York: Macmillan, 2013.

Robbins, Trina, and Catherine Yronwode. *Women and the Comics*. N.p.: Eclipse Books, 1985.

Tilley, Carol L. "Seducing the Innocent: Fredric Wertham and the Falsifications That Helped Condemn Comics." *Information & Culture* 47, no. 4 (2012): 383–413.

Tye, Larry. *Superman: The High-Flying History of America's Most Enduring Hero*. New York: Random House, 2012.

Weldon, Glen. *The Caped Crusade: Batman and the Rise of Nerd Culture*. New York: Simon & Schuster, 2016.

Wertham, Fredric. *Seduction of the Innocent*. New York: Rinehart, 1954.

Willaert, Kate. *Kirby without Words*. https://kirbywithoutwords.tumblr.com/.

Wright, Bradford W. *Comic Book Nation: The Transformation of Youth Culture in America*. Baltimore: Johns Hopkins University Press, 2001.

Index

Adams, Neal, 41–43, 69, 84
The Adventures of Superman, 35, 37
Albuquerque, Rafael, 129, 176
Allie, Scott, 165, 169
Alonso, Axel, 128–29, 139
Alterna Comics, 183
Altman, Teddy. *See* Hulkling
Amanat, Sana, 149
Angel, 31, 32
antiheroes, 65, 75–87
anti-semitism, 3
Ant-Man, 28–31, 119
Antos, Heather, 176–77, 182
Apollo, 135
Aquaman: in comics, 23, 45, 87, 103, 119; in film, 150, 161
Archie Comics, 16, 45
Asian superheroes, 145–47
Asselin, Janelle, 169, 176
Atlas Comics. *See* Marvel Comics
the Atom, 21, 23, 117–18
the Authority, 135
Avengers (comics), 28–31, 35, 47, 51, 57, 90, 118, 141, 145
Avengers (film), 150, 170
Ayala, Vita, 108
Ayer, David, 163
Azrael, 86–87

Balent, Jim, 93–95
Bane, 86
Banner, Bruce. *See* the Hulk
Barnes, Bucky, 7, 141
Baron, Mike, 78, 81
Bat-Girl, 20
Batgirl: Barbara Gordon, 38–39, 50, 74–76, 99, 112, 129, 130, 176; Cassandra Cain, 104; in film/ TV, 39–41, 154, 170; Stephanie Brown, 120
Batman: in comics, 4, 6, 8, 15, 18, 23, 35, 41–44, 46–47, 57, 69–72, 73–77, 86–87, 89, 97, 112–14, 119–20, 124, 135–36, 139, 141, 147, 166; in film/ TV, 35–41, 150, 153–54, 159–60
Batman: The Dark Knight Returns, 69–71, 73, 103, 160
Batman: The Killing Joke, 74–76, 113, 129, 154
Batman: Knightfall, 86–87, 119, 154
Batman: Year One, 72
Batman v Superman: Dawn of Justice, 159–60
Bat-Woman, 18–21
Batwoman, 104, 136–38
Batwoman (TV), 142
Baz, Simon. *See* Green Lantern

Bendis, Brian Michael, 109, 120, 139, 149
Bennett, Tara, 158
Berg, Jon, 150, 152
Berganza, Eddie, 165, 168–69
Berger, Karen, 103
Berry, Halle, 154, 155
Birds of Prey, 101, 103, 113
Birds of Prey (film), 141, 150, 161–62
Bishop, Kate. *See* Hawkeye
Black Canary: in comics, 90, 113, 119, 141; in film, 161
Black Lightning, 144
Black Lives Matter, 81
Black Panther, 48, 141, 144
Black Panther (film), 150
Black superheroes, 148–52
Black Widow: in film, 155, 157–58; Golden Age, 8; Natasha Romanoff, 54, 98
Black Widow (film), 157–58
Blackman, W. Haden, 137
Blade, 144, 150
Blue Beetle: Jaime Reyes, 147; Ted Kord, 72–73
Blue Lives Matter, 81, 182
Boden, Anna, 157
Bolland, Brian, 74–76
The Boys (TV), 185
Brackett, Leigh, 18
Braddock, Betsy. *See* Psylocke
Brite, Poppy Z., 166
Brown, Stephanie. *See* Batgirl; Robin; Spoiler
Brown, Tara Tiger, 126
Brownstein, Charles, 169–70, 172
Bumblebee, 133
Burton, Tim, 154
Buscema, John, 52, 82
Byrne, John, 58, 62, 66, 81, 85, 91, 134, 175
Byrne, Olive, 11

Cable, 82, 84
Cage, Luke, 144

Cain, Chelsea, 176
Campbell, J. Scott, 147, 149
Captain America: in film, 158; Sam Wilson, 148, 149; Steve Rogers, 4, 6, 8, 57, 78, 120, 134, 141, 148, 149, 175
Captain Marvel (Billy Batson), 45
Captain Marvel (Carol Danvers), 99, 108, 130, 177–78
Captain Marvel (film), 157–59
Carlin, Mike, 165, 167–68
Carol Corps, 108, 130
Carter, Lynda, 153, 160
Castle, Frank. *See* the Punisher
The Cat, 52, 54, 106
Catwoman: in comics, 8, 36, 38–39, 70, 72, 89, 93–95, 97, 103–4, 134, 137, 139, 148; in film, 154–55
Catwoman (film), 155
CBLDF. *See* Comic Book Legal Defense Fund
CCA. *See* Comics Code Authority
Cebulski, C. B., 147
Changeling, 63–64, 112
Charlton Comics, 72
Chavez, America, 177–78
Cheung, Jim, 135
Choi, Ryan, 146
civil rights movement, 31, 48–49
Claremont, Chris, 58–63, 82, 134
Cloonan, Becky, 104, 110
CMAA. *See* Comics Magazine Association of America
Coates, Ta-Nahesi, 178
Cockrum, Dave, 58
Cole, Kai, 170
Collins, Nancy, 103
Comic Book Legal Defense Fund, 169–70
comic book sales, 45, 58
Comics Code Authority, 16–17, 22, 49, 68, 77, 90–91, 133
Comics Magazine Association of America, 16–17
Comicsgate, 177–83

Constantine, John, 141–42
Conway, Carla, 103
Conway, Gerry, 52, 103, 106
Cooke, Darwyn, 182
Cooke, Marsha, 182
cosplay, 126–27
Craig, Yvonne, 39–41
crime comics, 13, 17
Cruz, Jessica. *See* Green Lantern
Cyborg: in comics, 63, 144; in film, 150, 152
Cyclops, 31–32, 58–63, 112

Danvers, Carol. *See* Captain Marvel; Ms. Marvel
Daredevil: in comics, 67–69, 77–78, 107, 112, 147; in film/TV, 150, 154–55
Daredevil (film), 155
Daredevil (TV), 150
Dark Horse Comics, 165, 169
Dark Knight film trilogy, 91, 101, 124, 154
Dark Phoenix. *See* Grey, Jean
Dark Phoenix Saga, 58–63, 90
Davis, Michael, 145
Dawnstar, 144, 146
Dazzler, 48, 58
DC Comics: Comics Code Authority, 16–17; creators by gender, 101–5; Golden Age, 1–5; new 52, 97–98, 104, 120, 127, 137, 143, 168; readership, 46–47; rebirth, 104, 128; sexual harassment, 166–69
DC Comics Bombshells, 104, 141
dead men defrosting, 119
Deadpool, 110, 121, 139
Death of Superman, 86, 119, 160, 167
Deathstroke, 64–66, 84, 90
DeConnick, Kelly Sue, 108, 130, 171
Dell Comics, 45
DeWitt, Alexandra, 111, 113
Dibny, Ralph. *See* the Elongated Man
Dibny, Sue, 117–18
DiDio, Dan, 104, 114
Dingle, Derek T., 145

direct market, 57–58
Ditko, Steve, 73
Doctor Fate, 145
Doctor Manhattan, 72, 74
Doctor Strange: in comics, 106, 146; in film, 158
Donenfeld, Harry, 3, 7
Donenfeld, Irwin, 35
Donner, Richard, 153
Doom Patrol, 103, 140
Doran, Colleen, 103, 167
D'Orazio, Valerie, 167–68
Dozier, William, 35–41
Dr. Light, 117
Drake, Bobby. *See* Iceman
Drake, Jessie, 140
Dreamer, 141
Drew, Jessica. *See* Spider-Woman
Duffy, Jo, 103, 107, 167
Dynamite Comics, 182–83

EC Comics, 16, 106
Eclipso, 84, 118
Edidin, Jay, 169
Elektra, 69, 89–90, 112, 120
Elektra (film), 155
Ellis, Warren, 165, 171–72
The Elongated Man, 117–18
Erin, Shvaughn, 140
Eternals (film), 141
Extraño, 134

Faith, 99
fake geek girls, 126–27
The Falcon, 48, 144
fangirls, 125
Fantastic Four, 23–28, 35, 47–48, 90
female characters, art, 89–99
female colorists, 108–9
female creators, 8–9, 101–10
Ferris, Carol, 21–22
Fiction House, 8
Fisher, Ray, 150, 152
Fite, Linda, 52, 106

The Flash: Barry Allen, 21, 23, 119, 143; in film, 160; Wally West, 89, 118, 143–44

The Flash (TV), 150, 170

Fleck, Ryan, 157

Flor, Yara, 148

Fowler, Tess, 171

Fraction, Matt, 98, 171

Fradon, Ramona, 103, 166

Freedom Ring, 135

Frost, Emma, 95

Gabriel, David, 101, 149

Gadot, Gal, 141, 160

Gaines, William, 16

Gamergate, 177

gatekeeping, 125–29

geek girls, 125

Ghost Rider, 82, 147, 154

Giant-Man, 31. *See also* Ant-Man

Gibbons, Dave, 72–74

Giffen, Keith, 84

GLAAD Media Award, 136, 137

Gold Key Comics, 67

Goodman, Martin, 4, 23, 31, 48

Gordon, Barbara. *See* Batgirl; Oracle

Gordon, James, 38, 74–75, 77, 141

Gore, Shawna, 169

Grace, Sina, 140

Grayson, Devin, 103, 136–37

Grayson, Dick. *See* Robin

Green Arrow, 23, 49, 87, 113, 118–19

Green Arrow: The Longbow Hunters, 113, 119

Green Goblin, 112, 119

Green Lantern: Hal Jordan, 21, 23, 49, 87, 119, 143, 154; Jessica Cruz, 147; John Stewart, 49, 143, 144; Kyle Rayner, 111, 134, 143; Simon Baz, 145, 147

Grell, Mike, 113

Grey, Jean: in comics, 31–34, 58–63, 90, 112, 139; in film, 154

Grimm, Ben, 23–28

Guardians of the Galaxy, 150, 157

Gunn, James, 157

Hall, Barbara, 8

Hamilton, Edmond, 18

Harley Quinn: in comics, 97, 139, 141; in film, 161

Harris, Tony, 126–27

Hawkeye: Clint Barton, 98, 113, 118, 120; Kate Bishop, 159

Hawkeye Initiative, 98

Heinberg, Allan, 135–36

Hercules, 139

Hitler, Adolf, 3, 4, 16, 179

Hodson, Christina, 161

homosexuality, 15–16, 17, 70, 133–42

horror comics, 13, 17

House of M, 118–19

Hudson, Laura, 98

The Hulk: in comics, 27–29, 41, 48, 81, 89–90, 134; in film, 154, 157

Hulkling, 135–36

Human Torch (Golden Age), 23

Human Torch (Johnny Storm). *See* Storm, Johnny

Hummel, Joye, 11

Iceman, 21, 139–40

Identity Crisis, 114, 116–18, 167

IDW Publishing, 180

Image Comics, 84–86, 89, 93

indigenous superheroes, 146

Infantino, Carmine, 38

Invisible Girl. *See* Storm, Sue

Iron Man: in comics, 28–29, 57, 120, 147, 149; in film, 157–58, 163

Ironheart, 149–50

Jameson, J. Jonah, 52

Janson, Klaus, 78, 82

Jenkins, Patty, 160

Jewish creators, 1, 3, 6

Johansson, Scarlett, 155, 157

Johns, Geoff, 109, 128–29, 144, 150, 152
The Joker: in comics, 26, 70, 74–77, 112, 129, 139, 147; in film, 143, 161
Joker (film), 161
Jones, Whitewash, 7
Jordan, Hal. See Green Lantern
Jordan, Michael B., 150
Jubilee, 146
The Judas Contract, 64–66
Juspeczyk, Laurie. See Silk Spectre
Justice League, 23, 46–47, 104, 117, 145
Justice League (cartoon), 101, 143
Justice League (film), 150, 152, 159, 162, 170
juvenile delinquency, 13–15

Kahn, Jenette, 103
Kane, Bette. See Bat-Girl
Kane, Bob, 4, 12
Kane, Kate. See Batwoman
Kane, Kathy. See Bat-Woman
Kanigher, Robert, 20, 49, 51
Kaplan, Billy. See Wiccan
Kefauver, Estes, 16
Kent, Clark. See Superman
Kent, Jonathan, 142
Khan, Kamala. See Ms. Marvel
Kid Flash, 63
Kimmel, Michael, 148
Kingkade, Tyler, 169
Kirby, Jack, 4, 23–28, 57
Kirby Without Words, 28, 32
Knight, Misty, 144
Koi Boi, 141
Kreisberg, Andrew, 170
Kwannon, 146–47
Kyle, Selina. See Catwoman

Lance, Dinah. See Black Canary
Lane, Lois: in comics, 8, 21–22, 47, 50, 97, 141, 148; in film, 85, 153, 159
Larsen, Erik, 84–85
Larson, Brie, 157–59

Latinx superheroes, 147–48
Latour, Jason, 165, 172
Lee, Jim, 84–85, 169
Lee, Stan, 23–34, 48–49, 51–55, 106
Legion of Super-Heroes, 140–41, 146
Letamendi, Drea, 125
letter columns, 27, 31, 42, 46–48 50–54, 58–59, 62, 65–66, 80, 91, 94, 135–36
Liefeld, Rob, 84–85
Lobdell, Scott, 97, 165, 171
Lobo, 84
Loeb, Jeph, 150
Loring, Jean, 21, 117–18
Luthor, Lex, 175

MacDonald, Heidi, 166
Madison, Julie, 8, 154
Magneto, 31–32, 59, 118, 154
Maines, Nicole, 141
Man of Steel, 159
Manara, Milo, 128–29, 176
Mantis, 145, 155
Marble, Alice, 11
MariNaomi, 171
Markov, Tara. See Terra
Marston, Elizabeth Holloway, 9, 11
Marston, William Moulton, 9–12, 20
Martian Manhunter, 23, 119
Marvel Cinematic Universe, 101, 124, 141, 150, 155–59
Marvel Comics: 1960s, 23–34; bankruptcy, 107; creators by gender, 105–8; Golden Age, 4–6; Marvel Knights, 113; MAX, 113, 135; NOW!, 108, 127; readership, 47–48; Ultimate universe, 107, 113, 119, 148
Marvel Girl. See Grey, Jean
Marvel Illustrated: Swimsuit Issue, 93–94
Mastermind, 59–60
Mazzucchelli, David, 68, 72
McDuffie, Dwayne, 145
McFarlane, Todd, 84–85
Meltzer, Brad, 66, 114
Meyer, Richard C., 177–80

Midnighter, 135
Mignola, Mike, 169
Milestone Comics, 145
Miller, Frank, 67–72, 75–77, 82, 154, 169, 179
Mills, June Tarpé, 8
Miss Fury, 8
MLJ Magazines, 4
Mockingbird, 113, 176
Momoa, Jason, 150, 161
Montoya, Renee, 120, 134, 137, 161
Moonstar, Dani, 146
Moore, Alan, 72–77
Moore, Demi, 91–92
Morales, Miles. *See* Spider-Man
Mr. Fantastic. *See* Richards, Reed
Ms. magazine, 50
Ms. Marvel: Carol Danvers, 48, 52, 90, 98–99, 106–7, 112; Kamala Khan, 108, 130, 149–50, 159
Murdock, Matt. *See* Daredevil
Mystique, 134, 141, 154

Nal, Nia, 141
Namor the Sub-Mariner, 13, 23, 25
Namora, 90
Nassour, Khalid. *See* Doctor Fate
Newell, Mindy, 103
Night Nurse, 51, 106
Nite Owl, 72–74
Nocenti, Ann, 107
Nolan, Christopher, 91, 124, 154
Northstar, 134, 139
Novick, Irv, 4, 41

O'Neil, Denny, 41–43, 49
Oracle, 75, 113
Ostrander, John, 75, 103
Ozymandias, 72–74

Page, Karen, 69, 112
Pantozzi, Jill, 128
Park, Linda, 143
Parker, Peter. *See* Spider-Man
patriotic superheroes, 4–5

Patton, Candice, 150
the Penguin, 36, 39
Pennyworth, Alfred, 15
Pérez, George, 63–66
Perlman, Nicole, 157
Perlmutter, Ike, 155, 175
Peter, H. G., 9, 20
Pfeiffer, Michelle, 154, 155
Phantom Lady, 8, 90
Phoenix, 118, 120. *See also* Grey, Jean
Pichelli, Sara, 107
Poison Ivy, 139, 154
Pollack, Rachel, 103
Polo, Susana, 69
Porcelain, 141
Portacio, Whilce, 84–85
Potts, Carl, 81
power fantasies, 12, 94–95
Power Girl, 95
Prince, Diana. *See* Wonder Woman
Professor X: in comics, 31–32, 60; in film, 154
Pryde, Kitty, 154
Psylocke, 98, 146–47
Punchline, 147
The Punisher: in comics, 77–81, 84, 89, 110, 147, 182; in film, 80, 154
The Punisher (film), 80
Pym, Hank. *See* Ant-Man

QAnon, 181
Quality Comics, 4
queer representation, 133–42
Quesada, Joe, 135
the Question, 72
Quicksilver, 118
Quinn, Zoe, 177

racism, 7–8, 143–52, 178
Raimi, Sam, 124, 154
Rambeau, Monica, 159
Ratner, Brett, 170
Raven, 63, 65, 113, 118
Rawhide, Kid, 135
Rayner, Kyle. *See* Green Lantern

readership, 91, 101, 45–49
Red Hood, 76
Red Wolf, 146
Reeve, Christopher, 124–53
Reeves, George, 35, 37
Renée, Lily, 8
Richards, Reed, 23–28
Riesman, Abraham, 185–86
Rivera, Gabby, 178, 182
Robbins, Trina, 166
Robin: Carrie Kelly, 69; Dick Grayson, 8, 15, 18–20, 41, 51, 63–65, 136; in film/TV, 36–41; Jason Todd, 76, 114; Stephanie Brown, 113–14; Tim Drake, 86, 113–14, 142
Roche, Ruth, 8
Rogers, Steve. See Captain America
romance comics, 13, 45–46, 57, 102, 205
Romanoff, Natasha. See Black Widow
Ronin, 68
Rorschach, 72–74
Ross, Betty, 8, 155
Roubicek, Dorothy, 11. See also Woolfolk, Dorothy
Rucka, Greg, 120, 137, 139, 168

Sandman, 101, 103, 140
Savage Dragon, 85
Sawyer, Maggie, 134, 137
Scarlet Witch: in comics, 118–19; in film/TV, 155, 159
Schumacher, Joel, 154
Schwartz, Julius, 35, 38, 41, 166–67
Scott, Nicola, 104, 139
Seduction of the Innocent, 13–16
Serano, Lee, 141
serialization, 25, 44
Seuling, Carole, 106
Seuling, Phil, 106
Severin, Marie, 52, 106, 108
sexual harassment, 165–73
sexual violence, 69–70, 75, 111–21
Shang-Chi, 144, 146
Shanna the She-Devil, 51, 54, 106

She-Hulk: in comics, 54, 90–92, 107; in TV, 159
the Shield, 4
Shinkoda, Peter, 150
Shooter, Jim, 62, 134
Shortland, Cate, 157
Shuster, Joe, 1–3, 12
Siede, Caroline, 157
Siegel, Jerry, 1–3
Silk Spectre, 74
Silver Sable, 82, 89
Silvestri, Marc, 84–85
Simon, Joe, 4
Simone, Gail, 103–4, 11, 133, 140–41
Simonson, Louise, 103, 107
Singer, Bryan, 170
the Snyder Cut. See Zack Snyder's Justice League
Snyder, Scott, 109, 169
Snyder, Zack, 152, 159–60, 162
Soma, Taki, 169
Soy, Dexter, 130
Spider-Girl, 107
Spider-Gwen, 120
Spider-Man: in film, 150, 154; Miles Morales, 148–50; Peter Parker, 28, 35, 41, 47–48, 67, 77–78, 84, 107, 112, 119, 124, 149, 165
Spider-Woman, 54, 99, 112, 120, 128–29, 176
Spoiler, 113, 120
Squirrel Girl, 99, 108, 128, 141
Stacy, Gwen, 112, 119–20
Star Sapphire, 22, 95
Starfire, 63, 90, 97
Stark, Tony. See Iron Man
Steinberg, Flo, 176
Steinem, Gloria, 50, 52
Stern, Roger, 59, 62
Stevenson, Noelle, 98, 123
Stewart, Cameron, 129, 165, 172
Stewart, John. See Green Lantern
Storm: in comics, 60, 134, 144; in film, 154
Storm, Johnny, 23–28, 150

Storm, Sue, 23–28, 54, 90, 95
Suicide Squad, 84, 97
Suicide Squad (film), 141, 150, 161, 163
Summers, Scott. *See* Cyclops
Superboy, 86
Supergirl, 22, 90, 97, 104, 112, 120, 134, 168
Supergirl (TV), 141, 170
Superman: in comics, 1–3, 6, 8, 23, 44–47, 69, 72–73, 85–86, 89, 97, 112, 119–20, 135, 141, 165–68, 175, 186; in film, 35, 85, 124, 150, 153, 159
Superman: The Movie, 85, 124, 153
Swamp Thing, 72, 103

Tamaki, Mariko, 104, 110
Tarr, Babs, 104, 129
Teen Titans, 63–66, 176
Teen Titans Go!, 101, 152
Terra, 63–66, 90, 112, 118
Testa, Jessica, 169
the Thing. *See* Grimm, Ben
Thomas, Dann, 103
Thomas, Jean, 106
Thomas, Roy, 103, 106
Thompson, Jill, 103, 166
Thompson, Kelly, 108, 110
Thor: in comics, 28–29, 59, 120, 128; in film, 158
Tilley, Carol, 15
Timely Comics. *See* Marvel Comics
Todd, Jason. *See* Red Hood; Robin
Tong, 141
toxic masculinity definition, viii
transgender characters, 140–41
Trevor, Steve, 20, 49, 139, 153
Trinary, 145
Trump, Donald, 175–76, 179, 181–83

Uncle Sam, 4

Valentino, Jim, 84–85
Valiant Comics, 99
Valkyrie, 51, 141

Valley, Jean-Paul. *See* Azrael
Van Dyne, Janet. *See* the Wasp
Van Sciver, Ethan, 179–80
Vanity Fair, 91–92
Vartanoff, Irene, 103
Vellani, Iman, 150
Vertigo Comics, 103
Villalobos, Ramon, 182
violence in comics, 6–7, 68, 72, 78, 80, 82, 84–87
Visaggio, Magdalene, 178, 182
Vixen, 144–45
Voodoo, 93, 97

Waid, Mark, 180
Walker, David F., 152
Walker, Patsy, 108, 113
Walters, Jennifer. *See* She-Hulk
Ward, Burt, 36–41
Wardlow, Ciara, 161–62
The Wasp: in comics, 18–31, 52, 90, 119; in film, 155, 157
Watchmen, 72–74, 103, 113
Watson, Mary Jane, 112, 154
Wayne, Bruce. *See* Batman
Wein, Len, 58, 72, 75, 81
Wertham, Fredric, 13–16, 90, 133, 136
West, Adam, 36–41
West, Iris, 21, 150
Whedon, Joss, 150, 152, 157, 160, 162, 170
Wiccan, 135–36
Williams, J. H., III, 137
Williams, Brittney L., 108
Williams, Riri. *See* Ironheart
Wilson, G. Willow, 104, 108, 130, 149
Wilson, Sam. *See* Captain America; the Falcon
Wing, Colleen, 59–60, 63, 144, 146
Wolfman, Marv, 63–66
Wolverine: in comics, 81–84, 89, 120, 134, 139, 147; in film, 154
Women in Refrigerators, 111–21
women's lib, 49–54
Wonder Girl, 21, 63, 65, 148

Wonder Woman: in comics, 9–12,
    15–16, 20–21, 23, 39, 45, 47, 49–50,
    87, 89, 93, 103, 120, 141, 146, 168,
    169; in film, 153, 160
Wonder Woman (film), 160
Wood, Brian, 165, 171
Woolfolk, Dorothy, 50–51
Word War II, 3, 6–7
Worthington III, Warren. *See* Angel
Wyngarde, Jason. *See* Mastermind

Xavier, Charles. *See* Professor X

X-Men: in comics, 31–34, 58–63, 81–82,
    84, 95, 101, 107, 118, 124, 134, 145,
    146; in film, 141, 150, 154, 170

Yale, Kim, 75, 103
Yan, Cathy, 161
Yeoh, Alysia, 140–41
Yoshida, Akira, 147. *See also* Cebulski,
    C. B.
Young Avengers, 135–36

Zack Snyder's Justice League, 162–63
Zatanna, 117

About the Author

Tim Hanley is a comic book historian and the author of *Wonder Woman Unbound*, *Investigating Lois Lane*, *The Many Lives of Catwoman*, and *Betty and Veronica: The Leading Ladies of Riverdale*. His work has also appeared in the *Atlantic*, *Los Angeles Review of Books*, and the *Comics Journal*. He lives in Halifax, Nova Scotia, between his massive stacks of comic books.

www.ingramcontent.com/pod-product-compliance
Lightning Source LLC
Chambersburg PA
CBHW030302100426
42812CB00002B/540